ARTIFICIAL INTELLIGENCE

IN THE TECHNOLOGIES SYNTHESIS OF CREATIVE SOLUTIONS

ALEXANDER V. ANDREICHIKOV
OLGA N. ANDREICHIKOVA

Academus Publishing
2018

Academus Publishing, Inc.

1999 S, Bascom Avenue, Suite 700 Campbell CA 95008
Website: www.academuspublishing.com
E-mail: info@academuspublishing.com

The work was carried out with the financial support of the Russian Foundation
for basic research and Russian Humanitarian Science Foundation,
project No. 16–02–00743 «Multicriterial analysis and forecasting of technical
and economic conditions and development trends of the world's leading
aerospace companies Contents

The right of Alexander V. Andreichikov, Olga N. Andreichikova
is identified as author of this work.

ISBN 10: 1 4946 0010 5
ISBN 13: 978 1 4946 0010 5
DOI 10.31519/1404

Abstract: Invention problem solving is connected to essential expenses of labour and time, which is spent on the procedures of search and ordering of necessary knowledge, on generation of probable variants of projected systems, on the analysis of offered ideas and decisions and understanding perspectiveness of them. The monograph present outlines the results of the developments in the field of creating computing technology of the synthesis of new engineering on the level of invention. The most attention is paid to problem of computer aided designing on initial stages, where synthesis of new on principal technical systems is carried out. Computer-aided construction of new technical system is based on using of data — and knowledge bases of physical effects and of technical decisions as well as different heuristic systematization procedures. The synthesis of principles of function of the technical new systems is carried out with using experts knowledge and requires the application of the artificial intelligence methods and the methods of the decisions making theory for invention's tasks. Considered approach has been used for synthesis of new technical systems of different functional purposes and had shown high efficiency in computer-aided construction.

Key words: artificialintelligence invention, creative solutions, database, knowledge base, knowledge systematization, decisions making, morphological synthesis, hierarchy analysis, fuzzy sets, invention software.

CONTENTS

CHAPTER 1.
Theory of Invention Problem-solving a creative process of developing new Technical Systems

1.1. Software for the inventive problem solving

Introduction.In the Theory of Invention Problem-solving a creative process of developing new Technical Systems (TS) may be characterised by the following basic stages, on which specialised processing of information is carried out:

• Preliminary statement of a problem, when the basic functions of the designed TS are formulated.

• Study and analysis of a problem. There is the study of the evolution and tendencies of development of the considered class of TS and classes which are functionally similar to it.

• Specification and elaboration of a problem. In the list of the requirements presented to the created TS, are joined operational, constructive, technological, economic, ecological and other requirements.

• Search for new technical ideas, decisions and physical principles of action. At this stage synthesis of an extended set of new technical and physical principles of action is realised.

• Choice of the best technical decisions. The versatile analysis and estimation of all found technical decisions is made for this purpose.

The most important procedures of information processing during the invention of new products are: knowledge systematization and classification; synthesis of the new technical decisions; the analysis and forecasting of rational decisions in conditions of uncertainty.

There are many scientific works devoted to decision regarding urgent problems of invention. The significant contribution in formation and development of invention methodology has been made by Hubka [1], Koller [2], Altshuller [3] and others [4-7]. Computer methods for invention support have received wide dissemination in the last two decades. For computer support of invention processes, optimisation methods, automatic methods for synthesis of TS, formal heuristic rules and algorithms of invention problem-solving [8]; automation of search designing [9-11] were used.

This article discusses a practical approach to computer support of invention processes, which in contrast to existing approaches allows:

- The achievement of complex automation of a large number of invention procedures;
- The inclusion of new methods and procedures for information processing;
- The use the approaches and methods of artificial intelligence (AI);
- The development of the methodology of creation and employment of the applications for invention problem-solving.

The main parts of inventions software are:
- Decision Support Systems (DSS);
- Software for knowledge extraction and systematization;
- Computer systems for the synthesis of the inventions.

Computer support allows for considerable reduction in expenditures for labour and time in routine design procedures. It also increases the probability of dawning upon designer during creation of the inventions.

Decision making tasks, techniques and systems Decision making tasks (DMT) may be divided into the following categories:
- Tasks relating to conditions of certainty, that is when the total and exact information about a problem is present. In this case it satisfies conditions necessary for the statement of an optimisation problem.
- Tasks relating to conditions of uncertainty, when the information is partial, inexact, incardinal, unreliable, illegible and so on. To solve such problems expert information is usually required and operations research methods, the methods of fuzzy sets theory and AI methods are applied. The approach to decisions making with the propositions of AI is considerably different from a mathematical one. Expert systems also ensure the support of choosing processes, but a strategy of problem-solving is different. The knowledge of experts are already incorporated in expert systems before their use.

DMT are differentiated in their degree of environmental influence. For example, there are tasks which slightly influence environmental parameters and there are examples to the contrary. Environmental changes can have various forms (smooth, sharp, qualitative and so on) as well as timed parameters. In accordance with this there are static and dynamic DMT. Invention problem-solving deals with dynamic decision-making processes in conditions of uncertainty. To dynamic DMT is related the problems of initial information being unstable in time. For such a task the following instabilities are typical:
- A change in the structure and properties of alternatives;
- A change in the set of choice criteria and their priorities;
- A change in the set of acceptable outcomes.

In dynamic DMT all categories of the initial information are subject to changes, as the changes in expert preferences reflect the tendencies of fluctuations occurring in the environment. These tendencies can be estimated on the basis of accrued statistics. Therefore the dynamic tasks in conditions of uncertainty require attraction, accumulation and multialternate processing of large volumes of expert information. Such information can be used for forecasting changes in considered variants preferences, an estimation of probable consequences of the accepted decisions and reception of new knowledge in areas researched.

In connection with the above, there is the urgent problem of development of such computer systems for decision-making, which satisfy the following common requirements:

- To provide the qualified support for the decision-making process on the adviser level, thus the task should be decided not by the system, but by the user;
- The support of decision-making processes should be multiform, i.e. the system grants to the user the set of various strategies and methods for making decisions;
- The system should have definite knowledge, necessary for decisions retaining to the presented task;
- The system should strive towards perfection, i.e. it should be able to supplement new knowledge, to accumulate them and integrate it into the problem-solving process;
- The system should be able to work with partial and indefinite information;
- The system should remain in working state in conditions of a rapidly varying environment;
- The system should be able to evaluate the consequences of decisions.
- The user of the system is an engineer or inventor, who should not need to have qualifications of an expert, knowledge-engineer and mathematician.

Most of these requirements are in accord with characteristics of second generation expert systems. The alternate approach is the concept of hybrid intelligent systems [12, 13], based on the connection of mathematical simulation methods with AI methods in frameworks of united systems. Such a connection is fruitful, both from the point of view of simulation and from the point of view of logical reasoning. On the one hand simulation methods can, to a certain degree, handle poorly structured and poorly formalised information in the

7

knowledge base, and, on the other hand, adding simulation components to expert systems expands the opportunities for representing and processing diverse knowledge. Apart from the difficulties, connected with the embodiment of such system, there are the principle difficulties of organisation, connected with conventional contradictions between system generality and its skill in aiding tasks in particular subject areas. The knowledge in such systems is heterogeneous and dynamic; therefore, the questions of its representation, processing and converting require theoretical and experimental study. In addition such systems must be applied to real life applications in order to acquire well referenced practical experience.

The DSS described incorporates two basic methods: the analysis of hierarchical processes [14] and the methods of fuzzy sets theory [15-17].

Hierarchy analysis method

The hierarchy analysis method supposes decomposition of a problem into simpler parts and processing of judgements of the accepting decision person. As a result, a vector of priorities of researched alternatives on all quality criteria, existing in the hierarchies, is defined. For estimation of hierarchy elements a pair comparisons technique is used, including a method of linguistic standards etc. By the use of pair comparisons an ordering of objects is carried out on the basis of calculating the right eigen vectors of pair comparisons matrixes, which is interpreted as a vector of priorities of compared alternatives. The main eigen vector w of a matrix A might be found from the equation:

$$Aw = \lambda_{max} w, \qquad (1.1)$$

where λ_{max} — maximum eigen value of a matrix A. The components of priority vectors on quality criteria are hereafter used as weight factors in a procedure of linear convolution on criteria hierarchy, the result of which is a priorities vector of alternatives concerning focus.

The hierarchy analysis method may be used for solving dynamic tasks. Forecasting experts' preferences is connected to reception of priority estimations of alternatives in the form of dependencies in time. Hence, the preference estimation may be given not by a constant, but by a function. The selection of such functions can be carried out alternatively:

– an expert selects the function from some functional scale [14];

– the function is formed by an approximation of expert estimations, which have been received in various moment of time.

The example of a functional scale is shown in Table 1, where the functions contain parameters, the selection of which allows for the description of varied judgements.

For dynamic tasks the pair comparisons matrixes contain functions of time as elements, therefore their maximum eigen values λ_{max} and eigen vector w will also depend on time, i.e.

$$A(t)w(t) = \lambda_{max}(t)\, w(t). \tag{1.2}$$

For equation (1.2) it is possible to obtain the analytical solution, if the order of a matrix $A(t)$ does not exceed four [14]. The priorities vector $w(t)$ may be calculated by solving the equation (1.2) for various moments of time with the subsequent approximation of obtained points. Such an approach allows the removal of the restriction on the order of a matrix $A(t)$ and allows to watch for consistency of experts' judgements in time. An alternate way is calculation of $A(t)$ and $w(t)$ numerically. For this purpose it is necessary to have information on experts' preferences for a certain period. If such information accumulates in the system, there is a possibility of forecasting the preferences and estimating the nearest consequences of the decisions.

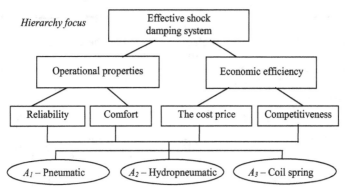

Fig. 1.1. Hierarchy of criteria for a choice of vibroisolation systems

Example of use of a hierarchy analysis method

Let us consider an application of a hierarchical analysis method with dynamic preferences for forecasting suitability of three alternate shock absorbers. Period of forecasting is $t = 1...5$ years. The hierarchy of quality criteria is showed on Fig. 1.1. Alternatives are: A_1 — pneumatic vibration damper, A_2 — hydropneumatic damper, A_3 — coil spring. The preferences, stated by the experts for criteria of quality and alternatives, are expressed by functions, being in Table 1.1, and are shown in Table 1.2.

9

Table 1.1. Expressed by functions

Function	The function description	Notes
Const	For any t $1 \leq const \leq 9$	Constancy of preference in time
$a_1(t) + a_2$	Linear function from t, inverse function — hyperbola	Linear increase of preference of one alternative before other in time
$b_1 log(t+1) + b_2$	Logarithmic growth	Fast increase of preference of one alternative before other up to some t, after which slow increase follows
$c_1 e^{c_2 t} + c_3$	Exponential growth or decrease $(c_2 < 0)$	Slow increase or reduction of preference in time, for which fast increase (reduction) follows
$d_1 t^2 + d_2 t + d_3$	Parabola	Increase up to a maximum, and then decrease (or on the contrary)
$f_1 t^n sin(t+f_2) + f_3$	Oscillatory function	Fluctuations of preferences in time with growing $(n > 0)$ or decreasing $(n < 0)$ amplitude
Accidents	Functions, having breaks, which it is necessary to specify	Extremely sharp changes of preferences intensity

Table 1.2. The preferences, stated by the experts for criteria of quality and alternatives

Reliability	Pneumatic	Hydropneumatic	Coil spring
Pneumatic	$y_{11} = 1$	$y_{12} = 1/y_{21}$	$y_{13} = 1/y_{31}$
Hydropneumatic	$y_{21} = 0.01 \cdot e^{1.1t} + 2$	$y_{22} = 1$	$y_{23} = 1/y_{32}$
Coil spring	$y_{31} = 0.5t+5$	$y_{32} = -0.5t+3$	$y_{33} = 1$

Comfort	Pneumatic	Hydropneumatic	Coil spring
Pneumatic	$y_{11} = 1$	$y_{12} = 1/y_{21}$	$y_{13} = 1.0 \cdot log(t+1)+3$
Hydropneumatic	$y_{21} = 0.01 \cdot e^{1.1t} + 3$	$y_{22} = 1$	$y_{23} = 1.0 \cdot log(t+1)+5$
Coil spring	$y_{31} = 1/y_{13}$	$y_{32} = 1/y_{23}$	$y_{33} = 1$

Cost price	Pneumatic	Hydropneumatic	Coil spring
Pneumatic	$y_{11} = 1$	$y_{12} = 3.8 \cdot log(t+1)+3$	$y_{13} = 0.4t+3.0$
Hydropneumatic	$y_{21} = 1/y_{12}$	$y_{22} = 1$	$y_{23} = 1/y_{32}$
Coil spring	$y_{31} = 1/y_{13}$	$y_{32} = -0.5t+7$	$y_{33} = 1$

Competitiveness	Pneumatic	Hydropneumatic	Coil spring
Pneumatic	$y_{11} = 1$	$y_{12} = 1/y_{21}$	$y_{13} = 0.25t^2+0.5t+1$
Hydropneumatic	$y_{21} = 1.0t+3$	$y_{22} = 1$	$y_{23} = 1.0 \cdot t^{0.7} \cdot sin(t+1)+5$
Coil spring	$y_{31} = 1/y_{13}$	$y_{32} = 1/y_{23}$	$y_{33} = 1$

Eigen vectors of pair comparison matrixes and convolution on the hierarchy were calculated numerically. It has enabled the achievement of functional dependenceof the priorities vector $w(t)$ concerning hierarchy focus (Fig. 1.2).

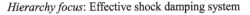

Hierarchy focus: Effective shock damping system

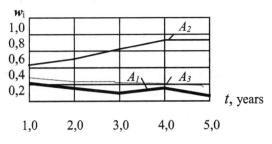

Fig. 1.2. Change of results priorities

The analysis of results show that the priority of hydraulic system (A_2) will grow; a coil spring (A_3) will monotonously be reduced; pneumatic (A_1) — will be wavy reduced.

Fuzzy sets in decisions making

The theory of fuzzy sets, as offered by [15], is applied to decision-making with success. The expert estimations of alternate variants on quality criteria may be submitted as fuzzy sets. For ordering fuzzy numbers there is a set of techniques, which differ from each other by the method used for convolution and construction of the fuzzy relations, which may be defined as the preference relations between objects. To choose the best variants on the criteria set it is necessary to have at one's disposal the information about criteria priorities and about the types of probable relations between them. The theory of fuzzy sets gives various means for taking into account the mutual relations of criteria: use of weight factors, fuzzy relations of preference, fuzzy logical reasoning on rules of definition of the best alternative and so on [16, 17]. Broad opportunities for representation of knowledge and the simplicity of computing procedures make this theory a very attractive tool for creation of computer applications for decision-making support. Thus it is necessary to carry out theoretical and experimental research of results obtained from systems with the purpose of checking their adequacy, consistency, reliability and so on. As described here, making decision systems involves a set of algorithms based on fuzzy set theory. One of the simplest approaches allows for determination of the best alternative by direct or weighed intersection of fuzzy sets, which describe quality criteria. The second approach uses fuzzy relations of preferences on a set of alternatives. A strict preference relation R expresses a degree of the superiority x_i over x_j; it has the following membership function:

$$\mu_R^S(x_i,x_j) = \begin{cases} \mu_R(x_i,x_j) - \mu_R(x_j,x_i), & \text{if } \mu_R(x_i,x_j) > \mu_R(x_j,x_i) \\ 0, & \text{if } \mu_K(x_i,x_j) \le \mu_R(x_j,x_i) \end{cases}, \quad (1.3)$$

where $\mu_R(x_i,x_j)$, $\mu_R(x_j,x_i)$ are the membership functions describing a fuzzy preference relation R defined on a set of alternatives $X = \{x_1, x_2, ..., x_N\}$. The fuzzy set of undominated alternatives is described by the next equation:

$$\mu_R^{UD}(x) = 1 - \sup_{x_i,x_j \in X} \mu_R^S(x_i,x_j). \quad (1.4)$$

Each preference relation R_k corresponds to some quality criterion. The resulting set of best alternatives $\mu_B{}^{UD}(x)$ is obtained by weighed intersection of initial fuzzy relations:

$$\mu_B^{UD}(x) = 1 - \sup_{x_i,x_j \in X} \sum_{k=1}^{m} w_k \left(\mu_{R_k}(x_i,x_j) - \mu_{R_k}(x_j,x_i) \right), \quad (1.5)$$

where w_k is a weight factor for corresponding relation R_k. When quality criteria are submitted as linguistic variables the different methods for ordering of fuzzy numbers are used. [15-17].

The methods of fuzzy logical reasoning are used in intelligent DSS, based on using expert knowledge. The facts in a such systems are submitted as fuzzy sets and fuzzy variables, and the rules are represented as fuzzy relations. A logical reasoning machine in such systems is based on the composition rule of inference and on the fuzzy correspondences. A rule of kind "If u is A then v is B, else v is C" is expressed by a fuzzy set R having the following membership function:

$$\mu_R(u,v) = \int_{U \times V} \left[(\mu_A(u) \to \mu_B(v)) \wedge (1 - \mu_A(u) \to \mu_C(v)) \right] / (u,v), \quad (1.6)$$

where

$$\mu_A(u) \to \mu_B(v) = \begin{cases} 1 & \text{if } \mu_A(u) > \mu_B(v) \\ \mu_B(v) & \text{if } \mu_A(u) \le \mu_B(v), \end{cases} \quad (1.7)$$

$\mu_A(u)$, $\mu_B(v)$, $\mu_C(v)$ are membership functions for the following fuzzy sets:

$$A = \int_U \mu_A(u)/u; \quad B = \int_V \mu_B(v)/v; \quad C = \int_V \mu_C(v)/v. \quad (1.8)$$

Decision making software application

The system of support for the dynamic decision-making processes in conditions of uncertainty described in the present work incorporate a database, a knowledge base, mathematical methods block, a knowledge extraction subsystem and multifunctional user interfaces. This system is built on application of known mathematical methods, which are developed and adapted for achievement of the following aims:

- The support of process multicriterial, multialternate choice, carried out on the basis of expert estimations, including automation of accounts, use of the information from a database, convenient user interface, formation of the problem-solving protocol, which is a detailed substantiation of received results;
- Formation of the databases, where initial information and results of problem-solving, relating to specific fields of knowledge are stored. Filling the database occurs in accordance with problem-solving in time;
- Maintenance of collective processes for making decisions;
- Estimation of the nearest consequences of the accepted decisions on the basis of forecasting experts' preferences, of possible changes of criteria priorities and alternative variants, establishment of tendencies of change of gravity of the factors, criteria, etc.;
- Reception of new knowledge on the basis of processing the information accrued in a database.

In the mathematical methods block described above, a decision-making system uses the standard procedures of a hierarchies analysis method. Application of this method to solve a number of practical problems has required essentially the expansion a set of previously used mathematical methods; therefore, the following procedures are included in the system:

- Calculation of a priorities vector of alternatives, having quantitative measurement;
- Calculation of a priorities vector of alternatives, measured with linguistic standards;

13

- Calculation of marginal priorities vectors;
- The procedure of linear convolution on incomplete hierarchy (in which criteria are connected to various subsets of alternatives);
- Selection of functions and building of polynomials, approximated dynamics of preferences and priority changes, on the basis of the information, kept in a database;
- The numerical decision of the equation (1.2) for matrixes of any dimension, the elements of which are given by functions from Table 1.1, and reception of dependencies, describing $w(t)$.

Decision-making systems based on fuzzy sets involves all the above-mentioned approaches and methods.

Knowledge systematization and optimization in invention problems

Knowledge systematization of the inventions, rules for the formation of search instructions for designing databases and expert estimations on quality criteria for invention classes and on individual inventions render powerful support to the inventor when deciding on invention problems. Important problems concerning the new technical decisions in designing are:
- Search in design databases of rational analogues to the inventions under the optimized technical instruction,
- Makeup of functional and constructive attributes; search of the rational inventions in databases;
- Building of systematization of researched classes of inventions and forecasting of perspective directions of development of the inventions subclasses;
- Search for new inventions by a method of functional — structural analogy.

The development of invention knowledge bases is closely connected to the question of knowledge representation. Information about inventions is very complex and heterogeneous, therefore its representation is complex, too. In created applications we have used the following approaches:
- Invention knowledge's representation by semantic networks, by frames and by production rules.
- Decision-making methods;

- Image recognition techniques;
- Cluster analysis.

A pithy basis of combined knowledge representation consists of:

- Classification attributes and meanings of classification attributes, reflecting functional properties and design peculiarities of the inventions;
- Relations of a type "whole — part", describing multilevel hierarchical decomposition of the inventions into subsystems;
- Relations of a type "sort — kind", describing a variety of subsystems with similar main function;
- Relations of a type "reason — effect", establishing consistent logic procedures for sorting inventions attributes and their meanings during formation of search images and of search instructions as a reference to the inventions database.

Formation of information models
for invention knowledge base building

The process of construction of information models, constituting a foundation for a knowledge base on inventions, is represented by a pyramidal stratified structure (Fig. 1.3). The pyramidal structure is developed from the base to the pyramid top. The relations between elements of levels specify directions of transformation of information from the description of individual elements to the description of sets of elements, and from general concepts to concrete ones from the point of view of engineering design.

Cause-effect relations are realised in the combined model by sets of rules: "If the meaning of an attribute A is selected, go to the meaning of an attribute B". The expert preferences are generated on set technological, economic and other quality criteria for the individual inventions, stored in a database, and for classes of the inventions described by alternate classification meanings for attributes. Processing expert preferences (expert estimations, membership function) is supported by the decision-making system. The search of the rational inventions descriptions on a database is performed on the basis of classification attributes and/or of quality criteria.

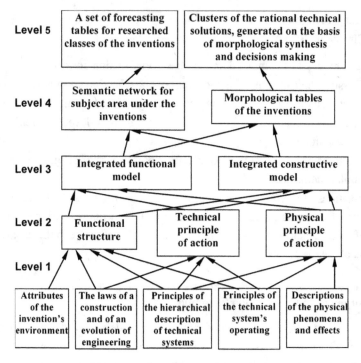

Fig. 1.3. Information models building

The search on classification attributes is carried out on the basis of the following relevance factors:

$$C_{F,K} = \frac{C_F \cdot \omega_1 + C_K \cdot \omega_2}{2}, \qquad (1.9)$$

$$m(R_1 \cap R_2) \ge \alpha \cdot m(R_2), \qquad (1.10)$$

$$m(R_1 \cap R_2) = m(R_2), \qquad (1.11)$$

where $C_{F,K}$ — measure of similarity on functional and constructive attributes simultaneously, which is calculated between a search image of the invention on a database and search instruction; C_F, C_K — measures of similarity for functional and constructive attributes determined independently; ω_i — weight factor; $m(R_i)$ — capacity of set R_i; R_1, R_2 — sets of classification attributes, describing search images of the current compared invention from a database and the search instruction; α — threshold factor, set by the researcher $(0 < \alpha < 1)$.

The search on quality criteria is reduced to the decision-making task. A set of quality criteria and their weight factors serves as the search instruction in this case. Alternatives of a choice are the descriptions of the inventions from a database. In this case the search images of the inventions are submitted by preferences of the experts on a set of criteria. With the help of a systematic dialogue mode, predicting systematics (Fig. 1.4 is an example) are built, allowing for new directions of search relating to the inventions.

Software for knowledge systematization

The computer application for invention knowledge ordering and optimization includes the following basic components:
- The user interface, ensuring convenient interaction of the designer with application;
- Knowledge base of subject area;
- Database of the textual and graphic descriptions of the inventions;
- Database functional-structural and functional-physical systematics for the inventions subclasses;
- Database of the descriptions of new physical principles of actions;
- Decision-making subsystem;
- Subsystem of image recognition and cluster analysis.

System for the synthesis of new engineering

The system of combinatorial morphological synthesis is used for solving the following problems:
- Synthesis of new original technical decisions on the basis of qualitative classification attributes, which describe functional and designed properties of the technical systems;
- Transformations of known analogues of designs to the new more rational decisions;
- Search in morphological sets finding the closest measure based on similarity criterion to the given reference decisions and classes of the technical decisions;
- Multicriterial synthesis of the multifunctional technical solutions concerning presence and/or absence of restrictions on the functional subsystems forming a complete design;

Function F(i)	Constructions of shock dampers			
	rubber	combined	torsion	pneumatic
F_1 — asymmetric characteristics 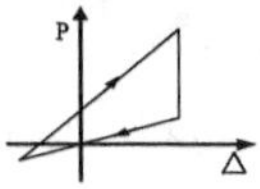		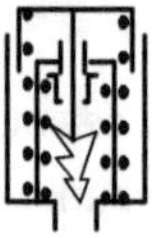		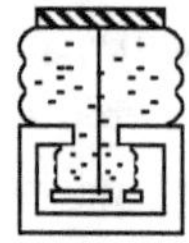
F_2 — adjustible curvature 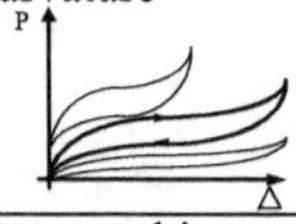	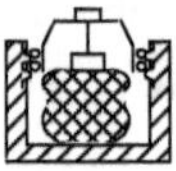	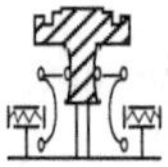	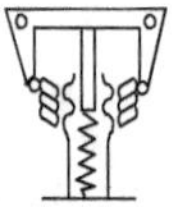	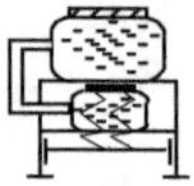
F_3 — multistep function 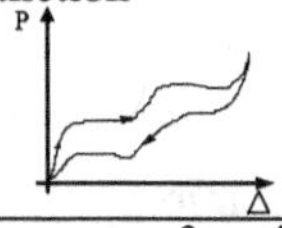				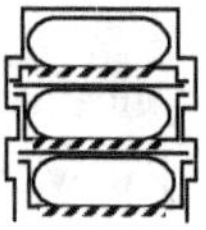
F_4 — step function 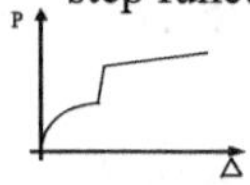	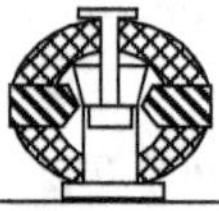	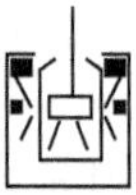		
F_5 — linear-piece function 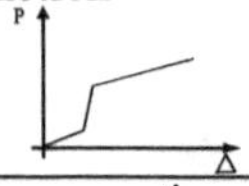	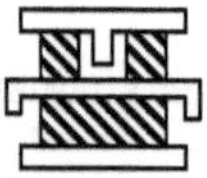			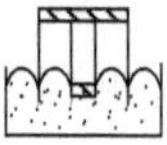
F_6 — negative rigidity 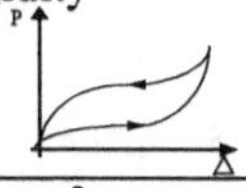	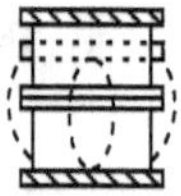	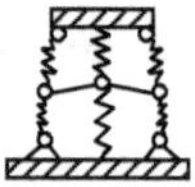	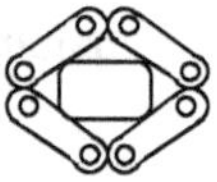	
F_7 — frequency dependent 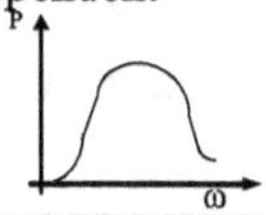				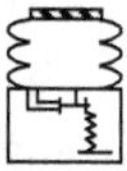
F_8 — amplitudes depression 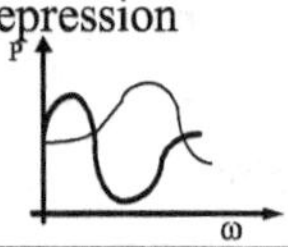	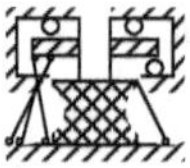	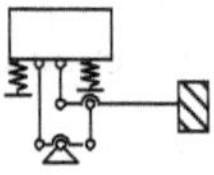		

Fig. 1.4. The functional-structural table for vibroisolation systems

18

- The analysis of morphological sets on various combinations of quality criteria with the purpose of revealing the strong and weak aspects in systems;
- The function-cost analysis and rational distribution of resources between alternatives.

The synthesis system is based on the following methods:
- Multicriterial morphological analysis and synthesis of systems;
- Intelligence synthesis on the rules of grammar;
- The theories of decision-making;
- Cluster analysis and recognition of images;
- Knowledge engineering.

Combinatorial morphological synthesis

The purposes of morphological synthesis of new rational technical systems consist of the following:
- generation and system research of a large set of known and new variants of technical systems from separate subsystems;
- realisation of diverse operations of variant's search for satisfaction with the requirements of the designer.

The morphological set of variants of the technical decision descriptions is represented in Table 1.3.

Table 1.3. Morphological set of variants of the technical decision descriptions

Functional subsystem (F_i)	Alternatives (A_{ij}) for realisation i	Number of realisation ways F_i
F_1	$A_{11} \, A_{12} \, ... \, A_{1k_1}$	k_1
F_2	$A_{21} \, A_{22} \, ... \, A_{2k_2}$	k_2
...	...	...
F_L	$A_{L1} \, A_{L2} \, ... \, A_{Lk_L}$	K_L

The general number of possible variants N, forming a morphological set is defined as the Cartesian product of alternative sets formed by each row of the morphological table.

The morphological synthesis is realised in a few stages.

Stage 1. Statement of the design purposes.

Stage 2. Building of the morphological table.

Stage 3. An estimation of alternatives in the morphological table (in a scale of the names of classified attributes or in a numerical scale on quality criteria).
Stage 4. Formation of the searching instruction and choice of target function.
Stage 5. Search of rational variants for problem-solving.

Synthesis of technical systems on the basis of quality criteria

It is possible to define two classes of problems soluble by a method of morphological synthesis on the basis of quality criteria. The first class of problems is connected to searching in a morphological set of the rational technical decisions on an additive or a multiplicate target function. The second class of problems is reduced to the problem of image recognition. The system variant that is most similar with the search instruction is found in a morphological set of subsets of technical system variants, in this case. The problem of searching in a morphological set of technical systems variants after the closest match to a given analogue is solved on the basis of a measure of similarity. It consist of finding subset $R \in \Omega$ elements of which are approximated by the following expression:

$$C(R_1^i, R_2) = \frac{2m(R_1^i \cap R_2)}{(1+u)[m(R_1^i) + m(R_2)] - 2um(R_1^i \cap R_2)} \to \max . \quad (1.12)$$

where $C(R_1^i, R_2)$ is a measure of similarity between the description of the synthesised variant R_1^i and the analogue or the technical project R_2; $m(R)$ — capacity of a set R; u — parameter of calculation technique of similarity measure $(-1 \le u \le \infty)$.

In the solution of applied design problems, the measure of similarity is formed in view of the various contributions from different quality criteria, by which functional subsystems are estimated and various contributions from a similarity measure are given by functional subsystems.

The target function in this case has the following form:

$$C(R_1^i, R_2) = \frac{2\sum\limits_{l=1}^{L}\sum\limits_{p=1}^{P} \rho_l w_{lp} \min(x_{lpm}^1, x_{lp}^2)}{\sum\limits_{l=1}^{L}\sum\limits_{p=1}^{P} \rho_l w_{lp} x_{lpm}^1 + \sum\limits_{l=1}^{L}\sum\limits_{p=1}^{P} \rho_l w_{lp} x_{lp}^2} \to \max . \quad (1.13)$$

where ρ_l is weight factor of functional subsystem or function (F_l); w_{lp} — weight factor of p'scriterion on estimation of subsystem F_l; L — the number of functional subsystems; P- the number of quality criteria; x_{lpm}^1 — estimation of alternative A_{lm}; x_{lp}^2 — estimation of functional subsystem F_l, belonging to the object representing the search instruction.

Synthesis of technical systems utilising classification of functional and constructive attributes

The classification attributes are used for the description of the technical system, but after problems relating to the inventions examination are solved. The examination is designed to reveal new functional and constructive properties of the system. It also searches the most original variants, having properties of essential novelty and competitiveness. In this case morphological sets of technical systems are described by classification attributes (functional — f_{ij} and constructive — k_{ij}). The rules of the description are the following: if an element (the alternative A_{ij}) is characterised by an attribute f_{ij} or k_{ij}, the search image of the given element contains unity, otherwise — zero. The analogue, that is which measure of similarity is calculated, is set in the same way. After determination of the analogue and morphological set, the generation of all variants on the basis of design elements contained in the morphological table, can be realised. The search attribute's images of generated variants are compared with attributes in the image of the analogue and a measure of similarity is calculated. Instead of quality criteria for comparison of TS variants classification functional fij and constructive kij attributes are used. Synthesised variants are sorted according to degree of affinity to the analogue. The variants closest to the analogue are given to the expert for more detailed analysis.

Morphological synthesis of technical systems on originality criterion

The progress in engineering is defined by innovation of new effective technical systems. Determination of the most original variant among a set of variants is a rather labour-consuming problem. Its solution is connected to the analysis and comparison of large numbers of classification attributes, describing functions and design features of TS.

The variant of a technical system, belonging to some set is the most original if it in the least degree is included in the structure of attributes found in all remaining variants from an examined set. The procedure of revealing procedure of the most original variants of TS is based on use of measures of inclusion (1.14) or of similarity (1.12) – (1.13). Measures of inclusion of set R_2 in R_1 and R_1 in R_2 is determined as follows:

$$V(R_2 ; R_1) = \frac{m\left(R_1 \cap R_2\right)}{m\left(R_1\right)}, \ V(R_1; R_2) = \frac{m\left(R_1 \cap R_2\right)}{m\left(R_2\right)}. \qquad (1.14)$$

21

The measures of inclusion are not symmetric, and inclusion of the description j into self is obviously:

$$m(R_j \cap R_j) = m(R_j).$$ (1.15)

The technique of revealing the most original variant of technical system in a morphological set is given by the following:

Step 1. On the morphological table the special algorithm generates all possible variants, forming a morphological set.

Step 2. For all variants forming a morphological set an asymmetric matrix of inclusion or a symmetric matrix of similarity is built.

Step 3. The eigen vector w of a matrix, constructed at the previous stage, is calculated.

Step 4. A subset of the minimum values in a vector w is found which correspond to the most original variants, that is *minima* of the target function are searched:

$$w = \{w_1, w_2, ..., w_n\} \rightarrow min.$$ (1.16)

The number of required elements n of a vector w is set by the researcher-designer.

Morphological synthesis on combinative novelty criterion

The criterion of combinative novelty numerically characterises for some classes of TS new combinations of functional subsystems, from which design is projected onto a complete and new system. This criterion is calculated under the following equation:

$$K_n = 1 - 2 \cdot \frac{\sum_{S=1}^{N-1} \sum_{P=S+1}^{N} K_{S_i, P_i}^{S,P}}{N \cdot (N-1)},$$ (1.17)

where N — number of functional subsystems or functions; S_i and P_i — are the numbers of elements in rows of the morphological table S and P accordingly, alternatives from $S \cup P$ have been integrated into the i's variant of TS; K — variable, which accepts value, equals 1, if the alternative from a row S and a column S_i has formed a known combination with an alternative of a row P and a column P_i, and the value of a combination was unknown earlier within the limits of a considered TS class.

The definition of combinative novelty criterion for each technical system is performed on the basis of matrixes of combinative links of alternatives. Principles for the construction of such matrixes follows. The morphological table, containing N rows is considered. Combinative links for every alternative from row i with alternatives contained in all other rows of the morphological table are marked. Further for alternatives of each pair of functional subsystems matrixes of combinative links for alternatives are built:

$$K^{ij} = \{ K^{ij}_{lr} \}, \, l = 1,\dots , n_i; \, r = 1,.., n_j \,, \qquad (1.18)$$

where n_i and n_j — accordingly number of alternatives in i and j rows of the morphological table. The number of matrixes $K = \{K^{ij}\}$ is determined under the formula:

$$N_k = N (N - 1)/ 2. \qquad (1.19)$$

Computation provides the designer with a subset of variants with the most significant values of combinative novelty criteria. From these variants the designer makes a final choice of the most acceptable decision.

Software for synthesis

An application synthesis contains the following algorithms:
- Multicriterial synthesis of rational variants and distribution of resources between alternatives;
- Synthesis of the new original decisions with use of classification attributes;
- Image recognition and identification of morphological sets on classes;
- Automatic construction of hierarchical classifications of morphological sets;
- Realisation of the diverse scripts from a choice of variations (lexicographic complete sorting, treelike, labyrinth and block-labyrinth search, evolutionary synthesis on the basis of cluster analysis).

The system includes knowledge and databases:
- Alternate functional subsystems of TS from various subject areas;
- Quality criteria;
- Classification attributes;
- Experts' preferences;
- Morphological tables and results of solved tasks.

Discussion

The development of computer approaches to the invention problem improves the efficiency of inventive labour and gives new opportunities for the research in this field. An improvement on inventive labour arises from automation of routine procedures for information processing.

Computer support of inventions enable researchers:
- To accept valid decisions;
- To carry out decisions forecasting;
- To implement the synthesis of rational TS variants;
- To perform the analysis of morphological sets of TS;
- To carry out a knowledge systematization of given TS class.

Formal methods of decision-making allow for the achievement of more objective evaluation of alternatives in comparison with the informal methods. This is connected with usage of the same methods and similar procedures for an evaluation of the alternatives. A formal approach permits generation of comparable results and the facility to see a difference between the experts. DSS sometimes cause a user to consider aspects which were not taken into account earlier. The main result of a such systems are the answers to the questions:
- What alternative is the best in view of a given set of quality criteria?
- Why is any alternative the best?

Intuitive decision-making by inventors does not often answer the second question.

DSS, filled knowledge, permits the carrying out of decision forecasting and the manufacture of a logical inference on the basis of this knowledge. Thus, DSS, filled knowledge, can work without an expert, consequently decision-making may occur automatically. Automatic decision-making is needed during the synthesis of TS. Computer support of a synthesis allows for an increase in the number of dimensions of a morphological set, therefore the important aspect of the problem is relieving the experts from evaluation of a huge number of synthesised TS variants.

The morphological synthesis method generates all possible TS variants, which are the combinations of considered elements. Some of the generated variants are unviable a *priori*, i. e. there are some restrictions on the combinations of some elements. So different kinds of restrictions on the elements combinations are present in developed applications for the TS synthesis. The simplest restriction is an addition to a database of an incompatibility matrix, that contains the numbers of elements which do not combine with each other. Incompatibility may be represented by a set of rules which is added to the set of rules describing a possible structure of synthesised TS. The synthesis utilising rules of grammar generates only viable TS variants. The most effective synthesis is realised by the intelligent synthesis system which generates TS variants at the base of a grammar including rules for building rational variants.

Software for the morphological analysis of generated TS variants allows one:
- To build hierarchical classifications for clusters determination of similar TS;
- To carry out an identification of generated TS variants to a given TS class or to some constructive standard;
- To reveal the most original TS variants in a given set of TS.

Software for knowledge systematisation allows for classification of inventive knowledge in functional and constructive attributes. Such an application also allows for the building of forecasting matrixes which characterise a probability density of different combinations of attributes. These matrixes show the most actively developing directions and poorly explored directions for considered TS classes. A probability of invention essentially increases in poorly explored areas of TS development. In addition multiaspect analysis and systematisation of a great number of inventions (thousands) is impossible without computer support. Software for knowledge systematisation ensures an opportunity to carry out searches of invention prototype descriptions on databases, with the aim of their further improvement. A search instruction is formed either as a set of classification attributes or as a set of quality criteria.

The described software for computer support of invention was used in designing of new shock dampers for an operator seat in a locomotive. Two rational variants were offered as a result of computer-aided designing. These new solutions and known variants of damper were tested in practice:
- Known pneumatic damper with a valve between pneumatic bellows and additional chamber (Fig. 1.5, pos. 4);
- New designed pneumatic damper with a valve of resonator type (Fig. 1.5, pos. 5);
- New designed pneumatic damper with a valve and inertial element (Fig. 1.5, pos.7).

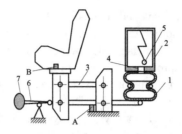

Fig. 1.5. A scheme of pneumatic shock damper:

1 — bellows; 2 — additional chamber; 3 — direction mechanism;
4 — a pneumatic valve; 5 — a resonator; 6 — transformation movement
mechanism; 7 — inertial element

In the process of research the accelerations in the vertical direction were registered by magnetic record system at the base of the system (Figure 1.5 point A) and at the mobile chair (Fig. 1.5 point B). The examined frequency was in the range from 0,5 Hertz to 40 Hertz. The dimensionless function for the absolute transfer coefficient $T_A(f)$ was calculated by the following equation:

$$T_A(f) = \sqrt{S_y(f) / S_x(f)}, \qquad (1.20)$$

where $S_y(f)$ and $S_x(f)$ are the estimations of spectrum density of accelerations at the entry (point A) and at the exit (point B) of the tested system. Results of the examination are shown in Fig. 1.6.

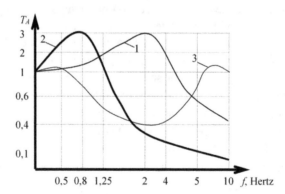

Fig. 1.6. The transfer function for transfer coefficient $T_A(f)$:

1 — Known pneumatic damper with a valve between pneumatic bellows and additional chamber; 2 — New designed pneumatic damper with a pneumatic valve of resonator type; 3 — New designed pneumatic damper with a valve and inertial element

The analysis of results demonstrates the improved vibroisolation properties of the new pneumatic dampers (variants 2, 3) in the range of low resonance frequencies in comparison with the known damper (variant 1).

1.2. Application of the AHP/ANP to invention problems

Introduction

Diverse technical devices and technologies determine the evolution of the technosphere that provides for the satisfaction of various needs of people including the quality of their lives. The rates of the technospheric evolution depend on the speed of creating both commercial use for the inventions and new spin-off technologies.

Until recently, inventing new subjects, including technical devices, was considered the destiny of prodigies, who use in the process their intuition, personal experience, the analogies taken from nature. However, in the middle of the 20th century the special methods for activating abilities and a systematizing procedures for analysis and synthesis of inventions began to thrive [18-20]. Most of these methods do not envisage an application of a formal method for quality assessment of the solutions created. Ways of applying the AHP/ANP for creative problem solving are given in [21-24].

This paper describes the outcome of applying the AHP/ANP to the solution of conceptual design problems including the following:

- Strategic forecasting the evolution of the mechanisms having a certain functional assignment;
- Choice of rational analogues and prototypes from databases;
- Synthesis and quality assessment of new conceptual solutions of the mechanisms;
- Evaluation of novelty by examining inventions.

Strategic forecasting of evolution of mechanisms

Forecasting challenging types of mechanisms

Such problem arises when it is necessary to determine what type of mechanism (or other device) is challenging with respect to further development and use. To answer this question a designer should have knowledge about different mechanisms with the same basic function. Databases containing information about mechanisms that have been studied are helpful in solving this problem. Making inventions databases containing the information on technical solutions of the mechanisms is one of the urgent problems in conceptual design. Descriptions of inventions often do not include parametric information. As a rule, they are represented by the text used and by graphic images. The most universal way of a representing such information in databases is the description of the technical solution by classifying the attributes, in particular the constructive and the functional ones [24]. In most cases, databases for storage and processing of information about the inventions are hierarchically organized. They contain thousands of descriptions of various mechanisms from different classes. Information on the inventions is represented with hierarchies of constructive and functional attributes and also by textual descriptions, graphic images, and expert estimates of different quality criteria.

There are two ways that can be used to determine the challenging types of mechanisms. First is to reveal the design directions that can lead to new solutions of the mechanisms. This task can be achieved through the use of a "discoveries matrix" that is the morphological table whose rows are the names of the basic functional attributes and whose columns include the names of basic constructive attributes. Basic attributes (functional or constructive) are those that are placed at the upper levels of the hierarchical database. Every cell of such a morphological table is a class of mechanisms that fulfils the function indicated in the row by means of the constructive mode indicated in the column. We look through the inventions in a database and put them into appropriate cells of the morphological table. After that we find out the empty cells that indicate possible directions for the "discoveries". If we wish to design a new mechanism we can select the most suitable direction using the AHP [21, 25].

The second way includes the following steps.

1) Cluster analysis of inventions from a database with the purpose to reveal the classes of mechanisms similar in constructive and functional attributes. Here we use the sets of attributes from the lower levels of a hierarchical database and classify the mechanisms, using appropriate similarity measures for comparing the attributes.

2) Revealing significant differences between the classes obtained by means of ANOVA/MANOVA. Here we try to find out the differences between classes with respect to various quality criteria, analyzing experts estimates of mechanisms from a database. Following that one can form a binary relation for the classes considered to discover what classes are better than others according to each criterion.

3) A choice of the challenging classes of mechanisms with use of AHP/ANP [26]. Thus we determine the direction for designing mechanisms with desirable properties and novelty.

We can use one of these ways or both to forecast the challenging mechanism types.

Forecasting change of requirements for inventions

The requirements for technical devices (mechanisms) change with time. This arises from appearance of new needs of people and also because of constant modification of the human values system. These reasons give rise to a changing of relative priorities of criteria used for quality assessment of the mechanisms and also an appearance of new criteria. The new inventions should be created taking into account the trends of the requirements changes if such trends are known. AHP can help to reveal trends of changing the requirements to the class of technical solutions under study [27]. For this purpose one can construct a hierarchy containing all the important criteria and then use it to evaluate an evolutionary set of alternatives, which includes the mechanisms created at different times with the same basic function. After evaluating the alternatives we can observe changes of their priorities with respect to the criteria. Usually the improvements by some criteria are accompanied by the deteriorations by other criteria. Thus the analysis of an evolutionary set of mechanisms helps to find out the trends of the criteria importance. These trends can change in future, therefore we carry out a marginal analysis of criteria by means of AHP.

Marginal analysis helps to reveal criteria that are most desirable for future improvements. By pairwise comparing the criteria, experts should answer the question: "Is an improvementthrough one criterion more preferred than a commensurate improvement by another, and how much more preferred?" If some important parameters deteriorate during the evolution it may be desirable to improve them in future. Thus we can determine the direction for perfecting the mechanisms.

The ANP is another mathematical method that can help to forecast changes in the requirements [26, 28, 29]. Analysis of the interdependence of various factors that influence the choice a challenging mechanism type by means of ANP enables us to find the type and the most important criteria (requirements).

Morphological synthesis and quality assessment
of new conceptual solutions of mechanisms

The synthesis of new mechanisms is needed when we cannot find required technical solution in the inventions database, or it is necessary to improve the properties of the existing prototypes. Let's notice that the search of rational analogues and prototypes in the inventions databases is carried out with use AHP for prioritization of selected attributes and criteria of quality.

Method of labyrinth synthesis

The method is meant for the invention problems with incomplete information on compatibility of the separate elements, which are included in a mechanism. The synthesis begins at a choice of the mechanism prototype, which is decomposed to the generalized functional subsystems ($GFSS_i$). After that one should form a morphological table whose rows names correspond to $GFSS_i$. The elements of each row are the alternative constructive embodiments of $GFSS_i$ indicated at the left.

Let's consider the example. Suppose it is necessary to design a vibroprotective mechanism for a car. This mechanism should satisfy the requirements of car users (drivers and passengers), manufacturers, and customers. The most important requirements of the drivers are: effective vibration isolation; safety; adjustment for different weight. The manufacturers require a high manufacturability, patentability, components availability and standardization. The customers requirements are: low cost; high reliability; compactness; low repair costs. Experienced designer has defined, what type of vibroprotective mechanism can fulfil these requirements. Such mechanism includes four functional subsystems: springing element ($GFSS_1$); guide mechanism ($GFSS_2$); vibration damper ($GFSS_3$); inertial vibration suppressor ($GFSS_4$). There are various constructive embodiments of these subsystems, which have different characteristics. We have selected the constructive embodiments shown in Fig.1.7 because of their off-the-shelf availability. The impact of each $GFSS_i$ into the quality (efficiency) of a whole mechanism was determined with use of AHP, therefore the rows of the morphological table are arranged according to decreasing of priorities of $GFSS_i$. We took into account two main criteria for $GFSS_i$: importance and effectiveness.

Morphological table

	Embodiments			*Priorities*
GFSS₁ Springing element	A₁ Air damper 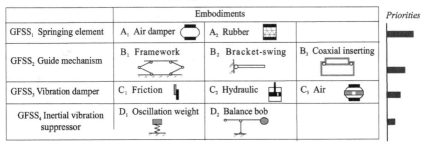	A₂ Rubber		
GFSS₂ Guide mechanism	B₁ Framework	B₂ Bracket-swing	B₃ Coaxial inserting	
GFSS₃ Vibration damper	C₁ Friction	C₂ Hydraulic	C₃ Air	
GFSS₄ Inertial vibration suppressor	D₁ Oscillation weight	D₂ Balance bob		

Fig. 1.7. Morphological table for the synthesis
of vibroprotective mechanism

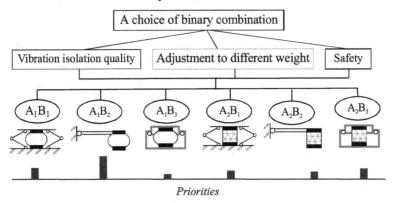

Fig. 1.8. The first step of labyrinth synthesis

An assemblage of new invention begins from joining GFSS₂ to GFSS₁, at that all pairwise combinations of alternative embodiments are generated. Then we make a choice of the best alternative, using AHP. In the Fig. 1.8 the best alternative is the combination A₁B₂, which is combined with all elements from the third row of the morphological table at the next step. A choice of the best ternary combination is made with use of a new hierarchy (see Fig. 1.9); such combination is A₁B₂C₃. The last step of labyrinth synthesis is shown in a Fig. 1.10, where we can see the hierarchy for a choice of the best vibroprotective mechanism composed of four functional subsystems.

The synthesis procedure continues until all the rows of the morphological table would be handled. The mechanism synthesized is examined for a satisfaction to the designing requirements. If these requirements are not fulfilled we can come back to the previous stages of the synthesis to take another alternatives.

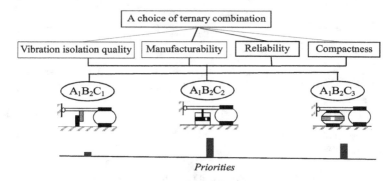

Fig. 1.9. The second step of labyrinth synthesis

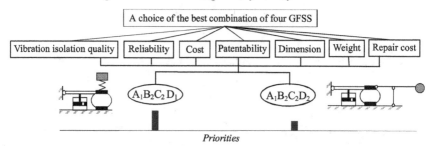

Fig. 1.10. The last step of labyrinth synthesis

Method of exhaustive treatment

An exhaustive treatment of all possible combinations, which can be synthesized in the morphological table, is reasonable at the invention problems with complete information. This implies the designer knows, what constructive elements embody each function by the best way and what of these elements can be combined together.

In this case the morphological table contains only compatible embodiments of $GFSS_i$. Every mechanism synthesized includes the only element from each row of the morphological table. The totality of mechanisms synthesized is called a morphological set; every element of this set differs from others at least by one constructive embodiment. We apply AHP to the analysis of a source information, using a proper hierarchy for each $GFSS_i$. Such hierarchies include the following levels:

1) Focus that is the main goal, namely: to find out the best embodiments for the $GFSS_i$;

2) Quality criteria level;

3) Alternatives level containing the embodiments of $GFSS_i$.

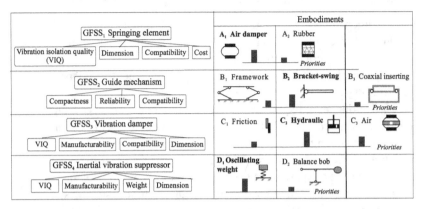

Fig. 1.11. Choice of the best embodiments for each GFSS

After pairwise comparing the criteria and alternatives we compute the priorities vectors and obtain priorities of alternatives concerning the hierarchy focus. Then we can find the best alternative embodiments for each GFSS$_i$. Since the embodiments of different GFSS$_i$ are compatible, then we can synthesize the best mechanism consisting of the best alternatives for each GFSS$_i$. Let's notice, that sometimes we can obtain several combinations if there is non-unique the best embodiment for some of GFSS$_i$. The alternatives with high and very close priorities values are supposed to consider as the best ones. Tendency to a high accuracy in this case can lead to a loss of challenging mechanisms. The mechanisms selected are developed at the further stages of designing.

Let's consider the example of synthesis with use of the morphological table shown in Figure 1. Suppose that all embodiments are compatible to a variable degree. We build the hierarchies for each GFSSi and choose the best alternative from the set of possible embodiments (see Fig. 1.11). The outcome is the mechanism that consists of the best alternatives. It is the same vibroprotective mechanism as in the previous example.

Let's notice that the exhaustive treatment of all possible variants, as well as the estimating them by the experts is not executed here. Application of AHP helps us to make simpler the problem of evaluating the synthesized (non-existent) mechanisms, reducing it to the estimation of existent constructive embodiments. Furthermore, this approach saves the experts from the time-consuming evaluation of a huge set of synthesized variants.

Synthesis method based on invention algorithm and AHP

Invention algorithm [18] includes the following main steps:

1) A choice of the subject researched (for example, a choice of a mechanism prototype from inventions database);

2) A revelation of shortcomings and engineering contradictions of the prototype;

3) Making up of requirements specification for the prototype improvement that is aimed at the shortcomings and contradictions elimination;

4) Determining the levels of requirements specification, i.e. desirable quantitative ratings for criteria characterizing a mechanism efficiency;

5) A choice of appropriate heuristic rules for the prototype improvement;

6) A transformation of the prototype with use of heuristic rules and then a forming a new set of inventions;

7) Analysis of new inventions and a choice the best of them.

Invention algorithm needs in information support in the form of a set of heuristic rules. The heuristic rule is a brief suggestion concerning a transformation of the prototype in order to improve its. In most cases the heuristic rule is not a well-defined instruction for a univocal transformation of the prototype, but a prompting, which can help to find a good solution without a guarantee. Any heuristic rule contains an advice for an improvement of certain properties of a mechanism and can be characterized by some estimate of its worth. The set of heuristic rules should be organized in some way for further using. This may be done by a generalization of the experience that the designers and inventors possess. We study inventors experience in the field of vibroprotective mechanisms, and the result of this study is the sets of relevant heuristic rules and important properties of these mechanisms. It was obtained by the following way. Vibroprotective mechanisms in the database were ordered in the form of some evolutionary chains (schemes) that demonstrate their historic development. The mechanisms in the evolutionary schemes were arranged so that each previous mechanism was a prototype for the next more perfect mechanism. Then the analysis of prototypes transformation in the evolutionary schemes was carried out. As a result of such analysis, the relations between the heuristic rules and the properties being improved were discovered. Besides, the expert estimates of a worth were assigned to each heuristic rule with respect to the improvements of certain properties. After that we could form the set of 150 heuristic rules, the set of 55 properties being improved, and the set of expert estimations of the worthof heuristic rules for an improvement of various properties of vibroprotevtive mechanisms.

34

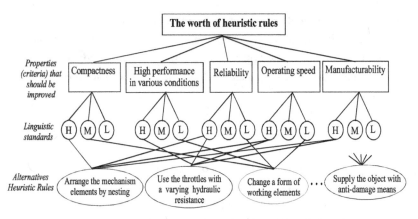

Fig. 1.12. General hierarchy for estimation of heuristic rules

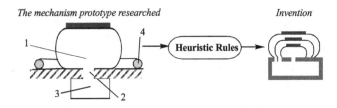

Fig. 1.13. Example of inventing the air damper

1 — compressed-air flask; 2 — throttle; 3 — auxiliary flask; 4 — buffer

Then heuristic rules and the mechanisms properties were systemized in the form of the general hierarchy shown in a Fig. 1.12. This hierarchy includes the following levels:

1 — Focus that defines the worth of heuristic rules for the improvement of mechanisms properties;

2 — Criteria level (criteria correspond to the mechanisms properties);

3 — Level of the linguistic standards, which are used for estimating alternatives;

4 — Alternatives level (heuristic rules).

At the solving of a specific invention problem we use a part of general hierarchy that includes only those criteria (properties), which should be improved for the mechanism researched.

Let's consider the example of invention problem. Suppose we wish to improve the competitiveness of the air damper (pneumatic vibroprotective mechanism) shown in a Fig. 1.13. Main shortcomings of this mechanism are a large overall dimension and low reliability. Our goal is the improvement of such properties (criteria) as a compactness, a reliability, and high performance at various conditions. For a solving of this problem we have used the part of general hierarchy that includes mentioned criteria and heuristic rules, which are connected with them.

For this problem the alternatives level includes the following heuristic rules:

1) Arrange the mechanism elements by nesting
2) Use the throttles with a varying hydraulic resistance
3) Replace a single object by a set of elements of the same type, but with various quantitative characteristics
4) Use the other mode of functioning
5) Replace a single-stage system by many-stage one
6) Use hydraulic fluids with electromagnetic properties
7) Change a form of working elements
8) Divide the object into two parts with different sizes, to place the part with large dimension outside the object workspace
9) Replace a reciprocation by a swinging movement
10) Use the materials having self-repair properties
11) Replace a monofunctional element by multifunctional one
12) Supply the object with anti-damage means

At first we determine the relative importance of criteria and then compute the priority vectors for heuristic rules. As a result we have found two heuristic rules: 1 — Arrange the mechanism elements by nesting; 2 — Use the throttles with a varying hydraulic resistance.

These rules help us to design a new air damper that includes the set of nesting flasks and some throttles with various hydraulic resistances.

Conclusion

Application of AHP to inventions problem gives an opportunity to analyse decisions researched with respect to multiple criteria. AHP/ANP are the effective mathematical method for systemic analysis and a formalization of poorly structured problems. Except decision-making support it can be used for a strategic forecasting, a searching of a relevant information in databases, and the analysis of mutual influences in complex systems.

1.3. An Intelligent System for the Evolutionary Synthesis of Compound Objects

Introduction

Evolutionary processes in natural systems were served as analogues of information processing methodsdeveloped for artificial systems. In this paper, the evolutionary approach to the problem of the conceptualdesign of compound objects is described. This problem is to develop a model of a certain system capable of performing specified functions with a given quality level. Requirements on the design object are formed in a higher level metasystem, which is an anthropogenic evolutionary system. For this reason, the purposes and requirements on the lower level system (subsystem) can change with time. Therefore, problems of the conceptual design of technical innovations, as well as of industrial or other systems, can be attributed to dynamical problems of making design decisions under conditions of uncertainty. In this case, uncertainty is characterized by multiversion and multicriteria nature and openness, i.e., continuous data exchange with the environment and the capability to change the properties and structure when environmental factors are changed (adaptability). Effective solution of such problems is based on the application of the evolutionary approach to design problems.

Information about changes in the environment is used to construct a pattern of behavior. Simulation data allows the generation of a time-dependent vector $R(t)$ of requirements on the designed system. On its basis, alternate systems $S1, S2, S3, \ldots$ are synthesized and a variant is selected such that it has the set of properties $P1=F(S1)$, $P2=F(S2)$, $P3=F(S3)$, $\ldots$, which are functions of the structure meeting the external requirements $R(t)$ in the best way.

When constructing the configuration of an entire system from simpler parts, environmental factors aretaken into account and the structure and composition of the system are selected so as to maximally satisfy the external requirements. In such a way, *natural selection*, one of the main principles of the evolutionaryapproach, is implemented. During the synthesis, separate elements are merged into larger objects, whichhave new properties and inherit some properties of the "parent" elements. Here, it is appropriate to use themechanisms of *inheritance, mutation*, and *interspecific recombination*, because the elements joined into the system can be described by different sets of properties. At every step, only elements that have no internal contradictions and good chances for "survival" in the environment are selected from the set of possible elements.

The problems of synthesizing compound systems differ from optimization problems. For this reason, inorder to solve them, it is necessary to modify wellknown genetic algorithms [30-32], because objects withvarious description structures are involved in the synthesis of a compound system, whereas only objectswith identical descriptions are considered in the optimization process. In other words, the composition of "populations" of synthesis objects is diverse; i.e., it contains a number of species, and interspecific crossing (recombination) is possible during synthesis. Moreover, the descriptions of synthesis objects are sets of structured data of various types rather than binary genetic sequences that are used in optimization algorithms. Therefore, synthesis involves the problems of generating description structures for descendants and choosing candidates for crossing, because crossing is possible only between certain species in a population. In well-known genetic algorithms, the problems of selecting parents and generating the descriptions of descendants are successfully solved by using random selection mechanisms. In synthesis problems, application of random selection and combination is limited.

The main stages of the evolutionary approach to the synthesis of a compound technical object are as follows.

(i) Creation of a population of initial objects of synthesis, which represents a set of alternative embodiments of functional subsystems (FSSs) that have certain properties and impose requirements on their environment within the system. A set of FSSs is formed on the basis of functional–structural or morphological analysis of the class under consideration [33]. The decomposition result may present an FSS set or a hierarchy of such sets.

(ii) Formation of a set of generalized requirements to the synthesized object that constitutes the viability or efficiency of this object. If the structure of the technical object is specified by a hierarchy, requirements on the subsystems having their internal structure are also formulated.

(iii) Generation of the criterion function for the variants of the technical object, which makes it possible to determine the degree to which the generated objects satisfy the specified set of external requirements. In the case of hierarchical representation, a set of such functions is used.

(iv) Selection of candidates and embodiment of the crossing operator, which allows both the creation of new objects (representatives of the next population) from the objects of the initial population and formation of their descriptions.

(v) Calculation of the criterion function for the variants generated and selection of the best variants from the new population on the basis of this function.

(vi) Testing of the conditions of synthesis process termination.

Presentation of knowledge about synthesis objects

We consider the representation of information in the evolutionary synthesis. Let the structure of the synthesized system S be specified by the graph shown in Fig. 1.14.

The variants of the complete system can contain no more than N elements Si, $i = 1, 2, …, N$. A variant of the complete system Vq uses $Nl < N$ elements if multifunctional elements appear in its structure. Knowledge involved in synthesis can include various characteristics described by the set of properties of every subsystem Si $Pi= \{Yi1, Yi2, …,\}$, where Ki is the number of properties of the i th subsystem, $i = 1, …, N$.

These characteristics are available, for example, from databases of engineering solutions [33]. In contrast to traditional binary genetic sequences, the properties of FSSs are represented by integer or real numbers, as well as by character strings or fuzzy sets. In addition to the set of properties, each subsystem is described by the set of requirements to its internal environment (to other elements): $Ri = \{Xi1, Xi2, …, XiMi\}$, where Mi is the number of requirements of the i th subsystem to other subsystems. The order of the mutual requirements of subsystems can be specified by a graph, which is exemplified in Fig. 1.15.

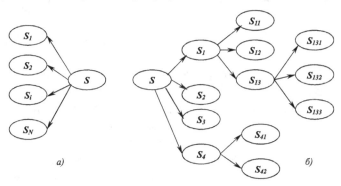

Fig. 1.14. Structure of the synthesized system

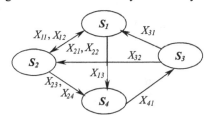

Fig. 1.15. Example of the graph of mutual requirements of the subsystems

39

In the matrix B representing the graph in Fig. 1.15, the elements correspond to the number of requirements that are imposed by the element Si indicated in the i th row on the element Sj indicated in the j th column. The first index of any requirement Xij coincides with the index of the subsystem (an element of the system) imposing this requirement, and the second index defines the ordinal number of the requirement in the list of requirements Rj.

It is important to specify the correspondence between the properties of an FSS and requirements that are imposed on it by other subsystems. To this end, correspondence matrices Ci are filled for every FSS Si. These matrices constitute an intermediate representation of synthesis objects, which is convenient for further processing. An example of the correspondence matrix is shown below:

$$
B = \begin{array}{c|cccc}
 & S_1 & S_2 & S_3 & S_4 \\
\hline
S_1 & 0 & 2 & 1 & 0 \\
S_2 & 2 & 0 & 1 & 0 \\
S_3 & 0 & 0 & 0 & 1 \\
S_4 & 1 & 2 & 0 & 0 \\
\end{array}
$$

$$
C_1 = \begin{array}{c|cccc}
S_1 & Y_{11} & Y_{12} & \ldots & Y_{1K1} \\
S_2 & X_{21} & X_{22} & \ldots & - \\
S_3 & X_{31} & - & \ldots & - \\
\ldots & \ldots & \ldots & \ldots & \ldots \\
S_N & - & - & - & - \\
X^*_1 & X^*_{11} & X^*_{12} & \ldots & X^*_{1K1} \\
\end{array}
$$

The first row of the correspondence matrix contains the properties of the i th subsystem. In the next $(N - 1)$ rows, the requirements imposed by other subsystems on the corresponding properties Si are given. The last row of the matrix Ci, $i = 1, 2, \ldots, N$, presents the results $(Xij\ ^*)$ of the combination of all requirements imposed on the j th property of the i th subsystem Xij, which are calculated after the substitution of specific values for the variables Xij during the synthesis. Alternative embodiments of every FSS are specified by a pair of arrays, where specific values of the properties $(yik j)$ and requirements $(xik j)$ are stored. The property values are numbers or text data, whereas the requirement values are constraints in the form of equalities or inequalities. In this representation, it is assumed that all alternative embodiments of the ith subsystem are described by the same numbers of properties Ki and internal requirements Mi. The total number of properties or requirements of every subsystem can be obtained by the combination of the respective characteristics of alternative embodiments Aij.

It is convenient to represent the descriptions of alternativeembodiments of an FSS in the form of the followingmatrices:

$$PA_i = \begin{array}{c|c|c|c|c|} S_i & Y_{i1} & Y_{i2} & \ldots & Y_{iKi} \\ \hline A_{i1} & y_{11} & y_{21} & \ldots & y_{K11} \\ \hline A_{i2} & y_{12} & y_{22} & \ldots & y_{K12} \\ \hline \ldots & \ldots & \ldots & \ldots & \ldots \\ \hline A_{iL1} & y_{1L1} & y_{2L1} & \ldots & y_{K1L1} \end{array}$$

$$RA_i = \begin{array}{c|c|c|c|c|} S_i & X_{i1} & X_{i2} & \ldots & X_{iMi} \\ \hline A_{i1} & x_{11} & x_{21} & \ldots & x_{M11} \\ \hline A_{i2} & x_{12} & x_{22} & \ldots & x_{M12} \\ \hline \ldots & \ldots & \ldots & \ldots & \ldots \\ \hline A_{iL1} & x_{1L1} & x_{2L1} & \ldots & x_{M1L1} \end{array}$$

Thus, the knowledge for evolutionary synthesis includes knowledge about an FSS from which the object is synthesized (vectors Pi, Ri, $i = 1, 2, \ldots, N$, matrix B, correspondence matrices Ci, $i = 1, 2, \ldots, N$); about particular embodiments of the FSS, which are represented by properties, requirements to the internal environment (sets of matrices PAi, RAi, $i = 1, 2, \ldots, N$); a set of external requirements on the synthesized object $RG = \{RG1, RG2, \ldots, RGM\}$, where M is the number of external requirements; and a set of rules and procedures for forming the descriptions of generated descendant objects.

The property values of the complete system that should meet the external requirements can be obtained by various methods. The attributes that are specified by quantitative estimates in the morphological synthesis approach are formed using additive and multiplicative convolutions [33, 34]. The logical approach to synthesis implies the application of predicate logic formulas (rules) for representing the characteristics of the complete system on the basis of the properties of elements, which expands the opportunities of information description but requires additional information [35]. The evolutionary synthesis approach allows various methods for obtaining parameters including mathematical and algorithmic functions and rules, as well as combined representation. The choice of a particular method depends on the amount of available information. Under lack of knowledge, the generalized additive or multiplicative criterion can be used to calculate the parameters. The procedure for calculating the components of the vector $PG = \{PG1, PG2, ..., PGK\}$ for the complete-system variant Vq can be specified, for example, as follows:

$$P_{G1} = Y_{11};$$

$$P_{G2} = \max_{si \in V_q}(Y_{i2});$$

$$P_{G3} = \sum_{i=1}^{N} Y_{i3};$$

$$(P_{G4} = \lambda_1) \rightarrow (Y_{21} \leq \lambda_2) \wedge (Y_{31} = \lambda_3);$$

$$\cdots \quad \cdots \quad \cdots \quad \cdots,$$

where λi are the constants determined in the synthesis specifications.

Implementation of the crossing operator

Let us consider the procedure of the combination of N elements with the different definitions that corresponds to the crossing operator in genetic methods for seeking optimal solutions. It is worth noting that a "descendant" in this case originates from N "parents." Selection of candidates for crossing is based on calculation of the degree of satisfaction of the mutual requirements of joined elements. For each element (FSS) of the synthesized object, the degree of satisfaction of the requirements of other elements that are candidates for entering the qth combination is calculated by the formulas

$$G_{qi} = \frac{1}{K_i}\sum_{j=1}^{K_i} L(X_{ij}^*, Y_{ij}) \quad \text{or} \quad G_{qi} = \sum_{j=1}^{K_i} w_j L(X_{ij}^*, Y_{ij}),$$

where $L(Xij^*, Yij)$ is a similarity measure between the jth property Yij of the ith FSS and the integrated set of requirements imposed on it by other elements, wj are the normalized weight coefficients of requirements on the jth property of the ith FSS, and Ki is the number of the properties of the i th FSS. A method for calculating the similarity measure depends on the type of description of the properties (descriptive, quantitative, or fuzzy) and on the kind of requirements (equality, inequality, or interval) and was presented in detail in [36].

Depending on the chosen compromise rule, a generalized estimate of the degree of satisfaction of mutual requirements of elements in the qth variant of the system is calculated either as the arithmetic mean

$$G_q = \frac{1}{N}\sum_{i=1}^{N}G_{qi} \quad \text{or} \quad G_q = \left(\prod_{i=1}^{N}G_{qi}\right)^{1/N}.$$

The additive function Gq vanishes only if all FSSs entering into the qth variant do not meet the requirements of other elements. The multiplicative function Gq vanishes when $Gqi = 0$ at least for one element in the combination. Therefore, the latter function is more effective for searching for alternatives with a high consistency of FSSs. When the additive function is used, the test for internal contradictions should be performed using some threshold Δ, $G_q \geq \Delta$. If the multiplicative function is used, the test may be realized for $Gq > 0$.

Thus, for every generated variant $Vq = \{A1i, A2j, A3k, ..., ANz\}$ of the system, the function Gq is calculated and, using the value of this function, one makes a decision whether such a combination of FSSs can exist. If this decision is negative, the variant Vq is not generated and is not included in the new population. Otherwise, the description of the resulting variant is generated using the corresponding procedure for determining the integrated properties of the object that will be involved in the further selection on the basis of the values of the function Fq reflecting the viability of the complete object in the environment. In such a way, the crossing of N heterogeneous objects is realized taking into account their consistency within a unified structure. It is worth noting that, in contrast to genetic algorithms, no exchanges of fragments of "chromosomes" occur in this case, because the definitions of elements are structured and diverse and mutual exchange by fragments of such definitions is senseless.

The description of a descendant obtained from N parents is generated using special procedures for calculating the properties incorporated in the knowledge base. If the combination of chosen embodiments of FSSs $(S1, S2, ..., SN)$ is allowed $(Gq > 0)$, the generation of the descendant Vq can be represented by the following grammatical rule:

$$S(P_{G1}, P_{G2}, ..., P_{GK}) \rightarrow S_1(Y_{11}, Y_{12}, ..., Y_{1K1}), S_2(Y_{21}, Y_{22}, ..., Y_{2K2}), ..., S_N(Y_{N1},$$
$$Y_{N2}, ..., Y_{NKN}), \{P_1 = Y_{11}; P_2 = \max(Y_{1j}, Y_{2j}); P_3 =$$
$$\sum_i Y_{i3}; ..., (P_L = \lambda_r) \rightarrow (Y_{3K3} < \lambda_u) \wedge (Y_{Nk} = \lambda_g)\}$$

$$\rightarrow S_1(Y_{11}, Y_{12}, ..., Y_{1K1}), S_2(Y_{21}, Y_{22}, ..., Y_{2K2}), S_3(Y_{31},$$
$$Y_{32}, ..., Y_{3K3}), \{P_1 = Y_{11}; P_2 = \max(Y_{1j}, Y_{2j}); P_3 = \sum_i Y_{i3};$$

$$..., (P_L = \lambda_r) \rightarrow (Y_{3K3} < \lambda_u)\}$$
$$\rightarrow ....,$$

where the braces contain examples of procedures for calculating the properties of a complete object in terms of the parameters of the elements. By means of such rules, information about the structure of descendants is represented. In the case of hierarchical synthesis, it is necessary to formulate the rules for generating the descendant descriptions for every population. With a lack of knowledge for rules construction, qualitative features can be combined and the values of similar quantitative features of the "parent" objects can be summed.

Selection of viable variants

After the procedure for determining the parameters of the complete system is formed, the criterion function for the variants can be calculated as a similarity measure between the vector of external requirements RG and the properties $PG(Vq)$ of a particular variant. The criterion function should present the viability of synthesized variants of the system in the environment. To construct it, it is necessary to formulate environmental requirements on the design object $RG = \{RG1, RG2, ..., RGM\}$, where M is the number of external requirements. These requirements are usually associated with the execution of a certain set of functions and with a specified quality level of the technical object. The requirements on the synthesized object can have the form of equalities or inequalities, which include the properties of the generated object $PG = \{PG1, PG2, ..., PGK\}$ and constants $\Lambda = \{\lambda_1, \lambda_2, ..., \lambda_H\}$, expressing the specificity of the synthesis specifications.

The generalized estimate of the satisfaction of the external requirements can be constructed as an additive or multiplicative combination of similarity measures

$$F_q = \sum_{j=1}^{L} w_j L(R_{Gj}, P_{Gj}^q) \quad \overset{\text{or}}{} \quad F_q = \prod_{j=1}^{L} [L(R_{Gj}, P_{Gj}^q)]^{w_j} \quad,$$

respectively, where wj are the normalized weight coefficients of external requirements and PGj is the value of the jth property of the qth variant of the system. The set of viable variants is constructed using the specified threshold Δ, and the best variants are determined by the maximum values $F^* = \max_{q \in \Omega} F_q$,

where Ω is the set of synthesized variants of the technical object. If the structure of the designed system is defined by a hierarchy, it is necessary to specify the criterion functions for all subsystems having a complex internal structure.

44

Evolutionary synthesis algorithms

Depending on the amount of information about the designed system and its complexity, evolutionary synthesis can be realized in various sequences. In the case of single-level representation of the designed system, the synthesis algorithm includes the following steps.

Step 1. Preparation and input of the initial information including the descriptions of FSSs in the form of a set of properties and requirements, a graph of mutual requirements of FSSs, and correspondence matrices of the requirements and properties. The procedure (grammar) of calculation of the parameters of the synthesized system in terms of the parameters of the components of the system is included in the knowledge base of the evolutionary synthesis system. A user should also generate a set of external requirements on the synthesized system.

Step 2. Generation of a variant Vq from N embodiments of functional subsystems randomly chosen from corresponding sets. If the cardinality of the sets of alternative embodiments of FSSs is low, a set of all possible variants of the complete system is generated by complete enumeration.

Step 3. Estimation of both the degree of satisfaction of requirements for every subsystem Gqi and the variant Gq.

Step 4. If $G_q \geq \Delta$, a description of the variant $V_q(P_{G1}, P_{G2}, \ldots, P_{GM})$ is formed using the procedure given for calculating the properties of the complete object. If $G_q < \Delta$, this variant is excluded from the population and the procedure returns to step 2.

Step 5. Calculation of the criterion function for the variant Fq and selection of viable variants on the basis of this function according to the condition $F_q \geq \Delta$ or by storing a given number of variants with the best Fq values.

Step 6. Repetition of steps 2–5 until the synthesis termination criterion is satisfied. Synthesis stops when the improvement of Fq values ends or when a certain number of steps is reached.

In the given algorithm, a single population consisting of the variants of the system that are obtained from N parents and contain N FSSs is formed. If the number of alternative embodiments of FSSs is large, this algorithm can include the preselection procedure of parents. It should be taken into account that parents have various descriptions. Therefore, their estimation requires the use of different criterion functions or estimates averaged over a set of quality criteria.

In the given algorithm, the presence of subsystems capable of performing several functions is disregarded. In the presence of such subsystems, the number of elements in the variants of the designed system can be $N1 < N$. The list of performed functions is included in the set of the properties of synthesis objects. The functions implemented by the complete system can differ from the joined set of functions performed by the subsystems. For this reason, the set of rules for forming the properties of the complete system (grammar) must be supplemented by rules for generating the complete system functions.

Furthermore, the presence of multifunctional elements is also disregarded. If such elements appear in the system, the number of its components can be reduced. For synthesis of objects with a variable numberof elements, the lists of functions performed by the synthesis objects are included in the description of these objects. If similar functions appear in this list, the elements providing duplication of functions can be eliminated from the design. In the list of requirements on the designed object, the functions for which the performance is obligatory are marked. When eliminating elements from the composition of the device, preservation of obligatory functions is controlled. These actions are performed at the second step of the given algorithm. Here, several variants differing in the number of elements are generated instead of one variant. Thus, synthesis objects are replaced by schemes in which free variables are optional functions.

The given synthesis algorithm is based on the simultaneous crossing of N elements and a one-step procedure for generating descendants. Let us consider an evolutionary synthesis mechanism using sequential combination of elements. In this case, the initial population of base objects and the set of populations of descendants are involved in the synthesis process. The sequential synthesis algorithm includes the following basic steps.

Step 1. Preparation and input of the initial information.

Step 2. Generation of the initial population of synthesis objects with or without the preselection procedure.

Step 3. Generation of new objects consisting of two elements. The process of combination of elements iscontrolled using the graph of mutual internal requirements. Two objects are combined if they are connected. If the requirement graph is disconnected, the disconnected nodes are involved in synthesis at the last stage. For problems of low dimension, synthesis of all combinations is realized. If the number of elements is large, a population of a limited size is randomly generated.

Step 4. Testing of the coincidence of functions performed by the elements of the resulting combination. Ifa set of functions performed by one element is the subset of functions of another one, the combination isreplaced with the latter element and control is passed to step 7. Otherwise, the list of functions for the newobject is created. If the functions performed by the combined elements partially coincide, the duplicatedfunctions are marked in the list with a special label.

Step 5. Calculation of the estimates of the degree of satisfaction of requirements for every subsystem Gqi entering into the resulting combination and calculation of the generalized estimate Gq calculated by multiplication. If $Gq > 0$, the combination description Vq is generated by uniting the descriptions of the elements, as well as by including the indices of the included subsystems and the value Gq. If $Gq = 0$, the combination is excluded from consideration and the procedure returns to step 3.

Step 6. Formation of the properties of the new object using the specified rules and the set of itsrequirements on the environment by uniting the requirements of the parents.

Step 7. The variants passed verification at step 5 are included in the new population. Here, it is possible toapply an additional selection condition based on the generalized estimate using quality criteria.

Step 8. Testing of fulfillment of the requirements of the new population objects on the internal environment. If requirements are not all satisfied, the object is involved in further synthesis. The procedure passes to step 3, where the search for candidates for crossing is governed by unsatisfied requirements. Otherwise, the procedure passes to the next step.

Step 9. Testing of the completeness of the functions that should be performed by the synthesized system. If the representation of the generated variant contains all the specified functions, the description of the resulting object is included in the population of the final variants and the procedure passes to step 12. Otherwise, the procedure passes to the next step.

Step 10. Return to step 3, where new objects are generated by the addition of the elements of the initialpopulation to the members of the new population (the process is controlled by the requirement graph).

Step 11. Iterations of steps 3–10 until the synthesis termination criterion is satisfied. Such a criterion is the termination of going through the requirement graph including separate nodes.

Step 12. Selection of variants from the population of complete systems on the basis of the criterion function Fq. If $F_q \geq \Delta$, the description of the variant Vq is written to the destination file. For problems of low dimension, it is reasonable to perform complete enumeration. Otherwise, a specified number of variants with the maximum values of the function Fq are randomly selected.

Software for the intelligent evolutionary-synthesis system

On the basis of the comparative analysis of different database management systems (DBMSs) and software development environments, we conclude that it is appropriate to use the Caché postrelational DBMS (InterSystems Corporation) and the Borland C++ Builder development environment. The postrelational DBMS Caché combines a server of multidimensional data and a multifunctional application server. The main advantages of Caché are developed object technology; high performance of Web development, which is achieved by using technology of the dynamic generation of pages on Caché Server Pages (CSP); advanced language SQL; and the unique technique of data acquisition. These advantages promote the achievement of higher performance and scalability than those in relational technology. The Borland C++ Builder system provides rapid program development and debugging combined with the high efficiency of the resulting code. Since modern database servers are highly efficient and the chosen DBMS supports the extended query language SQL, which realizes complex procedural algorithms including cycles, branching, etc., it is possible to combine the client and server almost without any performance loss and to change complex three-tier architecture, which is superfluous in this case, with simplertwo-tier architecture. Since it is necessary to organize remote access to the system, as well as to ensure the security of stored data and high efficiency, a Web interface for nonprivileged users and special client software for the coordinator are separately realized in the system (Fig. 1.16).

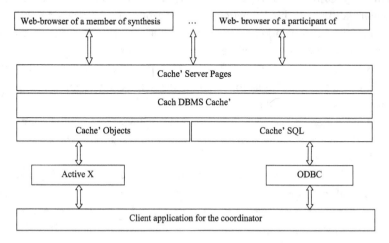

Fig. 1.16. Block diagram of the software system

The suggested structure of knowledge base was realized by creating a set of classes in the standarddesign tool Object Architect. The relational representation corresponding to an object model is automatically created by the system and is used when the SQL language for data access is more convenient. In other cases, the data is accessed using Active X technology. The main advantages of the suggested models for storing data and algorithms for accessing them that have been achieved at this design stage are as follows: recursive application of already created values of linguistic and fuzzy properties, as well as supersets for property sets, which makes it possible to save time of users for inputting the initial data and to reduce the size of the knowledge base; the cardinal number of the sets of properties and required values, as well as the cardinal number of the union and intersection of these sets, is calculated immediately on the server, which substantially reduces network traffic; the storage format developed for fuzzy values enables one to store the data very compactly in the form of membership functions and to access them very quickly; the pseudocode obtained by an optimizing interpreter when processing the calculated properties is stored in the database, which enables one to use it repeatedly and, thus, to considerably increase the system performance.

To create the Web interface for nonprivileged users, a standard tool Web Form Wizard, which uses the concept of Caché Server Pages (CSP), was applied. Pages are created and immediately filled with data (on-thefly); i.e., when they are demanded by a browser. Using this facility, templates have been created for CSP pages realizing the user interface with capabilities of data adding, editing, and searching.

The user interface of the client application of the coordinator is developed in Borland C++ Builder andincludes the following modules: the main module, task edit, properties of the class and requirement on the class, diagram, task execution, expression builder, and analysis of the outcomes. These modules enable the coordinator to create new tasks, to edit the data on properties and requirements of all objects, to perform diverse calculations, and to analyze the results effectively using both visual representation and sorting and filtering operations.

The use of caching of intermediate results and twodimensional indexation for access to the cache reducedthe time spent on performing tasks of medium complexity (about five different classes and five objects in a class) by a factor of 10 to 100 on average. For more complex problems, the gain is even greater and, if free main memory is sufficient, the efficiency of the cache (the ratio of the number of cases of the presence of a required value in the cache to the number of cases of its absence) increases almost exponentially. Caching of the properties and requirements, as well as the use of the optimizing interpreter, is aimed at excluding a sharp decrease in system performance when the calculated properties are actively used, which is often necessary when performing tasks. The developed representation format, as well as the transition to integer arithmetic in calculations, enables one to work very quickly and to deal with fuzzy representation of the initial data.

Example: synthesis of a vibration isolation system

Let us consider application of the evolutionary approach to structural synthesis of a vibration isolation system (VIS) for the operator of a locomotive. External requirements on the designed object are represented by the parameters of the performance specification, which are given in Table 1.4. Requirements of the specifications are imposed on the properties of synthesized variants of the VIS, which are calculated on the basis of data about the attributes of the elements of the VIS and connections between them. The calculated parameters of the complete VIS are presented in Table 1.5. The parameter *Func* is obtained in the process of synthesis by uniting the functions of subsystems. Redundant functions are excluded with the aid of the user performing the synthesis.

**Table 1.4. Requirements of the performance specification
on the synthesis of a VIS for the operator of a locomotive**

Characteristic of the VIS	Desig- nation	Possible values	Requirement of the specifications
Performed functions	Func	Generation of elastic force (EF), damping force (DF), stabilization (S), power control(PC), electric power consumption (EPC), pneumatic power consumption (PPC), hydraulic power consumption (HPC), energy absorption control (EAC), damage protection (DP), ...	$Func$ = [EF, DF, S, PC]
Fundamentalvibration frequency	FG	$0 \le FG \le 3.0$ Hz	$FG \le 1.2$ Hz
Transmission coefficient at resonance	TR	Low, medium, high	$TR \le$ low

Characteristic of the VIS	Designation	Possible values	Requirement of the specifications
Transmission coefficient beyond resonance	TN	Low, medium, high	$TN \leq$ medium
Intensity of damped vibration	U	Low, medium, high	$U \geq$ high
Energy control method	M	(1) Manual, (2) automatic	$M = 2$
Number of damped frequencies	KF	(1) One, (2) one and more	$KF \geq 1$
Possibility of rearrangement	VF	(1) No, (2) yes	$VF = 1$
Horizontal size	G_g	Small, medium, large	$G_g \leq$ large
Vertical size	G_v	Small, medium, large	$G_v \leq$ large

Table 1.5. Main parameters of the vibration isolation system

S	S_1	S_2	S_3	Specifications	Parameter	Possible parameter values
FG				FG^*	Fundamental vibration frequency	$FG = FS+FM+FD$
	FS				Natural vibration frequency of the resilient member	$0 \leq FS \leq 3.0$ (Hz)
		FM			Directing-mechanism-induced increase in the resilient member eigenfrequency	$0 \leq FM \leq 0.5$ (Hz)
			FD		Damper-induced increment in the resilient member eigenfrequency	$0.1 \leq FD \leq 0.5$ (Hz)
TR				TR^*	Transmission coefficient at resonance	$TR = T_1+DT_1$
TN				TN^*	Transmission coefficient beyond resonance	$TN = T_2+DT_2$

S	S_1	S_2	S_3	Specifications	Parameter	Possible parameter values		
T_1					Transmission coefficient of the resilient member at resonance	$T_1 \geq 5$ high (3)	$3 \leq T_1 < 5$ medium (2)	$1 \leq T_1 < 3$ low (1)
	T_2				Transmission coefficient of the resilient member beyond resonance	$T_2 \geq 0.8$ high (3)	$0.5 \leq T_2 < 0.8$ medium (2)	$0.1 \leq T_2 < 0.5$ low (1)
		DT_1			Damper-induced change in the transmission coefficient at resonance	No (0)	Small decrease T_1 (-1)	Large decrease T_1 (-2)
		DT_2			The increment of the transmission coefficient with the resonance due to the damper	No (0)	Small decrease T_2 (1)	Large decrease T_2 (2)
U				U^*	Intensity of damped vibration	$U = \max(U1, U2)$		
	U_1				Intensity of damped vibration for the resilient member	$0 \leq U_1 < 15$ low (1)	$15 \leq U_1 < 20$ medium (2)	$20 \leq U_1 < 30$ high (3)
		U_2			Intensity of damped vibration for the directing mechanism	$0 \leq U_2 < 15$ low (1)	$15 \leq U_2 < 20$ medium (2)	$20 \leq U_2 < 30$ high (3)
N			N	N^*	Energy-absorption control method	No control (1)	Manual (2)	Automatic (3)
M	M			M^*	System power control under change in mass	No control (1)	Manual (2)	Automatic (3)
KF				KF^*	Number of resonance frequencies damped by the VIS	$KF = \min(K_1, K_2)$		
	K_1				Number of resonance frequencies damped by the resilient member	One (1)	One and more (2)	

S	S_1	S_2	S_3	Specifications	Parameter	Possible parameter values		
				K_2	Number of resonance frequencies damped by the damper	one (1)		One and more (2)
VF	VF			VF^*	Structure change possibility	No (1)		Yes (2)
G_g				G_g^*	Horizontal size of the VIS, m	$G_g = \max(G_{lg}, G_2)$		
G_v				G_v^*	Vertical size of the VIS, m	$G_v = \max(G_{lv}, G_3)$		
	G_{lg}				Horizontal size of the resilient member, m	$0.3 \le G_{lg} < 0.5$ Large (3)	$0.15 \le G_{lg} < 0.3$ Medium (2)	$0 \le G_{lg} < 0.15$ Small (1)
	G_{lv}				Vertical size of the resilient member, m	$0.3 \le G_{lv} < 0.5$ Large (3)	$0.15 \le G_{lv} < 0.3$ Medium (2)	$0 \le G_{lv} < 0.15$ Small (1)
		G_2			Horizontal size of the directing mechanism, m	$0.4 \le G_2 < 0.6$ Large(3)	$0.2 \le G_2 < 0.4$ Medium (2)	$0 \le G_2 < 0.2$ Small (1)
			G_3		Vertical size of the damper, m	$0.3 \le G_3 < 0.4$ Large (3)	$0.2 \le G_3 < 0.3$ Medium (2)	$0 \le G_3 < 0.2$ Small (1)

The specificity of the given method is the representation of knowledge about the synthesis objects in the form of sets of properties and requirements. The graph of mutual requirements of the FSS of the synthesized system is shown in Fig. 1.17, where S_1 is the resilient member (RM), S_2 is the directing mechanism (DM), S_3 is the damper (D), S_4 is the power controller (PC), and S_5 is an external power source (PS). The properties of the resilient member, their values for sets of embodiments used in synthesis, and the requirements imposed by other subsystems on the resilient member are given in Table 1.6. Tables 1.7–1.10 present the properties of other FSSs and the requirements imposed on them by the other elements of the projected VIS.

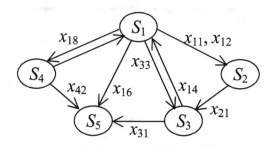

Fig. 1.17. Graph of mutual requirements of the VIS subsystems

Table 1.6. Properties of the resilient members ($S1$) and requirements imposed on them by the other functional subsystems

Property	Desig-nation	Properties of a resilient-member embodiment				
		A_{11}	A_{12}	A_{13}	A_{14}	A_{15}
Resilient-member type	Y_{11}	Pneu-matic	Pneu-draulic	Metallic	Metallic	Metallic
Operation methodof the resilient member	Y_{12}	Compre-ssion	Compre-ssion	Compre-ssion	Tension	Torsion
Elastic force	Y_{13}	[Small, medium, large]	[Small, medium, large]	[Small]	[Large]	[Medium, large]
Performed functions	Y_{14}	[EF; DF]	[EF; DF]	[EF, S]	[EF]	[EF]
Eigenfrequency FS	Y_{15}	1.5 Hz	1.2 Hz	2.0 Hz	2.0 Hz	1.5 Hz
Transmission coefficient at resonance T_1	Y_{16}	Medium	Low	High	High	High
Transmission coefficient beyond resonance T_2	Y_{17}	Low	Medium	Low	Low	Low
Intensity of damped vibration U_1	Y_{18}	Medium	High	High	High	High
Number of damped frequen-cies K_1	Y_{19}	2	2	1	1	1
Horizontal size G_{1g}	Y_{110}	1	2	1	1	1
Vertical size G_{1v}	Y_{111}	Medium	Small	Large	Small	Large
Vertical size G_{1v}	Y_{112}	Small	Medium	Large	Medium	Large
Requirements of the resilient member						
Damper S_3	X_{33}	(Y_{11}≠ rubber)∧(Y_{11}≠ pneudraulic)				
Energy source S_4	X_{41}	Y_{11}≠ rubber				

Table 1.7. Properties of directing mechanisms (S2) and requirements imposed on them by the other functional subsystem

Property	Designation	Values of the properties of a directing-mechanism embodiment		
		B_{21}	B_{22}	B_{23}
Increase in dynamic amplitude	Y_{21}	No (0)	Large (2)	Large (2)
Possible arrangements of the resilient member and damper	Y_{22}	[(1) vertical]	[(1) vertical, (2) inclined, (3) special]	[(2) inclined, (5) horizontal]]
Transmission ratio	Y_{23}	No (0)	High (3)	Medium (2)
Performed functions	Y_{24}	[S]	[S]	[S]
Increase in the eigenfrequency FM	Y_{25}	0	-0.5	-0.3
Intensity of damped vibration U_2	Y_{26}	Low	High	High
Horizontal size G_{2g}	Y_{27}	Small	Large	Large
Vertical size G_{2v}	Y_{28}	Medium	Large	Large
Requirements on the directing mechanism				
Resilient member S_1 on Y_{21}	X_{11}	$(Y_{12} \neq$ compression$)) \vee (G_{1v} =$ large$) \vee (Y_{21} > 0)$		
Resilient member S_1 on Y_{22}	X_{12}	$(Y_{12} \neq$ compression$) \vee (Y_{22} = 1) \vee (Y_{22} = 2)$ $(Y_{12} \neq$ tension$) \vee (Y_{22} = 2) \vee (Y_{22} = 5)$ $(Y_{12} \neq$ torsion$) \vee (Y_{22} = 3)$		
Resilient member S_1 on Y_{23}	X_{13}	$Y_{23} \leq m(Y_{13})$, where $m(Y_{13})$ — is the cardinal number of the set $Y13$		

The right column of Table 1.5 presents the methods for calculating the properties of the VIS on the basis of the attributes of its elements. In particular, the eigenfrequency of the system is calculated as the sum of the corresponding parameters of the elements, the number of dampened resonance frequencies is determined as their minimum, and the size is obtained as a maximum. Possible values of the parameters T_1, T_2, U_1, U_2, G_{1g}, G_{1v}, G_2, and G_3 are represented by the linguistic variables corresponding to the intervals of the measured quantities specified above them.

As embodiments of the resilient member, we use (A_{11}) a pneumatic cylinder vibration isolator with a throttle, (A_{12}) a pneudraulic vibration isolator, (A_{13}) a helical metallic compression spring, (A_{14}) a metallic tension spring, and (A_{15}) a metallic torsion element.

Table 1.8. Properties of dampers (S3) and requirements imposed on them by the other functional subsystems

Property	Designation	Properties of damper embodiment				
		D_{31}	D_{32}	D_{33}	D_{34}	D_{35}
Damper type	Y_{31}	Friction	Hydraulic	Hydraulic	Pneumatic	Electro-magnetic
Damping force	Y_{32}	[Small, medium, large]	[Small, medium, large]	[Large]	[Small]	[Small, medium]
Allowed spatial arrangement	Y_{33}	[(1) Vertical, (2) inclined, (5) horizon-tal]	[(1) Vertical, (2) inclined]	[(1) Vertical, (2) inclined]	[(1) Vertical, (2) inclined, (5) horizon-tal]	[(1) Vertical, (2) inclined, (5) horizon-tal]
Performed functions	Y_{34}	[DF, EAC]	[DF, EAC]	[DF]	[DF]	[DF, AC]
Increase in the eigenfre-quency FD	Y_{35}	0.5 Hz	0.3 Hz	0.3 Hz	0.1 Hz	0.2 Hz
Increase in the transmission coefficient at resonance DT_1	Y_{36}	-2	-2	-2	-1	-1
Increase in the transmission coefficient beyond reso-nance DT_2	Y_{37}	2	1	1	0	0
Number of damped fre-quencies K_2	Y_{38}	1	2	2	2	1
Number of damped fre-quencies G_3	Y_{39}	Small	Large	Medium	Medium	Medium
Requirements on dampers						
Resilient member S_1 on Y_{31}	X_{14}	($Y_{11} \neq$ pneumatic)$\vee$($Y_{31} \neq$ friction)				
Resilient member S_1 on Y_{32}	X_{15}	($Y_{13} \cap Y_{32}) \neq \varnothing$				
Directing mechanism S_2 on Y_{33}	X_{21}	($Y_{22} \cap Y_{33}) \neq \varnothing$				

Table 1.9. Properties of power controllers ($S4$) and requirements imposed on them by the other functional subsystems

Property	Designation	Values of the properties of a power-controller embodiment		
		E_{41}	E_{42}	E_{43}
Controller type	Y_{41}	Pneumomechanical	Electric	Mechanical
Control mode	Y_{42}	(2) Automatic	(2) Automatic	(1) Manual
Performed functions	Y_{43}	[PC]	[PC]	[PC]
Requirements on the PC				
Resilient member S_1 on Y_{41}	X_{18}	$(Y_{11} \neq$ metallic$) \vee (Y_{41} \neq$ pneumomechanical$)$		

Table 1.10. Properties of power sources ($S5$) and requirements imposed on them by the other functional subsystems

Property	Desig-nation	Properties of a power-source embodiment				
		K_{51}	K_{52}	K_{53}	K_{54}	K_{55}
Energy output type	Y_{51}	Pneumatic	Pneumatic	Electric	Hydraulic	Electric
Power	Y_{52}	High	Low	Low	High	High
Performed functions	Y_{53}	[PPC]	[PPC]	[EPC]	[HPC]	[EPC]
Requirements on the PS						
Resilient member S_1 on Y_{51}	X_{16}	$A_{11} : Y_{51} =$ [pneumatic] $A_{12} : Y_{51} =$ [pneumatic] $A_{13} : Y_{51} =$ not required $A_{14} : Y_{51} =$ not required $A_{15} : Y_{51} =$ not required				
Resilient member S_1 on Y_{52}	X_{17}	A_{11}: $[Y_{52} \geq$ low$]$ A_{12}: $[Y_{52} \geq$ high$]$				
Damper S_3 on Y_{51}	X_{31}	$D_{31} : Y_{51} =$ not required $D_{32} : Y_{51} =$ [hydraulic, electric] $D_{33} : Y_{51} =$ not required $D_{34} : Y_{51} =$ [pneumatic] $D_{35}:Y_{51} =$ [electric]				
Damper S_3 on Y_{52}	X_{32}	D_{32}: $[Y_{52} \geq$ high, $Y_{52} \geq$ low$]$ D_{34}: $[Y_{52} \geq$ high$]$ D_{35}: $[Y_{52} \geq$ medium$]$				
Power controller S_4 on Y_{51}	X_{42}	$E_{41} : Y_{51} =$ not required $E_{42} : Y_{51} =$ [electric] $E_{43}:Y_{51} =$ not required				

For synthesis of the VIS for the operator of a locomotive, we use the following three structures of the directing mechanisms: (B_{21}) a column, (B_{22}) a parallel link mechanism, and (B_{23}) a "scissors" link mechanism. As variants of the damper, we consider (D_{31}) a friction damper, (D_{32}) a hydraulic damper with controlled parameters, (D_{33}) a hydraulic damper without control, (D_{34}) a pneumatic damper, and (D_{35}) an electromagnetic damper. Three embodiments of the power controller, which are based on different operation principles, and five alternative external power sources are involved in the synthesis of the VIS. The number of variants of the five-element VIS that can be obtained by combination of alternatives is equal to 1125. If we consider various versions of the structure of the VIS with different numbers of elements, the number of variants increases significantly. As a result of evolutionary synthesis on the basis of the formulated performance specification (see Table 2) in the automatic mode with complete enumeration of all alternative solutions, 18 variants of the VIS were obtained, the characteristics of which are presented in Table 1.11.

Table 1.11. Characteristics of the synthesized variants of the VIS

Group of solutions	Structure of the variant	Characteristics of the variant
1	$A_{11}B_{22}D_{34}E_{41}K_{51}$ $A_{11}B_{22}D_{34}E_{41}K_{51}K_{52}$ $A_{11}B_{22}D_{34}E_{42}K_{51}K_{53}$ $A_{11}B_{22}D_{34}E_{42}K_{51}K_{55}$ $A_{11}B_{22}D_{34}E_{42}K_{51}K_{52}K_{53}$ $A_{11}B_{22}D_{34}E_{42}K_{51}K_{52}K_{55}$	$FG = 1.1$ Hz; $TR = H$; $TN = H$; $U = B$; $M = 2$; $VF = 1$; $KF = 2$; $Gg = B$; $Gv = B$ $Func = $ [EF, DF, S, PC, PPC] $Func = $ [EF, DF, S, PC, PPC, EPC]
2	$A_{11}B_{22}D_{35}E_{41}K_{51}K_{55}$ $A_{11}B_{22}D_{35}E_{41}K_{52}K_{55}$ $A_{11}B_{22}D_{35}E_{42}K_{51}K_{55}$ $A_{11}B_{22}D_{35}E_{42}K_{52}K_{55}$ $A_{11}B_{22}D_{35}E_{42}K_{51}K_{53}K_{55}$ $A_{11}B_{22}D_{35}E_{42}K_{52}K_{53}K_{55}$	$FG = 1.2$ Hz; $TR = H$; $TN = H$; $U = B$; $M = 2$; $VF = 1$; $KF = 1$; $Gg = B$; $Gv = B$ $Func = $ [EF, DF, S, PC, EAC, PPC, EPC]
3	$A_{12}B_{22}E_{41}K_{51}$ $A_{12}B_{22}E_{42}K_{51}K_{53}$ $A_{12}B_{22}E_{42}K_{51}K_{55}$	$FG = 0.7$ Hz; $TR = H$; $TN = C$; $U = B$; $M = 2$; $VF = 2$; $KF = 2$; $Gg = B$; $Gv = B$ $Func = $ [EF, DF, S, PC, PPC] $Func = $ [EF, DF, S, PC, PPC, EPC]
4	$A_{12}B_{23}E_{41}K_{51}$ $A_{12}B_{23}E_{42}K_{51}K_{53}$ $A_{12}B_{23}E_{42}K_{51}K_{55}$	$FG = 0.9$ Hz; $TR = H$; $TN = C$; $U = B$; $M = 2$; $VF = 2$; $KF = 2$; $Gg = B$; $Gv = B$ $Func = $ [EF, DF, S, PC, PPC] $Func = $ [EF, DF, S, PC, PPC, EPC]

All the synthesized variants are compatible and completely meet the requirements of the specifications.

The number of elements in the synthesized objects varies from 4 to 7. Among them, there are the variants containing three power sources. A pneumatic (A_{11}) or pneudraulic (A_{12}) resilient member with a high degree of vibration isolation and a wide range of the elastic force is used in the synthesized devices as the resilient member. We emphasize that the metallic resilient member whose quality parameters do not satisfy the performance specification does not appear in these variants. Only pneumatic (D_{34}) and electromagnetic (D_{35}) dampers, which are of high quality, are included in the resulting objects. The mechanical power controller E_{43} is not included in the results, because its manual control method does not satisfy the performance specification. The presence of power sources in the VIS is easily explained by the required types of energy and power.

The synthesized variants are grouped according to the values of the properties of the resulting system.

From the first group of solutions, it is reasonable to extrude the variants of the VIS with two pneumatic power sources $(K_{51}$ and $K_{52})$, suggesting that the highpower pneumatic source K_{51} is capable to provide power for both the resilient member and the damper. From the second group of variants, it is possible to exclude the variants with two electricity suppliers of different powers $(K_{53}$ and $K_{55})$, whose origin is explained by the presence of two FSSs requiring electric power supply: the damper D_{35} and power controller E_{42}.

The third group of solutions is characterized by the lowest eigenfrequency $(FG = 0.7$ Hz$)$. This group consists of the VISs with the pneudraulic resilient member (A_{12}) and parallel directing mechanism (B_{22}), which contain no dampers and differ from each other by power controllers and external power sources. Among the variants of this group, the variant A_{12} B_{22} E_{41} K_{51}, which requires no electric-power source and has the minimum number of elements, can be considered as most rational. The final choice of the best variant can be made using expert support systems [33] on the basis of the analysis of the set of relevant performance criteria.

The results evidently have shown the advantages of the evolutionary method, in which incompatible and ineffective variants are not synthesized. The use of the knowledge of designers during the synthesis enables one to overcome the difficult problem of the expert estimation of a huge set of non-existent objects. The knowledge incorporated into the intelligent system makes it possible not only to synthesize a foreseeable set of variants having the specified quality level, but also to solve the problems of examination of engineering solutions. To this end, it is necessary to realize the synthesis of the analyzed engineering solution in the "manual" mode, where the choice of acceptable embodiments is made by the user. If the variant under consideration contains some contradictions, they are found in the process of synthesis. If the variant is realizable, its characteristics are calculated.

Conclusions

An intelligent system has been proposed for the evolutionary synthesis of compound multivariate objects.

The system core is a method based on the application of the mechanisms of natural evolution for a combination of elements and selection of viable solutions. The feature of this method is that the descriptions of generated objects are created on the basis of the knowledge of experts, which is represented in the form of rules and functions, and the best solutions are selected using the generalized measure of similarity with specifications. The generated solutions have no self-contradictions and meet the external requirements. The system is invariant with respect to the synthesis object, and its application is the most actual for the synthesis of conceptual engineering solutions.

The expert knowledge that is incorporated into the system can be used repeatedly for solving problems in a certain subject region. The system enables one to obtain efficient and original solutions in a short time.

1.4. DSS for a collaborative decision-making with considering of mutual requirements of the choice subjects

Introduction

The traditional problems of collaborative decision-making are formulated as a choice of the best alternative from a set of possible alternatives (objects) on the basis of preferences expressed by the choice participants (subjects). Sometimes it is difficult to distinguish the objects from the subjects of a choice, as the inanimate objects often make certain demands to other subjects of collaborative decision-making. The individual choice may depend not only on decision-maker's preferences, but also on alternatives' requirements. An example is the known task about the grooms and brides [37]. Further we shall name such problems as the tasks with bilateral requirements. In practice such tasks are frequently reduced to the traditional ones by using the criteria, which describe requirements of the alternatives being chosen. For example, all the technical systems have some requirements to operation conditions, which in traditional tasks are taken into account by criteria *Operational properties, Resistance to mechanical damages* etc. Also the mutual requirements of the choice subjects may be represented as constraints [38]. The variants are supposed to be not acceptable, if the constraints are not fulfilled.

A representing of alternatives requirements in terms of constraints often leads to the elimination of alternatives making strong demands of the environment (decision-maker). Such approach is not always justified, because these requirements often are formulated with approximate or verbal values, which can be fulfilled in various degree for different decision-makers. Soft considering of the alternatives requirements allow to avoid a risk of rejecting the best alternatives.

The participants of collective choice can make demands not only to the alternatives being chosen, but also each other. Sometimes these requirements and the mutual influences determine a group choice, which can differ from the outcomes obtained without considering of such information. The approach taking into account mutual requirements of the choice subjects gives the results more feasible in practice. Besides, it enables to find out the reasons explaining why the group sometimes can choose alternative, which is not being the best objectively. At last, in collaborative decision-making problems we can generate and examine the various sets of complex alternatives. For example, when organizing of a joint enterprise one should consider a set of combinations, which include various output kinds being produced, industrial partners, investors, different technologies etc. Such problems emerge in virtual enterprises, both in a stage of their organization, and in a stage of functioning.

Decision making tasks with bilateral requirements

Let's consider a task with the bilateral requirements, where two sets A and B are described by properties and requirements. Each element from the set $A_i \in A$, $(i=1,\ldots, n)$ is characterized by a set of properties $P_{Ai}=\{P_{Aiz}\}$, where z is the index of a property, and makes certain demands $R_{Ai}=\{R_{Aiz}\}$ to the objects from the set B, where z is the requirement's index. Thus A is a set of the subjects (individuals) and B is a set the choice objects, which are described by the sets of properties $P_{Bj}= \{P_{Bjz}\}$. Each property is described by the name, type and value. The values may be expressed by the verbal, quantitative or fuzzy ratings.

The requirements are represented by the name, value's type, operation's type and value's range. The requirements correspond to desirable values of properties and are formed as the sets or the intervals given by equalities $P_{Bjz} = R_{Aiz}$ or inequalities $P_{Bjz} \leq R_{Aiz}$; $P_{Bjz} \geq R_{Aiz}$; $R_{Aiz}^{min} \leq P_{Bjz} \leq R_{Aiz}^{max}$, where z is index of a property (criterion), by which a comparison is carried out. The correspondence of the properties P_{Bjz} and requirements R_{Aiz} is based on the names coincidence, $Name(R_{Aiz}) \cap Name(P_{Bjz}) \neq \emptyset$.

The degree of the alternative's suitability is estimated as a generalized measure of subject requirements' compliance. To form a such estimation it is necessary to use dimensionless and commensurable values, for example, the similarity measures. When properties are represented with verbal ratings the similarity measure for the requirements of any kind can be calculated by the

formula $S_z(R_{Ai}, P_{Bj}) = \begin{cases} 1, & \text{if } R_{Aiz} \cap P_{Bjz} \neq \emptyset \\ 0, & \text{if } R_{Aiz} \cap P_{Bjz} = \emptyset \end{cases}$.

For quantitative values, a way of calculation of similarity measure depends on the kind of the requirement. For equalities $R_{Ai} = P_{Bj}$ one can use the measures

of similarity $S_z(R_{Ai}, P_{Bj}) = \dfrac{2\min(R_{Aiz}, P_{Bjz})}{R_{Aiz} + P_{Bjz}}$ or $S_z(R_{Ai}, P_{Bj}) = \dfrac{\min(R_{Aiz}, P_{Bjz})}{\max(R_{Aiz}, P_{Bjz})}$;

for inequalities $P_{Bjz} \leq R_{Aiz}$ and $P_{Bjz} \geq R_{Az}$, appropriate measures of inclusion

$I_z(P_{Bj}, R_{Ai}) = \dfrac{\min(P_{Bjz}, R_{Aiz})}{P_{Bjz}}$ and $I_z(R_{Ai}, P_{Bj}) = \dfrac{\min(P_{Bjz}, R_{Aiz})}{R_{Aiz}}$ can be applied;

for the requirements, given as intervals $R_{Aiz}^{min} \leq P_{Bjz} \leq R_{Aiz}^{max}$, the measure of par-

tial similarity $PM_z(R_{Ai}, P_{Bj}) = \min\left(\dfrac{\min(P_{Bjz}, R_{Aiz}^{max})}{P_{Bjz}}, \dfrac{\min(P_{Bjz}, R_{Aiz}^{min})}{R_{Aiz}^{min}} \right)$ can be

calculated.

When property P_{Bjz} is expressed by a fuzzy number, the similarity measures are calculated with use of the appropriate scalar indexes for fuzzy sets. Scalar index of similarity for equalities can be calculated as

$$S_z(R_{Ai}, P_{Bj}) = \frac{|R_{Aiz} \cap P_{Bjz}|}{|R_{Aiz} \cup P_{Bjz}|},$$

where $|X|$ designates the scalar potency of a fuzzy set X given on the basic set U: $|X| = \sum_{u \in U} \mu_X(u)$.

For inequalities, scalar indexes of inclusion are calculated as

$$I_z(P_{Bj}, R_{Ai}) = \frac{|R_{Aiz} \cap P_{Bjz}|}{|P_{Bjz}|} \text{ or } I_z(R_{Ai}, P_{Bj}) = \frac{|R_{Aiz} \cap P_{Bjz}|}{|R_{Aiz}|}.$$

The scalar index of partial similarity is applied for calculation of the compliance degree for requirements-intervals:

$$PM_z(R_{Ai}, P_{Bj}) = \min\left(\frac{|R_{Aiz}^{\min} \cap P_{Bjz}|}{|R_{Aiz}^{\min}|}, \frac{|R_{Aiz}^{\max} \cap P_{Bjz}|}{|P_{Bjz}|}\right).$$

We can use the various principles for obtaining of a general measure of requirements' compliance (sum, product, maximin). Let's consider additive principle for calculation of such generalized measure for i's participant A_i. This principle admits a compensating of low values by high ones, that is usually acceptable for one person. Then one can determine the best alternative for the subject A_i as

$$\max_j F_j^i = \max_j \sum_{z=1}^{l} w_z S_z(R_{Ai}, P_{Bj}),$$

where w_z is the weight factor for R_{Aiz}, and $S_z(R_{Ai}, P_{Bj})$ is calculated as measure of similarity, partial similarity or inclusion.

To find an alternative B_j, that is the best for all participants, we can use additive, multiplicative or maximin principle. This may be done by the following ways:

Additive: $\max_j \sum_{i=1}^{n} v_i \sum_{z=1}^{l} w_z S_z(R_{Ai}, P_{Bj})$ or $\max_j \sum_{i=1}^{n} v_i F_j^i$,

where v_i is the weight factor for i's participant.

Multiplicative: $\max_j \prod_{i=1}^{n} \left[\sum_{z=1}^{l} w_z S_z(R_{Ai}, P_{Bj})\right]^{v_i}$ or $\max_j \prod_{i=1}^{n} \left[F_j^i\right]^{v_i}$;

Maximin: $\max_j \min_i \left[\sum_{z=1}^{l} w_z S_z(R_{Ai}, P_{Bj})\right]^{v_i}$ or $\max_j \min_i \left[F_j^i\right]^{v_i}$.

In turn the objects from the set B can make demands to the subjects from A. Let's denote these demands as $R_{Bj} = \{R_{Bjk}\}$, $j=1,\ldots,m$. The scheme of such task is shown in Fig. 1.18, where the elements from both sets are the subjects and the objects at the same time.

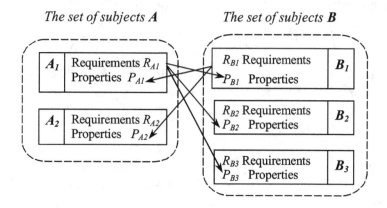

The set of subjects **A**   The set of subjects **B**

Fig. 1.18. The scheme of a task with bilateral requirements

In this case the following variants of the task statement are possible:

1. The ranking of all probable pairs composed from objects belonging to the sets A and B;

2. The ranking of the objects from the set B according to collective requirements of all subjects from the set A;

3. The ranking of the objects from the set A according to collective requirements of all subjects from the set B.

In the first case it is necessary to find the decisions $V_q \in A \times B$, which have the maximal degree of the mutual requirements satisfaction, i.e. max $F(V_q)$. The forming of an integral parameter characterizing the requirements' compliance includes two steps, which may be executed by different ways. The first step consists in a formation the generalized estimation F_j^i for each subject. The second step is a calculating of the degree of mutual requirements' compliance $F(V_q)$ for each variant $V_q \in A \times B$. We use additive principle for formation of F_j^i and multiplicative principle for computing of $F(V_q)$:

$$F(V_q) = \left[\sum_{z=1}^{l_i} w_z S_z (R_{Ai}, P_{Bj}) \right]^{v_A} \left[\sum_{z=1}^{l_j} w_z S_z (R_{Bj}, P_{Ai}) \right]^{v_B} \quad \text{or} \quad F(V_q) = [F_j^i]^{v_A} [F_i^j]^{v_B},$$

where v_A is the weight factor characterizing the contribution of A_i into general estimation, and v_B is weight factor for elements from the set B; l_i is the number of requirements for the subject A_i; l_j — the number of requirements for the

64

object B_j. The best variant V_q has a maximum degree the mutual requirements satisfaction $\max\limits_{A \times B} F(V_q)$.

If one would like to rank the alternatives from the set B, taking into account the requirements of all subjects from the set A and also the demands, which the alternatives make to these subjects, he can use the following formulas:

$$Additive:\ \max_j \sum_{i=1}^{n} v_i \left\{ \left[\sum_{z=1}^{l_i} w_z S_z(R_{Ai}, P_{Bj}) \right]^{v_A} \left[\sum_{z=1}^{l_j} w_z S_z(R_{Bj}, P_{Ai}) \right]^{v_B} \right\},$$

where v_i is the weight of i's subject from the set A.

$$Multiplicative:\ \max_j \prod_{i=1}^{n} \left\{ \left[\sum_{z=1}^{l_i} w_z S_z(R_{Ai}, P_{Bj}) \right]^{v_A} \left[\sum_{z=1}^{l_j} w_z S_z(R_{Bj}, P_{Ai}) \right]^{v_B} \right\}^{v_i}.$$

$$Maximin:\ \max_j \min_i \left\{ \left[\sum_{z=1}^{l_i} w_z S_z(R_{Ai}, P_{Bj}) \right]^{v_A} \left[\sum_{z=1}^{l_j} w_z S_z(R_{Bj}, P_{Ai}) \right]^{v_B} \right\}^{v_i}.$$

The ranking of the objects from the set A according to the collective requirements of all subjects from the set B may be done by the same way.

Example

Let's consider an example, which may be described by a scheme shown in the fig. 1.18. Suppose, a firm chooses employees for two kinds of activity. The set B includes three candidates, from which a choice should be made. The kinds of activity are the elements of a set A. Each candidate is described by the properties P_{Bj} (age, education, qualification, experience) and has certain requirements to the activity kind R_{Bj} (salary, responsibilities, location, opportunity of growth). Each kind of activity also is described by properties P_{Ai} and requirements to the candidates R_{Ai}. For shortness we do not give the concrete values of properties and requirements, and show only the values of additive measures of the requirements' compliance for each object from the sets A and B in the table 1.12.

The preferability of each candidate from B for each kind of activity A_i is shown in a Fig. 1.19. One can see, that the best candidate for A_1 is B_1, but this candidate prefers activity A_2 in comparison with A_1. The best candidate for A_2 is B_2, which prefers A_1.

Table 1.12. The additive measures of requirements' compliance

$F_j^i = \sum_{z=1}^{l_i} w_z S_z(R_{Ai}, P_{Bj})$		B_1	B_2	B_3
	A_1	$F_1^1 = 1.0$	$F_2^1 = 0.5$	$F_3^1 = 0.75$
	A_2	$F_1^2 = 0.3$	$F_2^2 = 0.83$	$F_3^2 = 0.5$
$F_i^j = \sum_{z=1}^{l_j} w_z S_z(R_{Bj}, P_{Ai})$		B_1	B_2	B_3
	A_1	$F_1^1 = 0.8$	$F_1^2 = 0.7$	$F_1^3 = 0.9$
	A_2	$F_2^1 = 0.9$	$F_2^2 = 0.5$	$F_2^3 = 0.7$

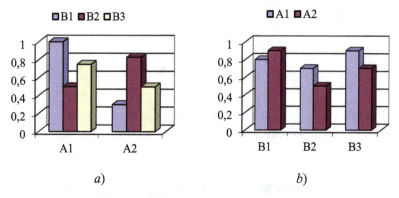

a)   *b)*

Fig. 1.19. The measures of requirements'
compliance for A_i (*a*) and for B_j (*b*)

Suppose, the choice of candidate is made with taking into account the requirements both of A_i. In other words, employer would like to select one person, who can manage both A_1 and A_2. Thus decision-making problem becomes collective. For combining of requirements of both subjects we can use different compromise principles. Besides, the subjects A_1 and A_2 can have unequal importance. Fig. 1.20 illustrates the results of collective choice.

One can see from Fig. 1.20, if the subjects A_1 and A_2 are equally important then all compromise principles give the same result, i.e. B_2 is the best alternative. But if A_1 is more important, we obtain another result: B_1 is the best decision by additive and multiplicative ways and B_3 — by maximin. The feature of maximin principle to select the alternatives with minimal disadvantages explains this fact.

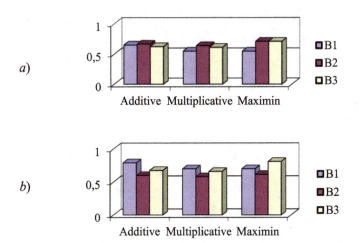

a)

b)

Fig. 1.20. The results of collective choice:
a) for equal importance of A_1 and A_2; b) for the case $v_{A1} = 0.7$ and $v_{A2} = 0.3$

Let's consider, what happens, if we take into account the requirements of the candidates from the set B. Suppose the employer's requirements are more important and have weight $v_A = 0.8$, while $v_B = 0.2$. A Fig. 1.21 demonstrates the results of collaborative choice with considering of candidates' requirements.

When taking into account the candidates' requirements, we can see that fitness of the alternative B_2 becomes less. It happens, because this candidate's requirements are satisfied less than others (fig. 1.19b). If $v_{A1} = v_{A2} = 0.5$, then the best alternative should be B_3, since it has the highest degree of compliance over all compromise principles. But if the weight of A_1 is more than A_2, then B_1 becomes the best candidate according to additive and multiplicative principles, although it is on the second place over maximin (B_3 remains the best).

So, we can conclude the following:

When one chooses the best candidate (B_j) for each activity (A_i), then the best for A_1 is B_1, and for $A_2 - B_2$.

If one selects one candidate for both of activities A_1 and A_2, the result depends on importance of A_1 and A_2 and on a compromise principle. Here we can say, that B_3 has the minimal disadvantages, but the overall evaluating by additive or multiplicative principle leads to the choice of B_1 in case when v_{A1} substantially more than v_{A2}. Otherwise the best candidate is B_2, even when $v_{A1} = v_{A2}$.

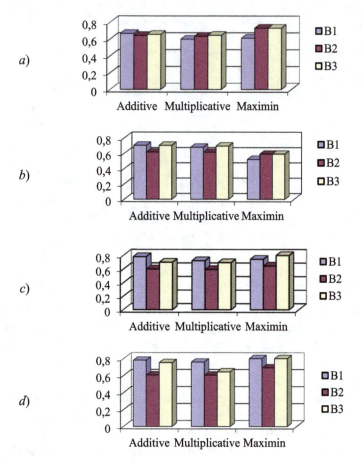

Fig. 1.21. The results of collaborative choice with taking
into account the alternatives' requirements:
a) v_A=0.8, v_B=0.2, v_{A1}=v_{A2}=0.5; *b*) v_A=0.8, v_B=0.2, v_{A1}=0.7 and v_{A2}=0.3;
c) v_A=v_B=0.5, v_{A1}=v_{A2}=0.5; *d*) v_A=v_B=0.5, v_{A1}=0.7 and v_{A2}=0.3

If taking into account the candidates' requirements, one should choose B_3 as
the best alternative by maximin and in case A_1 and A_2 have equal importance or
the weight factor for A_2 more than for A_1. When the weight of A_1 is substantially
more than A_2, the best candidate by additive and multiplicative principles is B_1.

Hence, the consideration of the alternatives' requirements can lead to
changing of a choice results. If alternatives' requirements are taken into account in decision-making, such decision is supposed to be more feasible in

practice. In example above, if the candidate B_2 will be taken, he can do his work without gusto or leave this job soon. Thus the firm, making wrong decision, can get losses and waste time.

Perspectives

The approach considered may be extended to the arbitrary number of subjects. Then we have a superset of subjects $Y = \{Y_1, Y_2, ..., Y_N\}$, where Y_i — a set of alternatives of i's subject. Each of alternatives is described by the set of properties $P_{Y_{iz}}$ and by the set of requirements to other subjects $R_{Y_{iz}}^j$, where z is criterion index; $i, j = 1, ..., N, j \neq i$ are indexes of the subjects. Collaborative decision is a combination of alternative subjects $V_q \in D$, $D = Y_1 \times Y_2 \times ... \times Y_N$ characterized by maximal degree of mutual requirements' compliance. Such way gives an opportunity to solve a problem of collective choice, and the result is complex decision being a tuple from relation D. The best decision may be found as $V_q = \max_D \prod_{\substack{i=1 \\ i \neq j}}^{N} \left[\sum_{z=1}^{Z_{ij}} w_z^j S_z(R_{Y_{iz}}^j, P_{Y_{jz}}) \right]^{v_i}$, where z is the requirement's index; w_z^i — weight factor for z's requirement of i's subject; Z_{ij} — the number of requirements from the subject Y_i to Y_j; $S_z(R_{Y_i^k}^z, P_{Y_j}^z)$ is the measure of similarity of the z's requirement from Y_i to the corresponding property of Y_j.

Making decisions under uncertainty we have to use expert information, which includes objective and subjective components. The representation of such information in terms of properties and requirements enables to distinguish the objective features of the decisions (properties) and the subjective preferences of the decision-makers (requirements). We can apply various techniques for information processing for the purpose of generating and ranking of collaborative decisions. Besides, approach proposed gives a chance to develop intelligent software based on structured knowledge bases containing objective data, subjective preferences, the rules for formation and evaluation of the decisions, and also the rules for the probable conflicts' resolution.

Discussion

The described technique is softer, than the known axiomatic methods for a collective choice [39], which often lead to the negative results. Suggested method is based on the concept of the requirements' similarity to properties, which is key in the designing problems. The requirements describe desirable properties' values and differ from the constraints in semantics. The best decisions are the closest to the given requirements. We have applied this technique in conceptual designing

[40], where sometimes it is impossible to compare real alternatives, because they do not exist at this stage. Thus a problem of the formation of technical solution's image, which has desirable properties, appears. For the solving of this problem it is necessary to determine the most important aspects of designing. After that one should create the set of project decisions and choose the best variant according with the certain compromise principle.

The representation of subjective preferences as requirements enables: 1) to avoid a labor-consuming procedure for direct comparison of the multidimensional alternatives; 2) to make a ranking of the alternatives on the basis of similarity with the collective requirements; 3) to take into account mutual dependences of the factors considered in decision-making problem.

1.5. International patent resources in the study of innovative technologies (at the example of GLONASS/GPS)

Background

Mankind has entered a new era when innovations determine the political, technological, economic strength of states and the quality of life of their citizens. In order that innovations to ensure increased labor productivity and commercial income, it is necessary at the pre-project stage of their creation to conduct system studies in the relevant technological subject area, to identify the general state and direction of innovative technologies development in the world and / or in the territories of individual countries, identify competitors and determine the directions of their activity, to collect information about what technological projects they are working on.

To solve such problems, innovative organizations around the world actively use international patent resources, since the patent is the first publication that can indicate a possible marketing plan of competitors, and 70–90% of information contained in patent documents is not published anywhere else.

The most complete collection of patents in the world, concentrating information from 67 countries and 37 international patent databases, is contained in the information resource Questel-Orbit [41].

Questel-Orbit is a division of the communications company France Telecom Group, which has been the leader of the information industry for more than twenty years, having a high rating in the field of providing data related to intellectual property and business.

This resource was used by us in researching innovations in the field of satellite navigation systems, which in the foreseeable future that will qualitatively change the situation not only in certain fields of activity, but throughout the world economy.

Objective

The objective of the authors is to consider international patent resources in research of innovative technologies development, using GPS — GLONASS samples as an example.

Methods

The authors use general scientific methods, comparative analysis, statistical method, evaluation approach, graph construction.

Analysis of GPS/GLONASS patents operating in the world

The market of global navigation systems is a market of goods and services using location and navigation based on GNSS (Global Navigation Satellite Systems) technologies. Active global satellite systems are GPS (USA), GLONASS (RF), DORIS (France), under construction: BeiDou (China), Galileo (European system).

GNSS is growing rapidly worldwide. The average annual rate of total revenue of the application market was 13% between 2010 and 2016. The global GNSS target market for segments is as follows: road sector — 54%, LBS — 43,7%, agriculture — 1%, surveying — 0,6%, aviation — 0,5%, shipping — 0,1%.

Thus, it can be stated that the bulk of the commercial revenues from space activities falls on telecommunications, television, navigation, etc., which are carried out using spacecraft and equipment installed on them. In this area (Global Navigation Satellite Systems) there is a large number of classes of the International Patent Classification (IPC), representing physics, electronics, information technology and mechanical engineering, so the search on the IPC does not allow selecting documents related to space. In this case, it is advisable to search for information on keywords, for example, GLONASS (GNSS, Global Navigation Satellite System) and GPS (Global Positioning System).

As a result of the query for the keywords «GNSS or GPS», the international patent resource Questel- Orbit issued 74439 documents 1, of which 53817 are valid documents, i. e. 72% of patent documents have legal force. Since all patent resources have limitations on the size of analyzed samples, the resulting set should be truncated, for which the priority date of the document was used — not earlier than 01.01.2004. As a result, 47 600 documents were received for the last 10 years (63% of the total), all of which are in force. The dynamics of the publication of information from this sample according to the «five-year plan» is shown inFig. 1.22 and Fig. 23, 1.24 show the leading countries of publication and rights holders.

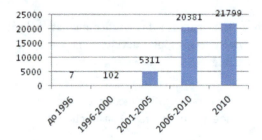

Fig. 1.22. Dynamics of publication of patent documents on GNSS / GPS

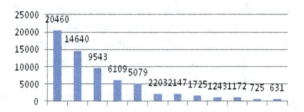

Fig. 1.23. Countries of publication of patent documents on GNSS / GPS

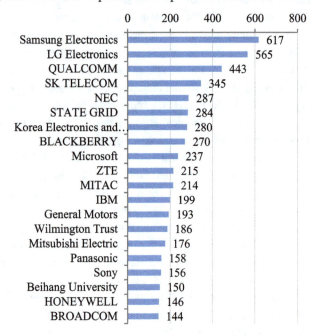

Fig. 1.24. Leading right holders of patent documents on GNSS / GPS

In the area under consideration, the largest number of patent documents is published in China, the United States is in second place, Japan is in the fourth after Korea, and Europe is in the fifth place. Russia occupies the 11th position with the number of publications 725.

The leading right holders are well-known manufacturers of electronics and telecommunications equipment from Korea, Japan and the USA.

Patents in force in Russia

From the sample of patents in the field of GNSS / GPS with priority after 01.01.2004, 1302 patents were published in Russia (without restriction on the priority date, 1628 documents were found, the analysis was conducted on a sample with a restriction).

The distributions of the patents published in Russia by the date of publication and the date of filing the first application are shown in Table 1.13. They show an almost exponential growth in the number of publications since 1998, with an annual number of primary applications half the total number of publications.

Table 1.13. Distribution of GNSS / GPS patents by the date of publication and the date of the firstapplication

Date	Number of patents		Date	Number of patents	
	by date of publication	by date of the first application		by date of publication	by date of the first application
1998	0	2	2006	91	39
1999	4	6	2007	117	62
2000	6	14	2008	137	70
2001	15	9	2009	191	87
2002	22	13	2010	230	121
2003	26	20	2011	285	122
2004	47	42	2012	285	95
2005	74	36	2013	258	43

Table 1.14 shows the distribution of patents by country of publication, from which it can be seen that almost half of the documents have international protection (WO, EP). The ranking by priority countries (Table 1.15) suggests that almost half of the published patents are foreign, since only 406 documents have priority of Russia (RU). Among the patents with the priority of Russia there are patents of the USA and other countries, which, as a rule, belong to foreign patent owners.

Table 1.14. Distribution of GPS / GNSS patents by country of publication

Country of publication	RU	US	WO	EP	CN	JP	CA	IN	AU	KR
Number of patents	711	337	334	327	297	227	218	190	187	163
Country of publication	RU	US	WO	EP	CN	JP	CA	IN	AU	KR
Number of patents	108	95	84	75	66	56	49	28	27	24
Country of publication	RU	US	WO	EP	CN	JP	CA	IN	AU	KR
Number of patents	23	23	20	17	17	14	8	8	7	7

Table 1.15. Distribution of GPS / GNSS patents by country of priority

Country of publication	RU	WO	OS	EP	DE	JP	KR	GB	AU
Number of patents	406	324	214	58	35	20	18	15	14
Country of publication	SE	FR	CN	IT	CA	BR	FI	NL	HU
Number of patents	9	7	6	5	5	3	3	2	2
Country of publication	NZ	AT	SG	LU	RT	TW	PL	ES	NO
Number of patents	2	2	1	1	1	1	1	1	1

The analysis of leading patent owners in the sample of Russian patents in the field of GPS / GNNS shows that foreign companies are leading in this area. Russian rights holders are relatively weak. Possible reasons may be related to the problem of the names of patent holders, as well as the inclusion of the term GPS in the request. Assuming that the Russian GLONASS navigation system (GNSS) is more relevant for Russian inventors, we made a selection of patents on the key word combination Global Navigation Satellite System (without limitation by priority date, but with restriction on the territory of the Russian Federation) and obtained a sample of 1364 documents. The distribution of these documents by publication date and priority date is presented in Table 1.16, where it can be seen that active patenting begins at the end of the 1990s and has an exponentially increasing trend, and the annual number of publications almost coincides with the number of primary applications, which leads to the idea of their domestic origin. Tables 1.17 and 1.18 show the distribution of

74

Table 1.16. Distribution of GLONASS patents by publication date and priority date

Date	Number of patents		Date	Number of patents	
	by date of publication	by date of the first application		by date of publication	by date of the first application
1994	0	3	2004	38	39
1995	1	9	2005	60	63
1996	7	10	2006	66	75
1997	10	9	2007	77	111
1998	16	12	2008	98	120
1999	13	24	2009	151	126
2000	24	25	2010	183	191
2001	24	27	2011	218	240
2002	29	30	2012	237	205
2003	31	33	2013	244	52

Table 1.17. Distribution of GLONASS patents by country of publication

Country of publication	RU	WO	US	EP	CN	JP	CA	IN	KR	AU
Number of patents	1349	90	61	58	52	39	39	37	26	24
Country of publication	TW	DE	ES	BR	AT	MX	FR	EA	IL	HK
Number of patents	18	18	13	13	10	9	8	6	6	4
Country of publication	NZ	PT	DK	SG	HR	ZA	AR	MY	NO	SE
Number of patents	3	3	2	1	1	1	1	1	1	1

Table 1.18. Distribution of GLONASS patents by priority countries

Country of publication	RU	WO	US	EP	FR	DE	CA	EA	JP	AU	SE	GR
Number of patents	1293	70	38	9	8	4	4	3	2	2	2	2

patent documents for the country of publication and the country of priority (origin) and confirms the hypothesis put forward, since out of the entire set, only 38 documents have priority in the USA, 9 in Europe, 8 in France, and so on. There are more patent publications in these and other countries, in particular in the United States, 61 patents, Europe — 68, China — 52.

Leading patent holders in the field of GNNS (GLONASS) on the territory — Moscow State Institute of Electronic Technology with 29 documents (without international protection), QUALCOMM (USA) with 22 patents, JSC Russian Railways with 18 patents of the Russian Federation, Russian Institute of Radio Navigation and Time (14 patents of the Russian Federation), the Open Russian Corporation for Rocket and Space Instrument Engineering (13 patents of the Russian Federation).

Analysis of technology patenting areas

In this section, the leading (with the greatest number of patents) subclasses, groups and subgroups of the IPC have been identified, in which inventions aimed at the application of GPS and GLONASS systems are patented. The analysis was carried out on territorial samples of patents received on requests with the keywords GLONASS, GNSS and GPS. Since detailed analysis is possible on a sample of not more than 15 000 documents, we have examined separately the samples of patents in the field of GNSS / GPS, published in different countries (in particular, Russia, China, the USA) and the world.

The total number of patents in leading subclasses is 1187 (sample size is 1364 documents). These subgroups are part of three sections of the IPC:

Section B — Various technological processes; Transportation (117 documents);

Section G — Physics (820 documents);

Section H — Electricity (250 documents).

The greatest number of patents is contained in the following subclasses and subgroups.

Subclasses:

G01S — Direction-finding; Radio navigation; Measuring distance or speed using radio waves; Locating or detecting objects using reflection or reradiation of radio waves; Similar systems using other types of waves (518 patents).

H04B — Signaling (170 patents).

G01C — Measurement of distances, horizons or azimuths; topography; navigation; Gyroscopic instruments; Photogrammetry or videogrammetry (92 patents).

G08B — Signaling devices or call devices; Command telegraph apparatus; Alarm system (63 patents).

B61L — Traffic control on railways; Safety equipment in railway transport (55 patents).

Subgroups:

G01S-19/00 — Satellite radio navigation positioning systems; Position, velocity or angular spatial position using signals transmitted by such systems (88 patents).

G01S-1/00 — Beacons and beacon systems that emit signals with characteristics that allow them to be detected by non-directional receivers and determine the directions and positions fixed relative to the beacons; Receivers for these systems (68 patents).

G01S-5/00 — Determination of the position by comparing two or more directions in one coordinate system; Positioning by comparing two or more distances in one coordinate system (54 patents).

G01S-5/14 — Definition of absolute distances to several spaced points with a known location (65 patents).

G01S-5/02 — Position determination using radio waves (64 patents).

H04B-7/26 — Radio communication systems, i. e. Systems using radiation for communication between two or more stations, of which at least one mobile (50 patents).

G08B-25/10 — Alarm systems with the transmission to the central station of signals that determine the location of the point at which the conditions that triggered the alarm have occurred, for example fire or police telegraph systems using radio communication systems (48 patents).

Table 1.19 shows the presence of patents in subgroups for the three samples studied: 1 — by the keyword GLONASS (1364 documents, all patents published in the Russian Federation); 2 — sampling by keywords GNSS or GPS in the territory of the Russian Federation; 3 — sampling by keywords GNSS or GPS in the United States. The decoding of the patent classes from Table 1.19 can be found in the patent database of the Federal Institute of Industrial Property (FIPS) [42].

The empty cells in Table 1.19 can be considered as potential technological (and commercial) niches. For example, in Russia there are 20 patent publications in subgroup B60R-25/00 (Vehicle equipment for preventing or detecting unauthorized use or theft of vehicles) with the use of GLONASS, and in the United States there are no such patents, and therefore, there is an opportunity to seize this niche.

Table 1.19. Comparative analysis of the leading IPC subgroups for patents in the samples GLONASS, GNSS / GPS (RF) and GNSS / GPS (USA)

Leading subgroups, included in top-50	Type of search query			Leading subgroups, included in top-50	Type of search query		
	GLONASS	GNSS/GPS in RF	GNSS/ GPS in the USA		GLONASS	GNSS/GPS in RF	GNSS/ GPS in the USA
	Number of patents				Number of patents		
B60R 25/00	20			G06F 17/00		29	924
B61K 9/08	12			G06F 17/30		19	773
B61L 25/00	33	19		G06F 17/50			849
B61L 25/02	12			G06F 19/00	11	37	
B61L 25/04	10			G06K 9/00			342
B63G 8/00	19			G06Q 10/00			478
B64G 1/00	11			G06Q 30/00			599
G01C 21/00	36	71	1608	G06Q 50/00			310
G01C 21/24	19			G07C 5/00	14	17	
G01C 21/26		25	452	G07C 5/08	12		
G01C 21/28		20	285	G08B 1/00			385
G01C 21/32		15		G08B 1/08			486
G01C 21/34		22	442	G08B 21/00			303
G01C 21/36		15	314	G08B 25/00	15		
G01C 23/00	37			G08B 25/10	48	22	
G01S 1/00	68	65	1053	G08G 1/00		14	365
G01S 1/02	12			G08G 1/01	16		
G01S 5/00	54	29	409	G08G 1/123	28	22	288
G01S 5/02	64	42	517	G09B 29/00		17	
G01S 5/14	65	72	746	G09B 29/10		17	
G01S 13/00	24			G09G 5/00			269
G01S 15/00	10			H01Q 1/00	10		
G01S 19/00	88	88	1947	H01Q 1/38	11		
G01S 19/01	13	15		H04B 1/00	14	15	367
G01S 19/05		18		H04B 1/06	15		
G01S 19/07	11			H04B 1/38	21	19	328
G01S 19/12		15		H04B 7/00	32	25	443
G01S 19/13	22			H04B 7/185	38	24	310
G01S 19/14	14	16		H04B 7/26	50	45	339
G01S 19/24	12			H04L 12/28		17	272
G01S 19/25	17	31	286	H04L 29/06			314
G01S 19/33	20	15		H04L 29/08			289

Leading subgroups, included in top-50	Type of search query			Leading subgroups, included in top-50	Type of search query		
	GLONASS	GNSS/GPS in RF	GNSS/GPS in the USA		GLONASS	GNSS/GPS in RF	GNSS/GPS in the USA
	Number of patents				Number of patents		
G01S 19/42	12	22	401	H04M 1/00		27	601
G01S 19/46		18		H04M 3/42			340
G01S 19/48		15	347	H04M 11/00	12	18	284
G01S 21/26		25		H04M 11/04			296
G01V 1/00		14		H04N 7/18			362
G01V 1/38	15			H04W 4/00			1155
G01V 9/00	12			H04W 4/02		32	1020
G01W 1/00	13			H04W 24/00		28	996
G05D 1/00	14	15		H04W 48/00		20	
G06F 3/00			384	H04W 56/00		17	
G06F 7/00			462	H04W 64/00	25	56	781
G06F 13/00	12			H04W 88/00		23	460
G06F 15/00			506	H04W 88/02		16	346
G06F 15/16			673	H05K 1/00	11		
				H05K 3/46	11		

We estimate how similar the leading subgroups of patents for each of the territories are to each other. We will define three classes of subgroups of patents. The first class «GLONASS» comprises leading subgroups of patents from the corresponding sample, the second and third classes are the leading subgroups of patents from GNSS / GPS samples published in the territories of the Russian Federation and the USA (classes GNSS / GPS RF and GNSS / GPS USA). For the analysis of classes, two types of signs are used: qualitative — the names of subgroups and quantitative — the names of subgroups and the number of patents in subgroups. Matrices of similarity of the classes considered, constructed for qualitative and quantitative characteristics using the Chekanovsky-Serensen similarity measure [43], are illustrated in Table 1.20.

Table 1.20. Matrices of similarity

Qualitative signs			
classes	GLONASS	GNSS / GPS RF	GNSS / GPS USA
GLONASS	1	0.46	0.3
GNSS / GPS RF	0.46	1	0.58
GNSS /GPS USA	0.3	0.58	1
Qualitative signs			
classes	GLONASS	GNSS/ GPS RF	GNSS/GPS USA
GLONASS	1	0.514	0.045
GNSS / GPS RF	0.514	1	0.072
GNSS /GPS USA	0.045	0.072	1

On qualitative grounds, the GNSS / GPS RF and GNSS / GPS USA classes are the most similar (0,58), the less similar are GLONASS and GNSS / GPS USA (0,30). The GLONASS and GNSS / GPS RF classes (0,514) show the greatest similarity in terms of quantitative characteristics, while the lowest is observed between the classes GLONASS and GNSS / GPS USA (0,072). A significant difference in the composition of patent subgroups in Russia and the US can suggest promising directions for development and take decisions on the international protection of domestic inventions abroad.

The analysis of the dynamics of the patenting of leading subgroups in the United States from 2000 to 2014 made it possible to identify the most promising subgroups (with the largest number of patents) over the past five years (2009–2013):

G01S-19/00 — Satellite radio navigation positioning systems; Position, velocity or angular spatial position using signals transmitted by such systems;

G01C-21/00 — Navigation; Navigation instruments;

H04W-4/00 — Services or features specifically designed for wireless communication networks;

H04W-4/02 — Services provided at the location of users or terminals;

H04W-24/00 — Control, monitoring or testing devices;

H04W-64/00 — Determine the location of users or terminals for network management, for example, mobile management;

G06F-15/00 — Digital computers in general;

G06F-15/16 — Combination of two or more computers, each of which is equipped with at least an arithmetic device, a software device and a register, for example for simultaneous processing of several programs;

G06F-17/00 — Devices or methods of digital computing or data processing specifically designed for specific functions;

G06F-17/30 — Information search; Database structures for this purpose;

G06F-19/00 — Devices or methods for digital computing or data processing for special applications;

G06Q-30/00 — Trade, such as shopping or e-commerce.

The analysis of patent groups revealed 68 leading groups in the samples studied. At the same time, groups that are absent in the territory of Russia are found, but are represented in the patent samples of other countries. Such groups are few in number, and most of them are related to electronics and information technology. The analysis allows to see the most current trends and competing countries, identify areas that are patented primarily in one country (for example, in group G05B19 (Program Management Systems) of 999 patents in the world sample 858 are published in China and do not fall into the top 50 patent groups in the samples for Russia and the USA).

The most promising in the US subclasses of the IPC (with the largest number of patent publications over the past twenty years) are as follows:

G06F — Digital data processing by electrical devices;

G01S — Direction-finding; Radio navigation; Measuring distance or speed using radio waves; Locating or detecting objects using reflection or reradiation of radio waves; Similar systems using other types of waves;

H04W — Wireless communication networks;

G01C– Measurement of distances, horizons or azimuths; topography; navigation; Gyroscopic instruments; Photogrammetry or videogrammetry;

H04B — Transmission of signals;

G06Q — Data processing systems or methods specifically designed for administrative, commercial, financial, managerial, supervisory or prognostic purposes; Systems or methods specifically designed for administrative, commercial, financial, managerial, supervisory or prognostic purposes not provided for in other subclasses;

H04M — Telephone communication;

H04L — Transmission of digital information, e. g. telegraph communication;

G08B — Signaling devices or call devices; Command telegraph apparatus; Alarm systems;

G08G — Vehicle traffic control systems;

H04N — Image transmission, e. g. television;

G06K — Data Recognition; Data representation; Data reproduction; Manipulation of information carriers; information carriers.

Conclusions

1. The international patent resource Qustel-Orbit allowed to reveal the state of innovative activity and patenting in the sphere of satellite navigation GPS-GLONASS for the entire period of patenting of inventions in the world until 2014. It was established that 74439 patent documents were issued, of which 53817 (72% of the total number of patents issued for the entire period) are in force today (have legal effect).

2. Dynamics of publications of patents in the field of GPS-GLONASS has an increasing trend. Inventions based on the use of satellite navigation systems have a wide range of practical applications. In the territory of the Russian Federation, such systems are used in 63 fundamentally different areas.

3. In the area under consideration, the largest number of patents is published in China, the United States, and Korea. Russia occupies the eleventh position in this row.

4. The leading right holders are manufacturers of electronics and telecommunications equipment from Korea, Japan, the United States.

Positioning algorithm

The method of positioning of patent holders is based on stage-by-stage processing of information according to the following algorithm.

Stage 1. Defining the scope of research and searching for patents in databases.

The identification and analysis of the areas of patenting of GNSS / GPS technologies by domestic and foreign organizations was carried out on patents published in the territory of Russia in the last ten years. A selection of patents was carried out using the patent resource Questel-Orbit and the system of the Federal Institute of Industrial Property (FIPS) [41, 42]. 236 patents have been revealed. During the analysis, for each of them, the year of publication, class, subclass, group and subgroup of the International Patent Classification (IPC), the patent owner, the scope of application and the technical result achieved — the objective of the invention have been recorded. All patent owners were divided into three groups: 1 — Russian patent owner organizations; 2 — foreign organizations-patent owners; 3 — patent holders — natural persons. A fragment of the preliminary systematization of patents is given in Table 1.21.

Table 1.21. Structure of preliminary systematization of patents

№ of patent (RU) Classes, subclasses, groups, subgroups	Name	Objective
2478049 B60M3/00	Power supply system ofelectriied AC railays	Establishment of an electric power supply systemfor electrified AC railways, which makes it possible to increase the accuracy of control over electric power consumption by electric vehicles by the movement, the condition of the track and the operating mode of the traction network and traction substations at the expense of control over the consumption of electricity by the electric rolling stock when moving along a separate section between adjacent traction substations of various power supply distances.

№ of patent (RU) Classes, subclasses, groups, subgroups	Name	Objective
2446065 B60M3/02	Information system for electricity accounting in traction networks	Increase in the accuracy of metering electricity consumption of traction networks.
2505861 G07C5/08	Device for control and registration of fuel consumption on a vehicle	The technical result of the invention is the creation of a device for control and recording of fuel consumption with a minimum measurement error, equipping it with protection from unauthorized access to ensure data reliability and fuel overexpenditure, and equipment safety; acceleration and simplification of data processing by storing them in the database format in the device itself, with the possibility of subsequent transmission of data selected according to a specified criterion to a stationary computer (server), in particular, in the event of accidents or mergency situations.
2513338 B61K9/08 E01B35/12	Method for assessing the state of the railway track	The technical result is to increase the reliability and efficiency of estimation of the rail track state by taking into account the synchronous action of the longitudinal forces in the train and the forces of interaction of the individual wheel and the railway track.

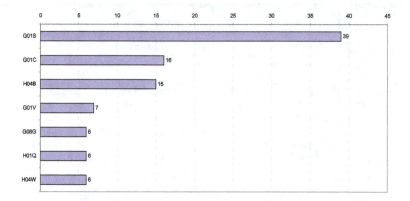

Fig. 1.25. The number of patent owners in classes

In Table 1.21, patent owners are ordered by classes, subclasses, groups and subgroups of IPC. This method of systematization shows potential competitors who patent GNSS / GPS technologies in the same patent classes, subclasses, groups and subgroups. Subclasses with the largest number of patent holders are shown in Fig. 1.25.

Based on the information summarized in Table 1, the total number of IPC classes patented on the territory of the Russian Federation can be established: classes — 29, subclasses — 63 (of which 50 cover organizations and 27 are individuals), groups — 116, subgroups — 194. For each class, subclass, group, subgroup, matrices of conformity with patent holders were established.

Matrix analysis showed that the range of coverage by individual organizations and individuals is: for subclasses — from one to eight, for groups — from one to twelve, for subgroups — from one to twenty-one. The range of coverage characterizes the level of diversification of organizations in various technological areas. The number of patent holders in one class indicates the importance and relevance of this direction. It can be considered as an indicator of the level of competition (scientific and technological and/ or market). Moreover, it should be noted that the directions that are relevant for the industry may have a low level of competition at the stage of formation (as a rule, during a short period).

It is of interest to compare the categories of patent holders by patent classes, which are common for them. For example, out of 63 subclasses, only 14 (22 %) are common for patent owners-organization and patent owners-individuals, which implies that individuals develop technological solutions that will rather not compete but complement technological solutions of strong market players in the form of organizations. A mutually beneficial «supplement» can be implemented through the patent licensing procedure.

Comparison of Russian patent owner organizations with foreign ones gives about 20 % of the total subclasses, which indicates a rather wide variety of Russian GLONASS applications, where there are no foreign patents on our territory yet. Large shares of foreign rights holders take place in subclasses G01C, G01S, H04B, H01Q, H04W, which cover the most significant features of satellite navigation — satellite positioning systems, navigation devices, signal transmission technologies, antennas, wireless communications.

Stage 2. For each organization, the nomenclature and the number of subclasses of the IPC are determined, for which it has patent publications in the territory of Russia. In this case, the total number of identified non-recurring subclasses is 63. The set of all non-recurring subclasses forms a set of attributes that are used to determine measures of similarity between organizations. The number of subclasses of IPC in patents of one organization characterizes the level of diversification of its scientific, technological and patent activities.

Stage 3. The pair-wise comparison of organizations is carried out and a measure of similarity is calculated for each pair, for example, according to the Chekanovsky–Sorensen formula [43]:

$$C(S_i, S_j) = \frac{2m(S_i \cap S_j)}{m(S_i) + m(S_j)},$$

where S_i, S_j, are the sets of subclasses of the IPC in the patents of organizations i and j respectively, $m(S_i)$ — cardinality of the set S_i.

Stage 4. The obtained values of similarity measures are recorded in the matrix of similarities of organizations.

Stage 5. The right main eigenvector of the similarity matrix is calculated, the values of which represent the levels of relative similarity of organizations.

The positioning of patent holders was based on indicators of the relative similarity of names and the number of areas in which patent holder organizations (individuals were not considered) patented inventions on the territory of Russia.

The field of patenting was defined as a subclass of the IPC. The category «subclass» is the most informative for conducting such an analysis. Analyzing subclasses, it is possible, on the one hand, to fully reflect the breadth of the organization's activity in terms of the diversity of application areas, and on the other hand, to obtain a fairly detailed idea of functional and constructive features of patented technical solutions. Descriptions of subclasses reflect the principal distinctive features characterizing the fields of application and the functional and structural features of inventions. In the descriptions of classes of IPC, insufficient and in the descriptions of groups and subgroups an excessive level of specification of inventions is used to obtain an informative map of positioning of patent owner organizations.

The characteristics of patent owners — organizations in the number of areas (in particular, subclasses) in which they patent invention, makes it possible to assess the level of diversification of their patent activities. Thelevel of diversification shows to a certain extent the level of the scientific and technological potential of the organization. If an organization patents its inventions in a large number of areas, it can be assumed that it has a fairly wide range of strategic technologies and its level of competitiveness in the market will be high in the long term.

The relative level of similarity shows how similar (close) is some object from the considered set to all its other objects according to a certain set of characteristics. In this case, the relative similarity of patent owner organizations was determined by a set of subclasses of IPC. Organizations with a high level of relative similarity have patents in subclasses that are present in a significant number of other organizations. The more organizations patent inventions in one subclass, the higher is the level of potential competition between them. Consequently, the indicator of relative similarity of patent owner organizations to the IPC subclasses allows to judge the level of existing or future competition in its sector. An organization with a high relative similarity index operates in an environment with a high level of competition and, conversely, an enterprise with unique technologies has a low relative similarity and operates in an environment with a low level of competition.

Stage 6. Individual organizations are grouped into clusters and groups. The organizations included in the group have the same or very close values of relative similarity index and the same number of characteristics — subclasses of IPC. Clusters are formed from groups of enterprises that have the same number of characteristics — subclasses. 15 such clusters were formed.

Stage 7. A map of positioning is being created, on which groups of enterprises are designated. The positioning map clearly shows in which area in terms of the level of diversification of patent activity and the level of competition (determined by relative similarity) are groups and clusters of organizations.

The positioning map of the patent owner organizations by indicators of the relative similarity of names and the number of subclasses of IPC is shown in Fig. 1.26. The values of relative similarity are plotted along the abscissa axis, and the number of subclasses and diversification levels are plotted along the ordinate axis. All 98 organizations in the analysis are grouped into 35 groups and 15 clusters in terms of relative similarity.

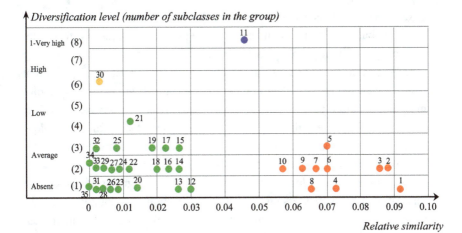

Fig. 1.26. Map of the positioning of groups of enterprises by the level
of diversification and relative similarity

Stage 8. The selected groups and clusters of organizations are described. Descriptions of formed clusters characterize the environment (patent) in which the enterprise is located. One or more groups may be present in one cluster. The groups in Pic. 1.26 are indicated by Arabic numerals, but can be described by the characteristics of the cluster to which they belong, with the addition of the semantics of the IPC subclasses included in the group. It should be noted that each of the IPC subclasses has the right to enter more than one group.

Types of patent owner organizations

On the positioning map (see Fig.1.26), it is possible to distinguish four types of patent owner organizations that differ in the level of diversification of technologies using GLONASS/GPS satellite navigation systems and the level of competition between them:

1 — organizations that own a large number of fundamentally different technologies and have a small number of competitors-patent holders of this type of technology; such organizations operate in the low-risk zone from the point of view of their displacement from the market or absorption by other organizations operating in the field of satellite navigation GLONASS/ GPS.

2 — organizations that own a large number of fundamentally different technologies, but have a large number of competing patent holders with similar technologies and therefore operate in a rather risky market segment.

3 — organizations that own a small assortment of fundamentally different technologies and have a small number of competitors with similar technologies, and therefore operate in the same risky segment as organizations of the second type, because in the long term they may lose in technological development to the more knowledge-intensive and innovative diversified organizations of the first and the second type.

4 — organizations located in an extremely risky segment of market and innovation activity, possessing a small diversification of technological activities and having a large number of competitive organizations with similar technologies.

Among the considered patent owner organizations using GLONASS/GPS satellite navigation systems, there are those, that are directly connected with railway transport. Table 1.22 shows the organizations and technologies (of corresponding IPC subclasses) that they own, organizations-competitors that have similar technologies, and groups and clusters that include all these organizations in accordance with the positioning map (see Fig. 1.26).

All organizations, patent owners in the field of GLONASS/GPS rail profile belong to the third type of organizations, that is, they own a small assortment of fundamentally different technologies and have a small number of competitors.

The most innovative technological competition in the field of GLONASS/GPS systems can be made by Russian patent holders possessing a higher level of technological diversification: Russian Open Society of Rocket and Space Instrument Engineering and Information Systems (JSC Russian Space Systems) (RU); 27th Central Scientific Research Institute of the Ministry of Defense of the Russian Federation (RU); JSC Avangard (RU); Taganrog Research Institute of Communications (FSUE TNIIS) (RU); International Academy of Ecology, Human and Nature Safety (RU).

On the other hand, when organizations that are directly connected with rail transport carry out an innovation strategy oriented at cooperation, competitors can become their strategic partners, having a synergistic effect from jointly created technologies and strengthening competitive positions in the territory of the Russian Federation, which will allow more effectively to prevent the penetration of foreign patent owners on the domestic market.

Table 1.22. Positioning of patent holders of GLONASS/GPS systems in the field of railway transport

Patent holder is directly connected with the railway transport (PRT)	Cluster (group), in which the patent holder is located on the positioning map (IPC subclasses, in which PRT inventions are patented)	Competing organizations that possess GPS / GNNS / GLONASS technologies similar to those of PRT	Cluster (group), in which the competing organization is located; (subclasses of IPC)
JSC Russian Railways (RU)	O (30) (B61K, B61L, E01B, E04G, G01M, H04M)	Joint-stock company Russian Corporation for Rocket and Space Instrument Engineering and Information Systems (JSC Russian Space Systems) (RU)	F (11) (B61L, G01C, G01M, G01S, G06F, G06G, G08G, H04B)
		Federal State Public Institution 27th Central Research Institute of the Ministry of Defense of the Russian Federation (RU)	L (27) (H04M, H04W)
State Educational Institution of Higher Professional Education Omsk State Transport University (RU)	L (33) (B60M, B63C)	State Educational Institution of Higher Professional Education Far Eastern State Transport University (FESTU) (RU)	K(31) (B60M)
State Educational Institution of Higher Professional Education Far Eastern State Transport University (FESTU) (RU)	K (31) (B60M)	State Educational Institution of Higher Professional Education Omsk State Transport University (RU)	L (33) (B60M, B63C)
Joint Stock Company Tver Wagon Works (JSC TVZ) (RU)	P (35) (B61D)		
Joint-Stock Company Research and Design and Technological Institute of Rolling Stock (JSC VNIKTI) (RU)	K (26) (G07C)	Joint-Stock Company Avangard (RU) Federal State Unitary Enterprise	F (11) (B60R, G01C, G01S, G01V, G07C, G08B, G08G)
		Taganrog Research Institute of Communications (FSUE TNIIS) (RU)	K (26) (G07C)
		International Academy of Ecology, Human and Nature Safety (RU)	K(26) (G07C)

Conclusions

1. With the use of the patent resource Qustel-Orbit and the system of the Federal Institute of Industrial Property (FIPS), 236 patents in the field of GLONASS/GPS, operating in the territory of the Russian Federation, have been identified. On the basis of this information, a systematization of patent holders was developed for classes, subclasses, groups and subgroups of the IPC, which allows to identify potential competitors who patent technologies in the same classes.

2. A technique for positioning of patent holders on the similarity indicators and the number of fundamentally different inventions relating to different subclasses of the IPC has been developed. In accordance with the methodology, the positioning of patent holders in the field of GLONASS/GPS in the territory of the Russian Federation was carried out.

3. The organizations-patent owners directly connected with railway transport have been revealed. It has been established that they own a small assortment of radically different GLONASS/GPS technologies on the territory of the Russian Federation. The main technological competitors for them are Russian organizations, which rather act as potential strategic partners in the development of innovative technologies based on GLONASS/GPS for rail transport.

1.6. Making decisions on substitution of imported equipment based on the analysis of patent and financial information

Background

The subject of our analysis is the situation at the enterprises producing high-tech products with a long supply chain, including foreign, connected with breaks of these chains because of the bans on imports, which could come from both the exporting country and the importing country. It should be noted that the ban on imports concern mainly food production, and export bans from European countries and the United States — products, usually related to defense. It is obvious that such bans are detrimental to producers and consumers, and become a shining example of deviations from rational economic behavior of decision-makers. The consequences of such decisions put economic actors in a new environment in which they must develop rational management strategies to ensure their survival. At the same time the development of long-term strategies is problematic due to a high degree of uncertainty of the future in times of crisis, as well as a large number and difficulty of the urgent tasks.

It is almost impossible to quickly replace necessary items, even if there are alternative providers, as it will take time to make test and to conclude contracts, not to mention the launch of own production. Therefore, in these circumstances, it is advisable to conduct exploratory research in order to identify possibilities of import substitution.

These studies include the following milestones:

1. Feasibility analysis of imported goods by the subject of technological complexity.

2. Patent search for analogues of imported products.

3. Research of license purchase options for the production of products in Russia.

4. Search for new suppliers of products on world markets.

5. Investigation of production capacity of products in Russia.

It should be noted that in this case any theoretical and statistical models are not suitable, and logic and analysis of empirical data, unfairly deprived of attention, are the only reliable scientific tools to solve problems.

The general scheme of feasibility study

To conduct a feasibility study, it is necessary to involve patent engineers, economists, marketers and experts in the field of art to which the product belongs. Possible results of this analysis can be represented by a situation tree shown in Pic. 1.27.

If an import-substituted object has no patent protection on the territory of Russia, it is theoretically possible to manufacture it on its own, if there are resources for it. Such an outcome is presented in Pic. 1.27 by Make option, where it can be seen that it is present in the tree branches with low technological complexity, and sometimes accompanied by competing alternatives. For example, in the case of availability of analogues on the market in the absence of patent protection it will be necessary to make a choice between the options Buy or Make, taking into account a time factor, as well as specific economic and technological opportunities of the enterprise. If the object in question or its close analog is patented abroad, then there is an additional possibility — Buy a license and make. With high technological complexity and the availability of analogues in the world markets the preferred option is Buy. Although there is a variety of issues related to the choice of supplier and contract options. At the same time the possibility of creating a domestic counterpart is not rejected, and can be implemented in parallel with the procurement of imported products for a certain period of time.

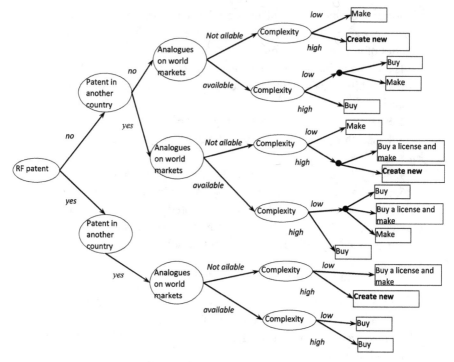

Fig. 1.27. Possible outcomes of a feasibility study

If there is a patent protection in Russia, it is reasonable to assume the existence of a foreign patent. In this case, there are less alternatives: if the markets have available analogues, it is advisable to purchase them (Buy), otherwise there is an option of buying a license and option — Create new, possible in the case of high and low technological complexity. This option is the most difficult to be implemented, as it implies the creation of new production, from the stage of development work. It occurs as and when the product is not protected by patents of Russia in case of unavailability of analogues in the world markets.

Patent search for analogues

A patent search can be performed with the assistance of information from national patent offices or international patent resources, for example, Questel-Orbit, Thomson Innovation, etc. [44, 45]. In practice, it is usually necessary to use all available sources of information, as the international patent resources allow fast search, sufficient to get an overall picture of patenting in the area of interest, but do not give an adequate idea of many patent holders because of distortion of names and frequent renaming. The first steps of the patent studies typically involve search for patents on the product imported by the name of the patent owner, if there is no accurate information on the availability and patent numbers. It should be borne in mind that the patent owner name can be different from the name of the manufacturer and the supplier of the product.

Patents of alleged patent holders found in international patent resources should be checked in the national patent offices. Patent protection may extend to certain parts of the product or the materials from which it is made. In such cases, it makes sense to carry out a series of searches in the international patent resources on the main functional and design features of the product to see what decisions and who patents in the field of art under consideration.

The first step is to establish the existence of patent protection on the territory of the Russian Federation. If it does not exist in relation to the object in question, the results of this search allow us to determine the class of similar technical solutions protected by Russian patents and to identify patent holders. In the next phase it is advisable to perform a patent search on the main design and functional features of products without limitation to the area of protection, to identify the world's leaders.

Patent research results provide valuable information for marketing and financial analysis with the assistance of Russian and international information resources on financial statements and economic indicators. In particular, it is possible to analyze the direction of economic activity of identified patent leaders in Russia and in the world and to draw conclusions about the likelihood of interaction with them as suppliers, licensors and / or industrial partners. In addition, analysis of production and economic performance of Russian companies allows to evaluate the prospects of production of desired products on them.

In addition to possible producers the patent search results provide information about the inventors and institutional organizations-developers of new technical solutions, which is important when you select the option Create new (product) in Fig. 1.27. The main stages of the proposed methods of analysis are described below with reference to the specific problem at import substitution.

Example of substitution possibilities research

Let's consider the main stages of the developed method of technical and economic analysis by the example of the problems that arose for the manufacturers of aviation and automotive equipment as a result of termination of contracts with the French company GAMMA SAS for the supply of elastomer shock absorbers to protect the electronic equipment of vehicles.

The shock absorber SEA 5A (Fig. 1.28), produced by the company GAMMA SAS is made of elastic material and covered from opposite sides with a metal frame. The elastomer part is made from high quality silicone and fror-silicone rubber. The official website of the manufacturer specifies the following characteristics of a given series of shock absorbers:

- shock absorbers operate in compression, tensile and shear;
- oscillation amplitude is up to ± 1,5 mm, the natural frequency is from 10 Hz;
- load range from 0,5 to 15 kg;
- standard embodiment of silicone;
- possible temperature for operation: from –55 to +150°C;
- shock absorber can damp dynamic loads with force coefficient of less than 4 at any surface;
- low natural frequency of oscillations allows the use of shock absorbers for helicopters.

Fig. 1.28. Shock absorber SES5A

In the shock absorber as a damping element a resilient plastic — elastomer is applied. Such a shock absorber is more reliable, but has the temperature dependence — at a low temperature the elastomer freezes and begins to operate differently. In this regard, the patent study material should be further carried out.

Shock absorbers of GAMMA SAS are fault tolerant and are primarily designed to provide effective vibration insulation of electronic devices, communications, navigation, various displays (shock absorbers are fixed on the dash board of aircraft, marine vessels, all-terrain vehicles and dampen fluctuations that occur during the movement); electronic circuits and small electronic devices with a high natural frequency; flight control systems, orientation and stabilization systems, weapons systems, inertial systems, and heading.

In this case the situation requires from manufacturers to take urgent decisions on replacement of such products, because without them, the products cannot pass tests and be transferred to the buyers. The complexity of the products is low, so the study of branches of the tree in Pic. 1.27 corresponding to such a situation leads to the option Make (analog, copy), if the product is not protected by RF patent. That is at the first stage of the study it is advisable to search for patents, by which a shock absorber can be protected, if such information is not available in the technical documentation prepared by the manufacturer from the supplier. When the number of patents are known and have not expired, then the best solution is Buy (product) from a new supplier, subject to the availability on the world markets. If it is impossible to find a new supplier, it is advisable to Buy a license to manufacture or Create new (private) product. This option corresponds to a high complexity in Pic. 1.27 and option Buy a license — low that, generally speaking, is conditional, because both of them can be viewed at any complexity, as their position in Fig. 1.27 corresponds to the case where the acquisition of licenses for production of complex products is not meaningful due to the impossibility of organizing such production in Russia in the foreseeable future.

Search for patents by the right holder name

In this example, information on patents for supplied elastomer (rubber) shock absorbers was absent, so the necessary action is to search for patents on the specified device in the territory of the Russian Federation. It is reasonable to start with a search for patents by the name of the supplier, it should be borne in mind that merger, acquisition and renaming of companies occur constantly in the global market.

GAMMA SAS company was founded in 1948 in France. To date, it has many years of experience in the application of its own know-how in the development and production of anti-vibration and vibration-damping shock absorbers for military and civil equipment. Due to the high quality of its products the company is involved in numerous international projects.

In 1993, according to Thomson Reuters [46], GAMMA SAS was acquired by EFFBE. In 2000, it became a part of WOCO group (Germany). In the early 1990s EFFBE began serial deliveries of its products to the Russian market. Now in Russia there are more than 30 regular consumers of its products in various industries. It is noteworthy that, after 90ies the number of domestic producers of elastomeric shock absorbers decreased steadily [47], i. e., the domestic market was given to EFFBE and other foreign firms. Data on companies EFFBE and WOCO group [48] are shown in Tables 1.23 and 1.24.

Table 1.23. Information about the company GAMMA SAS

Date of foundation, country	1948, France
Data of financial accounting	absent

Table 1.24. Information about the company EFFBE

Date of foundation, country	1949, France
Information about the company	The company specializes in the production of (http://www.effbe-diaphragm.com/en/): • rubber-textile membrane fabric with high resistance to mechanical and chemical stress. The membrane is made of high quality rubber. • produces molded rubber products that are used in the production of anti-vibration equipment. • produces elastomeric spring.(Two types of elastomers: EFFBE295 — on the basis of chloroprene rubber and EFFBE URELAST — based on enriched polyurethane
M&A	Since 2000 Effbe company is a part of production group of firms WOCO Gmbh & Co
Financial indicators (TR)	Revenue — 37 mln US dollars (2010), 36 mln US dollars (2012) Net income 3 mln US dollars (2010) Total assets — 23 mln US dollars (2010)

Patent search by the name of the right holder was conducted on all known names (GAMMA SAS, EFFBE, WOCO Group) and gave results, indicating that they have no Russian patents. This conclusion is based on research in the international patent resources and data base of Rospatent [49]. Therefore, further steps of the study will be determined by the top part of the tree in Pic. 1.27. Lack of patents by the supplier does not give full confidence in the fact that they are absent. If it is decided to Make the domestic analogue, it is necessary to clarify the idea what and by whom is patented in the art under consideration.

Search by functional and design features

The main function of a shock absorber is vibration isolation; basic element of the structure is an elastic rubber. Let's search for patents that contain these characters in the title and description of the invention. On 27.06 2015 the query on these features in Questel- Orbit gave 1436 documents, almost half of them were acting (47,5%). The average number of filed patent applications from 1990 to 2015 grew about four times (from 20 to 80). Distribution of patent documents for the publication countries and priority countries is shown in Fig. 1.29, 1.30. According to the number of patent publications the first place is occupied by China (573), followed by Japan (542) and the USA (505). The second echelon of leaders — European countries: Germany with 339 patents and France with 264. In Russia 116 patent documents with the desired features are published.

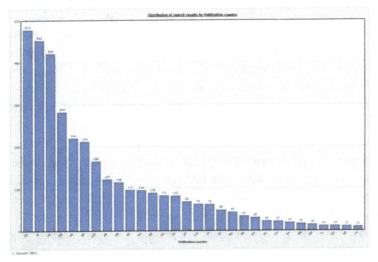

Fig. 1.29. Distribution of patents by publication countries

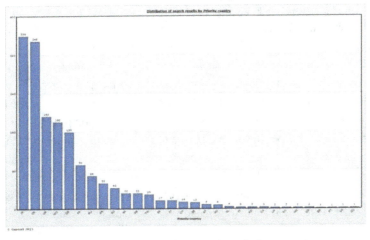

Fig. 1.30. Distribution of patents by priority countries

Distribution of patent documents by publication countries and priority countries differ. The first place in the number of initial applications is occupied by Japan (66,1% of all published), slightly ahead of China (60,7%). The USA, Germany and France have more than double backlog of Asian leaders in the number of priority applications, and also have a smaller share of the priority applications in the total number of patent publications (USA — 38%, Germany — 46,9%, France — 34,5%). This evidences particularly mass movement of production facilities to China and the concomitant rapid growth of patenting rates in this country, and that the US and European patent holders may give preference to international patent protection (WO, EP). More accurate conclusions can be made after a detailed analysis of the patent holders.

The analysis of the level of capitalization of companies in the industry «Car parts» has shown thatthe first place belongs to the European countries with the absolute leadership of Germany, followed by Japan, China and the United States. The number of companies in Europe is much less.

Comparison of rankings of capitalization and patent activity led to the conclusion that there is no direct link between them; patent leaders (in this case the countries) occupy high positions in the economic rankings, but economic leaders may have a low patent activity. It turns out that in the industry high patent activity of the subjects does not provide economic leadership in the world markets.

The leading patent holders in the study sample are shown in Fig. 1.31, where it is possible to see the famous Japanese, European and American companies, as well as lesser-known Chinese representatives. The only representative of Russia in the top 30 is the inventor O. S. Kochetov.

The graph of cooperation of patent holders in Fig. 1.32 shows which companies co-patent their developments. The numbers on the arcs correspond to the number of joint patents of patent holders. For example, Honda Motor has them in the field of vibration isolation with known chemical companies Sumitomo Riko and Tokai Rubber Industries, Toyota Motors — with Sumitomo Riko, etc. Such patents describe likely shock absorbers with rubber elastic elements designed for cars. The sought-for French firm (EFFBE, GAMMA) in the test sample is not determined, and representatives of WOCO Group are presented with a joint patent with Audi, Volkswagen and WOCO Franz Josef Wolf.

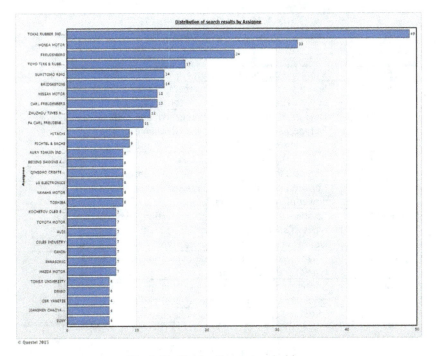

Fig. 1.31. The leading patent holders

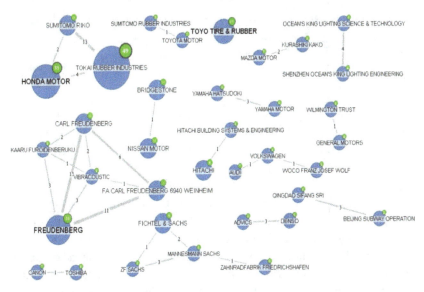

Fig. 1.32. The graph of cooperation of patent holders

Table 1.25. Leading groups of IPC

Group code	Group name	Number of documents
F16F-015	Vibration damping in systems	170
F16F-009	Springs, dampers, shock absorbers, that use a liquid or gas as an absorbing medium for amortization	128
F16F-013	Devices, including elastic elements of non-hydraulic type, as well as dampers for vibration damping, shock absorbers or hydraulic shock absorbers	124
F16F-001	Springs (hydraulic and pneumatic)	108
F16F-007	Dampers for vibration damping; shock absorbers	72
B60K-005	Location or installation of internal combustion power plants or jet-propulsion	62
B60G-015	Elastic suspension, different in location, layout or types of shock absorbers, combined with dampers, for example, of a telescopic type	53
B60G-011	Elastic suspension, different in location, layout or type of shock absorbers	51
F16F-003	Spring devices, composed of several springs, for example, to get the desired characteristic of elasticity	44
B61F-005	Structural elements of railway bogies	44

Distribution of search results by Concepts

Elastic rubber (151) | Shock absorber (140) | Damping (120) | Vibration (237) | Vibration isolation (69) | Vibration damping (62) | Elastic body (57) |

Damper (72) | Engine mount (34) | Vehicle body (79) | Elastic material (62) | Vulcanization (54) | Vibration isolator (28) | Elastic member (64) | Rubber elastic (20) | Elastic deformation (60) | Resilient rubber (28) | High frequency vibration (22) | Elastic rubber member (16) | Vibration input (20) | Equilibrium chamber (16) | Shock (70) | Rubber elastic material (18) | Vibration frequency (38) | Vibration damper (23) | Non compressible fluid (17) | Damping property (25) | Vibration transmission (23) | Fluid filled vibration (11) |

Elasticity (87) | Damping effect (21) | Orifice passage (17) | Vibration amplitude (31) | Pressure receiving chamber (11) | Damping element (24) | Axial direction (100) | Statement vibration proof (10) | Rubber material (27) | Spring constant (21) | Low frequency vibration (13) | Damping fluid (16) | Shock absorption (21) | Idling vibration (11) | Piston rod (51) | Fluid chamber (31) | Wheel suspension (18) | Vibration proof (16) | Flexible rubber (18) | Rubber member (14) | Rubber (25) | Rubber layer (22) | Elastic element (27) | Hydraulic shock absorber (14) | Elastomer (58) | Engine vibration (17) | Hydraulic damper (14) | Vibration absorbing (16) | Partition member (18) | Damping force (11) | Circumferential surface (40) | Elastic (28) | Automobile suspension (11) | Riding comfort (13) | Damping material (14) | Circumferential direction (53) | Outer peripheral (47) | Damping action (11) | Elastomeric material (36) | Mounting member (20) | Damping performance (10) | Car body (25) | Spring element (29) | Suspension (44) | Spring rigidity (10) | Resonance (43) |

© Questel 2015

Fig. 1.33. Cloud of concepts

Ten leading groups of International Patent Classification (IPC) in the study sample are presented in Table 1.25 and Fig. 1.33 shows the «cloud of concepts» — key words with the frequency of their occurrence inpatent documents of the sample. Such information indicates the relevance of the found documents according to the query, but in order to understand whether there are patents among them that are close to the product in question, it is necessary to analyze the texts of patent documents. Teh analysis carried out by an expert in the art of vibration-proof equipment shows that in the considered sample patents have very little resemblance to the specified device. This is due to the simplicity of the latter and, consequently, low patentability, as the solution is standard [50], and the novelty can be possessed by material, of which the elastic element is made.

Patent landscape of studied art field is shown in Fig. 1.34 as a map ThemeScape that allows to select classes of patent documents most similar in occurrence of concepts. On the map it is possible to see the class Damping-Elastic Body-Vibration damping, containing 57 documents, to the greatest extent corresponding to the query. It can also be noted that the technical field, we are interested in, is characterized by a low patent activity when compared to some others, which are on the map (Engine, Magnet Rotor Electrical, etc.).

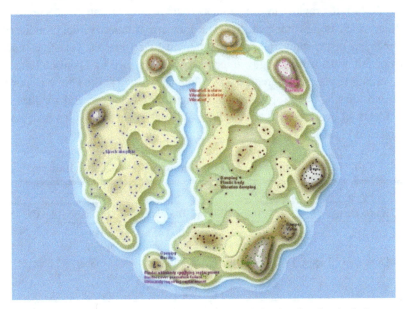

Fig. 1.34. The patent landscape in the field of elastic vibration isolation devices

Elastomeric shock absorbers are a special class of devices, as closely related to the materials used, and hence patent subclasses from the section C (chemistry), in particular C08L — the composition of high molecular compounds (based on polymerizable monomers). At the same time, most complex inventions in the field of vibration protection do not fall here, because the improvement of these devices involves the use of hydraulic, pneumatic, electropneumatic, hydraulic, and other dampers, magnetic fluids and engineering solutions of a combined character.

The quality of the inventions described in the patents is taken to be assessed by their citation. The analysis of citation of patents by elastomeric dampers revealed the most reputable producers (developers) of materials (Tokai Rubber Industry, Freudenberg) and devices (Porche, Honda Motor).

Analysis of activity of leaders

As a result, patent research revealed companies that develop, patent and produce the devices of a specified class, so it is advisable to analyze their economic performance. Patent leaders are Japanese companies Tokai Rubber Industry, Sumitomo Riko, Honda Motor and the German company Freudenberg SA.

Table 1.26 provides information on Tokai Rubber Industry and Sumitomo Riko, which are now merged [51]. The company Sumitomo Rubber Industry, a member of the industrial group Sumitomo Riko, over the past five years, twice fell into the top 100 global innovators, determined by Thomson Reuters according to patent resource Thomson Innovations [52]. The Group has over 80 subsidiaries, many of which are foreign representatives, and supplies its products all over the world, providing its patent protection, which is demonstrated in Fig. 1.35.

Table 1.26. Information about the company Tokai Rubber Industry

Date of foundation, country		1929, Japan	
Name change		Since 2014 is a part of Sumitomo Riko Group	
Directions of activity		• production of rubber, polymers and flexible materials for shock absorbers; • manufacture of various rubber and plastic parts for automobiles; • manufacture of electronic equipment	
Financial indicators (bln yen)		2013 FY (the tax period from 01.04.2013 to 31.03.2014)	2014 FY
	Total assets	383.005	406.777
	Intangible assets	34.326 (9%)	26.39 (6,5%)
	Revenue	369.093	400.93
	Net profit	4.076 (1,1%)	4.429 (1,1%)
	Costs of R&D	11.673 (3,16%)	12.821 (3,2%)

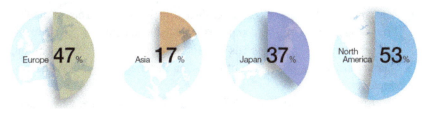

Fig. 1.35. Patent protection of exported products by regions

Financial indicators show an innovative company profile, which can certainly be considered as a potential supplier of the right shock absorber.

Table 1.27 shows a summary of the transnational industrial group Freudenberg [53], which has officesin Russia and can be considered as a potential supplier of elastomeric dampers.

Table 1.27. Information about Freudenberg group

Date of foundation, country		1870, Germany	
Information about the company		Freudenberg group designs and manufactures filters, seals, technological components for vibration control, non-woven materials, chemical products for surface treatment, lubricants, medical and mehatronic products.The product range includes thousands of titles in 30 market segments.The group consists of almost 500 companies in 57 countries, employing more than 30000 employees	
Financial indicators (mln euro)		2013	2014
	Total assets	5872.6	6666.5
	Intangible assets	786.7 (13,4%)	860.6 (12,9%)
	Revenue	5646.1	5982.3
	Net profit	398.8 (7,0%)	477.8 (8,0%)
	Costs of R&D	270.3 (4,8%)	246.3 (4,1%)

Authoritative patents for devices of this class are also owned by Honda Motor and Porsche.

Leaders of the industry, who are not patent-leaders, may hold high positions in the market, which is confirmed by the ranking of countries in terms of capitalization of companies in the industry «Spare parts of cars». Therefore, along with the patent studies it is necessary to conduct also marketing studies. As a result of the market analysis of elastomeric dampers the following potential suppliers of the required products were identified:

- The company Hutchinson (France), which is included in the Total group that brings together nearly 100 companies. The main activities — development and production of new materials for protection against noise and vibration, thermal insulation, production of insulation materials, seals, hydraulic systems, etc.
- Transnational corporation LORD (USA) with a wide range of products, consisting of elastomeric shock absorbers for aviation.

Possibilities to purchase a license

Purchase of a license for production in Russia is especially important in the event that a patentee has a Russian patent, and therefore it makes sense to carry out a detailed analysis of Russian patents from the described sample. From 1436 documents only 116 are published on the territory of the Russian Federation; their distribution by year of filing the application is shown in Fig. 1.36, where it can be seen that the publication peak falls on the period from 2004 to 2010.

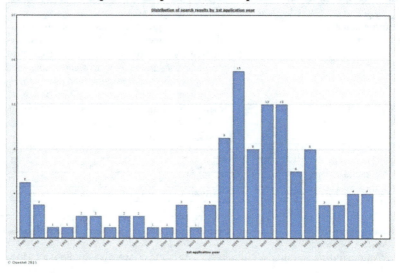

Fig. 1.36. Distribution of Russian patents by year of publication of the first application

Analysis of the distribution of patent documents by the country of publication and country of priority leads to the conclusion that in this field more than 40% of Russian patents are owned by foreign right holders. However, the analysis of that resource is complicated by the problem of resource names in international databases. Leading patent holders are shown inin Fig. 1.36, where we

104

can see foreign companies, Russian enterprises, universities and inventors directly. It should be noted that the leaders in the considered art shown in Fig. 1.31, 1.32, practically do not patent their inventions in Russia.

The results of the analysis of Russian patents of foreign patent holders provide a basis for decisionsabout the appropriateness of acquisition of licenses for the product. The question of the existence of a patent on an elastic material of a shock absorber requires a separate study and is not affected.

The possibility of organizing production

The studies provide information on Russian inventors and companies with patents in the studied art. The greatest interest among right holders amounts to organizations with production capabilities.

In Fig. 1.37, we can see the company FSUE «NPO Progress» and LLC «ATP-Holding», which are useful to be analyzed as both potential producers of relevant products. Information about them obtained from the database SPARK [54], is shown in Tables 1.28, 1.29 and suggests that two companies could be considered as potential producers, but their patents and manufactured products are substantially different from the imported device, so for decision-making more complete information and negotiations are required.

Patents of individuals and universities can be useful when selecting the option Create new (product) in Fig. 1.27

Databases of financial accounting of Russian companies [47, 54] allow us to find manufacturers of shock absorbers, which either have not patented their development, or are not included in the sample under study for various reasons. This search allowed to form a very broad list of possible manufacturers, which requires clarification by means of negotiations, analysis of manufactured products and patent activity.

The studies lead to the conclusion that the production of the desired product in Russia is possible.

Conclusion

Extraordinary situations, that require urgent decisions, often occur in the economy. It is known that theoretical and statistical models in such cases do not work, so these are usually the leaders of enterprises, who are forced to make decisions without any scientific support, using only their own experience and intuition. This is difficult under high uncertainty. Reducing its extent is necessary and possible through the involvement and analysis of empirical data from available sources, which include patent databases and financial information.

The name of the patent owner	Amount
KOCHETOV OLEG SAVEL EVICH	7
VORONEZH STATE UNIVERSITY OF ENGINEERING TECHNOLOGIES	3
FEDERAL NOE GUP NPP PROGRESS FGUP NPP PROGRESS	2
OOO ATR KHOLDING	2
AQUATIC	2
EIFELER MASCHINENBAU	2
GATES	2
GATES MECTROL	2
WILMINGTON TRUST	2
LANXESS	2
VOENNO MORSKAJA AKADEMIJA IM A	2
KHODAKOVA TAT JANA DMITRIEVNA	1
NATIONAL RESEARCH UNIVERSITY — MPEI	1
KLEIN IBERICA	1
OILES INDUSTRY	1
MAN TRUCK & BUS	1
MANCA STOCK	1
G OBRAZOVATEL NOE UCHREZHDENIE VYSSHEGO PROFESSIONAL NOGO OBRAZOVANIJA	1
DO PLANT OF MINE RESCUE EQUIPMENT OPEN JOINT STOCK	1
LA NACION MINISTERIO DE DEFENSA FUERZA AEREA COLOMBIANA	1
LG ELECTRONICS	1
TOYO TIRE & RUBBER	1
GERRESHEIMER REGENSBURG	1
MAKITA	1
SHAPE	1

Fig. 1.37. Leading holders of Russian patents (based on a screenshot)

Table 1.28. Brief information about LLC «ATR-Holding»

Name, adress	LLC «ATR-Holding», Saratov region, Balakovo, Sadovaya street, 119/1
Manufactured products	• Manufacture of spare parts and belongings of cars and their engines • Manufacture of rubber and plastic products • Manufacture of other rubber products
Financial indicators	Revenue — 157 mln rubles (2013), 160 mln rubles (2012) Fixed assets — 16,5 mln rubles (2013), 17,6 mln rubles (2012) Current assets — 38,8 mln rubles (2013), 29,4 mln rubles (2012) Stocks — 19,7 mln rubles (2013), 19,0 mln rubles (2012)

Table 1.29. Brief information about FSUE «Progress»

Name, adress	FSUE SPE «Progress», Omsk region, Omsk, 5-ya Kordnaya, 4
Manufactured products	• Molded rubber products • Shock absorbers rubber-metal plated ARP-150 (for drilling platforms) • Conveyors, feeders, transporters • Production of tires, cameras • Production of other rubber products.
Some financial indicators	Revenue — 497 mln rubles (2013), 420 mln rubles (2012) Fixed assets — 298,5 mln rubles (2013), 249,9 mln rubles (2012) Current assets — 1477 mln rubles (2013), 404 mln rubles (2012) Stocks — 339,1 mln rubles (2013), 136,0 mln rubles (2012)

Application of the method proposed in the article provides a systematic approach to the development of managerial decisions in difficult situations, and can significantly reduce the degree of uncertainty, taking into account various aspects of decisions, generate alternative solutions, obtain quantitative data for evaluation of the options under consideration.

References of chapter 1

1 Hubka, W. and Eder, W.E. (1992) *Engineering Design, General Procedural Model of Engineering Design,* Heurista,Zurich.

2 Koller, R. and Kastrup, N. (1994) *Prinzipl□sungen zur Konstruktion techniseher Produkte,* Springer Verlag, Berlin.

3 Altshuller, G. (1996) *And Suddenly the Inventor Appeared,* Technical Innovation Centre, Worcester.

4 Pahl, G. and Beitz, W. (1996) *Engineering Design: A Systematic Approach,* Springer Verlag, Berlin.

5 Andreasen, M.M. (1992) "The Theory of domains", *Proceedings Workshop Understanding Function Function-to-Form Evolution,* Cambridge Engineering Design Centre.

6 Hundal, M.S. (1997) *Cost-based Mechanical Designing and Product Development,* ASME Press, New York.

7 Suh, N. (1993) *Principles of Design,* Oxford University Press, USA.

8 Andreichicov, A.V. (1995) "Computer Simulation and Modelling Synthesis of New Technical Decisions on the Invention Level", *Problems of Engineering and Automation,* No.1-2, pp. 11-18.

9 Andreichicov, A.V. and Andreichicova, O.N. (1998) *Computer Support of Invention,* Machine Building Publisher, Moscow.

10 Alexeyev, A., Borisov, A., Vilums, E., Slyadz, N., and Fomin, S. (1997) *Intelligent Decision-Making Systems in Computer-aided Design*, Zinatne Publishers, Riga.

11 Blessing, L.T.M. (1994) *A Process-Based Approach to Computer Supported Engineering Design*, Cambridge UK.

12 Tomiyama, T., Xue, D., Yoshikawa, H. (1985) "Developing an Intelligent CAD Systems", *Artificial Intelligencein Optimal Design and Manufacturing*, Prentice Hall, Englewood Cliffs NY USA, pp.83-112.

13 Andreichicova, O.N. (1998) "Consequences estimate of taking decisions in computer systems", *Information Technologies*, Machine-building Publisher, Moscow, No.3, pp. 21-29.

14 Saaty, T.L. (1990) *The Analytic Hierarchy Process*, RWS Publications, Pittsburgh, PA.

15 Zadeh, L.A. (1973) *The Concept of a Linguistic Variable and Its Application To Approximate Reasoning*, American Elsevier Publishing Company, New York.

16 *Fuzzy Sets and Possibility Theory: Recent Developments*, (1982) Yager, R. (Ed.), Pergamon Press, New York.

17 Sanc, E., Hrubes, Z., Hospergrova, M. (1997) "The use of fuzzy numbers in the design of machine parts", *Proceedings of the 11th International Conference on Engineering Design*, Tampere, Finland, vol.3, pp. 691-696.

18 Altshuller G.S. (1988) *Creativity as an exact science*, New York, Gordon & Breach.

19 Jons J.C. (1984) *Essays in design*, New York, Toronto etc.

20 Zwicky F. (1948) *The morphological method of analysis and construction*, Courant, Anniversary Volume.

21 Saaty T.L., Vargas L.G. (1994) *Decision making in economic, political, social and technological environments: The Analytic Hierarchy Process*, Pittsburgh, RWS Publications.

22 Saaty T.L. (2001) *Creative thinking, problem solving and decision making*, Pittsburgh, RWS Publications.

23 Saaty T.L. (2001) *Decision making with dependence and feedback: the Analytic Network Process*, Pittsburgh, RWS Publications.

24 Andreichicov A.V. and Andreichicova O.N. (1998) *Computer support of invention*, Moscow: Machine Building (in Russian).

25 Saaty T.L. (1994) *Fundamentals of decision making and priority theory with the Analytic Hierarchy Process*, Pittsburgh, RWS Publications

26 Andreichicov A.V. and Andreichicova O.N. (2001) "A choice of a perspective system for vibration isolation in conditions of varying environment", *Proceedings of the Sixth International Symposium on the Analytic Hierarchy Process ISAHP'2001*, Bern, 13-24.

27 Andreichicov A.V. and Andreichicova O.N. (2003) "The analysis of the technical system's evolution", *Proceedings of the Sixth International Symposium on the Analytic Hierarchy Process ISAHP'2003*, Bali, Indonesia, 121-126.

28 Saaty T.L. (2001) *Creative thinking, problem solving and decision making*, Pittsburgh, RWS Publications.

29 Saaty T.L. (2001) *Decision making with dependence and feedback: the Analytic Network Process*, Pittsburgh, RWS Publications.

30 G. S Stetsyura, "Evolutionary Methods in Problems of Control, Choice and Optimization," Prib. Sist, Uprav. No. 3, 54–62 (1998).

31 I. P. Norenkov and O. T. Kosachevskii, "Genetic Algorithms for Combining Heuristics in Problems of Discrete Optimization," Informatsionnye Tekhnologii, No. 2, 2–7 (1999).

32 V. M. Kureichik, *Geneticheskie Algoritmy* (Tag.Rad. Tekh. Univ., Taganrog, 1998).

33 A. V. Andreichikov and O. N. Andreichikova, *Computer Support of Invention (Methods, Systems, and Examples of Application* (Mashinostroenie, Moscow, 1998) [in Russian].

34 A. V. Andreichikov and A. S. Kiselev, "Morphological Tables-Based Evolutionary Synthesis of Novel Technical Systems," Izv. Vuzov. Mashinostroenie, Nos. 2–3, 44–48 (2002).

35 A. V. Andreichikov, "An Intelligent Method for Synthesis of Technological Innovations," Izv. Vuzov. Mashinostroenie, No. 10, 47–62 (2003).

36 A. V. Andreichikov and O. N. Andreichikova, *Intelligent Data Systems* (Finansy i Statistika, Moscow, 2004) [in Russian].

37 Gardenfors P. 1975. Match making: assignments based on bilateral preferences. *Behavioral Science*, 3(20): 166-173.

38 Faltings B., Haroud D., Hua K., Kimberly G., Smith I. 1992. Dynamic constraint satisfaction in a bridge design system. In G. Gottlob, W. Nejdl (ed.) *Expert systems in engineering principles and applications*, 462: 217-232.

39 Moulin H. 1988. *Axioms of cooperative decision making.* Cambridge: Cambridge University Press.

40 Andreichicov A., Andreichicova O. 2001. Software for inventive problem-solving. *Int. Journal of Technology Management,* 3-4(21): 277-297.

41 [Electronic resource]: http://www.orbit.com. Last accessed 26.08.2016.

42 [Electronic resource]: http://www.fips.ru. Last accessed 26.08.2016

43 Andreichikov, A.V., Andreichikova, O. N. System analysis and synthesis of strategic solutions in innovation: Models of multicriteria analysis of innovative organizations [Sistemniy analiz I sintez strategicheskih reshenii v innovatike: Modeli mul'tikriterial'nogo analiza deyatel'mosti innovacionnyh organizacii]. Moscow, Librocom publ., 2013, 360 p.

44 [Electronic resource]: http://www.orbit.com. Last accessed 27.06.2016.

45 [Electronic resource]: http://www.Thomsoninnivation.com. Last accessed 27.06.2016.

46 [Electronic resource]: http://www.Eicon.com. Last accessed 27.06.2016.

47 [Electronic resource]: http://www.spark-interfax.ru. Last accessed 27.06.2016.

48 [Electronic resource]: http://www.effbe-diaphragm.com/en. Last accessed 27.06.2016.

49 [Electronic resource]: http://www.fips.ru. Last accessed 27.06.2016.

50 Vibration in equipment: A Handbook. In 6 Vol. Edboard: V. N. Chelomey (introd.) [*Vibracii v tehnike: Spravochnik. V 6-ti t./ Red. Sovet: V.N. Chelomej (pred.)*]. Moscow, Mashinostroenie publ., 1981, 456 p.Vol.

51 Protection against vibration and shock / Ed.by K. V. Frolov, 1981, 456 p.

52 [Electronic resource]: http://www.sumitomoriko.co.jp.Last accessed 27.06.2016.

53 The Future is Open: 2015 State of Innovation / Thomson Reuters. [Electronic resource]: http://www.stateofinnovation.com. Last accessed 27.06.2016.

54 [Electronic resource]: http:// www.freudenberg.com. Last accessed 27.06.2016.

CHAPTER 2.
New paradigms of decision-making

Introduction

The decision-making theory as a science has appeared in the 19th century. During the last two centuries, a lot of methods for searching for optimal decisions have been developed in frameworks of this theory. Its initial stages were connected with the development of methods for a finding of the best decisions on the basis of exact mathematical models with a quantitative information. rather soon the methods for the analysis of statistical decisions have appeared, which used the probabilistic models instead of deterministic ones. Researchers began widely to apply the concepts of risk and lotteries in decision-making problems with probabilistic data. now the most urgent decision-making problems are the problems with uncertainty, which take place, when there is no information on probabilities, and the decisions are being accepted on the basis of subjective judgments of decision-maker.

New century will demand making more difficult and more crucial decisions from people living on the planet. The rising complexity of the choice problem is caused by increase of their dimensionality and also by the necessity of their nearing to reality. For these reasons it's necessary to abandon some assumptions, convenient in view of theory, and to take into account a number of new factors and tendencies. In spite of the fantastic computer progress, the most difficult problems unlikely will be solved by quantitative methods. Main decisions in human history were subjective, as they have been made by the persons. Making a choice from a set of alternatives, a person evaluates their quality, connecting the objective aspects with his (her) personal values. This fact explains an impossibility of an "objective" choice in principle, even if there is exact quantitative information for decision-making. Therefore, further we shall imply the decision-making problems under uncertainty.

The traditional multiple criteria decision-making problems are usually reduced to a choice of the best alternative from the set of possible variants or to a ranking of the finite set of alternatives given. Main features of decision-making problems in administrative sciences are continuous evolution and unpredictable character of probable changes in the systems researched. These features essentially influence the statements of decision-making tasks. In evolutionary systems, the result of choice has dynamic character in connection with emergence of new criteria and alternatives, and also because of preferences' inconstancy, which reflect the changes happening in a system and outside it. Therefore, it is difficult to distinguish the independent elements, as the active participants (actors), purposes, criteria, policies, alternatives and so on influence each other. Besides, in the systems simulating social phenomena, the conflicts between the participants of decision-making processes can take place.

2.1. New approaches to decision making

In traditional decision-making problems the simple alternatives are examined, i.e. each of them is considered as indivisible essence and is evaluated by each criterion as something whole. Along with the simple alternatives in decision-making tasks there can be complex ones obtained by a combination of simple alternatives. For example, the policies, plans or projects are the sets of certain actions arranged in various sequences, and some of these actions can simultaneously be presented in different alternatives. Thus the decision synthesis problems arise in the decision-making tasks.

Except the traditional ranking tasks it is possible to formulate the following problems in socio-economic systems:

1. A ranking of a finite set of simple alternatives with taking into account the mutual influence of the purposes, actors, criteria, subcriteria and alternatives.
2. A ranking of a finite set of simple alternatives with varying preferences including importance of criteria and purposes.
3. A collective choice with considering of different actors' preferences and also of the alternatives' requirements.
4. Generating and ranking of complex alternatives in the collective choice problems with considering of mutual requirements of the participants.

Besides, the decision-making task may consist in a choosing not one the best alternative (or ranking of a finite set), but in a choosing of the best subset (combination) of variants. The task of resources allocation and the task on assignments are the examples of such problems in operations research.

Mutual Influence's Problem

Axiomatic methods of the Utility Theory [1-3] suggests new decision-making paradigm, which takes into account dependence and feedback between the elements of the decision. Analytic Network Process (ANP) represents a complex problem by the hierarchy or network, whose elements can influence each other. Integral influence ratings for each element are the limit priorities, which are calculated by expert judgments on relative influence intensity. The example of hierarchy containing 3 levels is given in a Fig. 2.1a. If the actors, criteria and alternatives influence each other, the hierarchy turns into the network shown in a Fig. 2.1b.

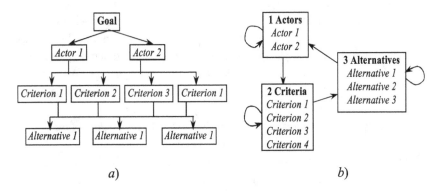

a)   b)

Fig. 2.1. Hierarchical (*a*) and network (*b*) models for a representation of decisionaking problems

The AHP (Analytic Hierarchy Process) enables to obtain the relative priorities for the alternatives concerning a main goal by means of consecutive pair comparison of the lower levels' elements with regard to the elements of upper levels [4].

The network structure is described by a supermatrix, whose elements are the matrixes formed from the priorities vectors for the elements of appropriate clusters.

Clusters	Actors	Criteria	Alternatives
Actors	W_{11}	0	W_{31}
Criteria	W_{12}	W_{22}	0
Alternatives	0	W_{23}	W_{33}

Supermatrix =

These priorities are calculated from pair comparison matrixes for the elements of a cluster indicated at the left, concerning the elements of a cluster at the top. The raising of a supermatrix to the limit powers enables to obtain the limiting priorities for all elements of considered problem with taking into account the dependences and feedback between them.

The ANP outcomes obtained with considering of mutual influence of decision elements can differ from the results of a hierarchical synthesis of priorities.

113

The hierarchical approach enables to find out the best alternative at the moment of decision-making. The mutual influence of decision elements leads to priorities' change, therefore in this case the limit result should be considered as a forecast, which indicates the alternative to be the best in the future.

Expert Preferences Varying in Time. AHP can be applied [4] to the decisions' priorities forecasting, with use of judgments varying in time. In this case the elements of pair comparison matrixes $A=\{a_{ij}\}$ are the dynamic judgments, i.e. the functions describing a change of $a_{ij}(t)$, where a_{ij} shows how much i's object is more preferable than j's at the point of time t. Let's consider an example of decision-making task with dynamic judgments [5].

Choice with Considering of Requirements of Decision-Makers and Alternatives. In decision-making problems it is accepted to assign a set of alternatives (objects) and one or more decision-makers (subjects), which should choose the best alternative using a set of relevant criteria. Sometimes it is difficult to select the objects and the subjects in the socio-economical systems, as the participants of decision-making process simultaneously choose each other. Examples of such tasks are: a choice of the business partners, a selection of the employees to a firm, a choice of strategy of enterprise development and so on. The solving of similar problems by traditional methods of the Decision Theory may lead to the conflicts between the participants and the ignoring of essential information describing various kinds of the relations between the subjects and the objects of a choice.

We propose a new approach to the problems of collaborative choice [6] based on a representation of the expert information by the sets of properties and the requirements, which subjects make to other participants of decision-making process. The representation of information in terms of properties and requirements (demands) enables to separate the objective features of the decisions (properties) from subjective preferences of the decision-makers (requirements). It gives an opportunity for the application of different methods for information processing during a formation and analysis of collaborative decisions, and also an opportunity for the development of intelligent software based on structured knowledge bases containing the objective data, subjective preferences, the rules for formation and evaluation of possible decisions, and the rules for the probable conflicts' resolution.

In the problems of collective choice the participants can make demands not only to alter-natives being chosen, but also to each other. Sometimes these requirements and the mutual influences determine a group choice, which can differ from the outcomes obtained without considering of such information. The approach taking into account mutual requirements of the choice subjects gives the results more feasible in practice. Besides, it enables to find out the reasons explaining why the group sometimes can choose alternative, which is not being the best objectively. At last, in collaborative decision-making problems we can generate and ex-amine the various sets of complex alternatives. For example, when organizing of a joint enterprise one should consider a set of combinations, which include various output kinds being produced, industrial partners, investors, different technologies etc. Such problems emerge in virtual enterprises, both in a stage of their organization, and in a stage of functioning.

Let's consider an example of the collaborative decision-making problem, where the enterprise — producer chooses the output kind for manufacturing with considering of probable consumers, investors and accessible technologies. The structure of the task is presented in a Fig. 2.2.

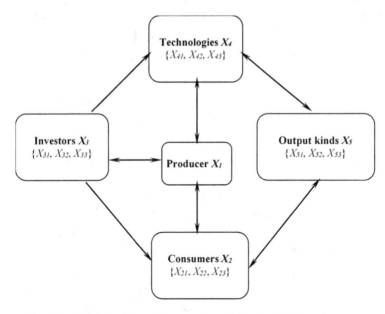

Fig. 2.2. Mutual requirements' graph for the collaborative decision-making problem

The arrows in the fig. 2.2 correspond to the requirements directions. Each element of the task is described by a set of properties, which may be expressed by numerical, fuzzy or verbal ratings. Each subject can make some demands to others. Requirements may be expressed by equalities, inequalities or ranges. The degree of requirement satisfaction is calculated as a measure of similarity to the value of appropriate property. To estimate a degree of compliance over all requirements, which a subject make to another, the weighed sum is used. The outcomes of problem solving are the values of generalized measure of mutual requirements compliance for each possible combination, which can be calculated as following:

$$F(d_z) = \prod_{\substack{i=1 \\ i \neq j}}^{N} \left[\sum_{k=1}^{K_{ij}} w_k^j S_k (R_{Y_ik}^j, P_{Y_jl}) \right]^{v_i}, \quad d_z \in D$$

where $D = X_1 \times X_2 \times \ldots \times X_N$; N — the number of subjects; $R_{Y_ik}^j$ – k's requirement, which a subject Y_i make to l's property of subject Y_j (P_{Y_jl}); K_{ij} — the number of requirements from i's subject to j's; w_k^j – a weight factor for k's requirement of i's subject; v_i — a weight factor of i's subject; $S_k (R_{Y_ik}^j, P_{Y_jl})$ – a measure of similarity of $R_{Y_ik}^j$ to P_{Y_jl}. The way of calculating of similarity measures depends on a form of representation of properties and requirements [6].

The society evolution results in the changing of the management tasks in socio-economical systems, where decision-making processes play the main role. In our opinion, the appearance of new approaches to decision-making is caused by the following reasons:

1. The complication of decision-making problems because of increasing of amount of information used.

2. The attracting of more participants to the decision-making processes, collective character of complex decision-making problems.

3. The necessity of a comprehensive evaluation of probable consequences of the decisions being accepted.

4. Progress in computer science and in the Decision Theory.

In this connection the decision-making problems become more difficult. The increasing of amount of information leads to the dimensionality enlargement in decision-making tasks. Besides, the nontrivial tasks of the preliminary analysis and structuring of such information emerge. Obviously, the most urgent decision-making problems relate to weakly structured problems, which may be solved with support of the intelligent software capable to accumulate

116

the information needed, to discover knowledge in it and to apply such knowledge to the problem solving.

In this paper we've considered three new approaches to complex problems of decision-making. The novelty is main factor, which unites them. Each of these techniques is destined to solving of certain task: ANP gives an opportunity to determine the factors of decisions, being the most influenced or influencing others; AHP with dynamic judgments allows to forecast the decisions' consequences; and collaborative approach enables to find out compromise decisions.

The collective character and complication of decision-making processes give rise to a number of new problems, namely: the synthesis of complex decisions, conflicts resolution, taking into account of a mutual influence of the factors determining the decision.

The natural resources exhaustion, ecology deterioration, the growing number of man-caused catastrophes, terrorism as a consequence of an economic inequality and other factors should force the people to be careful and responsible in evaluating of probable consequences of the decisions being accepted in political, socio-economic and socio-technical fields. The considering of the environment's reaction, prediction of its probable changes, forecasting of the variations of preferences and priorities, and also of the possible consequences of the decisions are becoming the most urgent problems of today. We hope a computer progress and efforts of the scientists and experts will enable to manage with these problems in 21 century.

2.2. The analysis of technical systems' evolution

Designing and the manufacture of competitive engineering requires the analysis of development prospects for devices created. The solution of this problem is connected to the analysis of large databases, where the information on devices of the considered class and close to it classes are stored. The application of formal methods for the information analysis promotes increase of productivity of designers' labour in early designing stages. As it is known from the evolution theory, the value of the information is determined by its use. In this connection the software made for the analysis of design databases enables to make the information use more effective and also to receive new knowledge.

In the paper the analysis of an evolution of pneumatic vibration isolators with use of Analytic Hierarchy Process (AHP) is considered. A number of the perspective technical decisions created in different moments of time was analysed on the set of quality criteria being incorporated in the hierarchy. The purpose of the analysis was formulated as follows: "To reveal the most perspective devices for perfection".

The second hierarchy level contains the following criteria groups: functional, layout, technological, economic, innovative. At the third level there are criteria connected with the appropriate functional groups. They are: vibroisolation quality, reliability, cost, operational expenses, complexity, adaptability to manufacture, patentability, competitiveness, spatial orientation, opportunity for setting-up different frequencies, compactness.

The marginal analysis for criteria has revealed criteria and groups important for perfection of pneumatic vibration isolators. These criteria are: quality of a vibration damping; spatial orientation; adaptability to manufacture; opportunity for setting-up different frequencies; the complexity and the operational expenses. The most important groups for development are functional criteria, layout criteria and innovation criteria.

We have considered above 500 patents of USSR on pneumatic vibration isolators. This information was processed with use of the decision-making software. In result 6 the most perspective devices created in different moments of time were chosen. The expert estimation of quality for these devices was made by a pair comparison method on quality criteria mentioned above. On the basis of calculated priorities for alternatives the following tendencies of criteria estimations changes in time are established:

- Improvement of the vibroisolation quality.
- Improvement of layout properties.
- Deterioration of economic parameters.

Thus the results of the marginal analysis for criteria have been completely proved at the analysis of evolution of the systems examined.

The outcomes reveal criteria groups exerting the most influence on the development of systems examined, and also criteria being more important for further perfection. In this case the best prospects for development have devices with good parameters of functional properties and layout. Their perfection is connected with the improvement of economic and technological parameters.

Introduction

The analysis of evolution of the technical systems (TS) with identical main function, is made with the purpose of revealing criteria, which determine a development of TS, and laws of their change. The TS' evolution is considered as consecutive transformations represented by an evolutionary chain or an evolutionary tree. Each previous decision is the prototype for the improved subsequent decision in TS' evolution.

The laws of TS' development are the certain steady changes of some criterion (attribute) during many generations. The criteria in this case reflect functional, technical and economic properties of systems.

During an evolution the improvements of a number of important quality criteria can be accompanied by significant deterioration of other criteria. The technical systems executed as the inventions, are characterized by uncertainty in criteria values. Therefore a multicriteria analysis of the inventions included in evolutionary chain is the important task which is directed to revealing of alternatives lacks with the purpose of mistakes prevention in a choice of rational variants for more detailed design and experimental study.

The statement of a task

Let's consider the analysis of evolution with use AHP [5, 6] on an example of the pneumatic dampers with controlled throttling device ensuring a vibrations damping by the certain law. The evolutionary chain includes six pneumatic dampers $A_i(i = 1...6)$, protected by the USSR patents (Fig. 2.3). These alternatives were selected on the basis of the preliminary analysis of 102 patents, which related to the examined class.

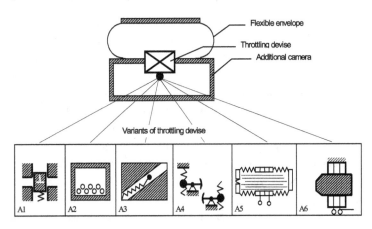

Fig. 2.3. The schemes of considered pneumatic dampers

The basic functional criterion of development in this case is the amplitude-frequency characteristic for the fluctuation transfer factor $T_z(f)$. The experimental amplitude-frequency characteristics for $T_z(f)$ for the considered dampers are shown in a Fig. 2.4. The analysis of these characteristics demonstrates there is a steady tendency to improvement of vibroisolation properties, i.e. the maximum of function $T_z(f)$ at passing from the previous generation to subsequent becomes less and it is displaced to the area of lower frequencies [6].

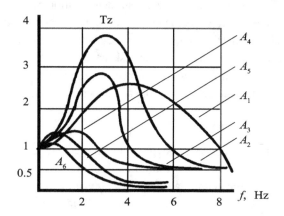

Fig. 2.4. Experimental amplitude-frequency characteristics for $T_z(f)$
in different pneumatic dampers

The experts in the field of vibroisolators designing have offered the following set of quality criteria for the analysis of evolution: K_1 — quality of the vibration damping; K_2 — patentability; K_3 — reliability; K_4 — quality and opportunity of a system reorganization for various required frequencies spectra; K_5 — constructional, technological and operational complexity of a system; K_6 — cost of a system; K_7 — operational expenses; K_8 — vibroisolation quality in various orientation of a system in space; K_9 — opportunity of realization of the various damping laws; K_{10} — conformity of a system to the best analogues; K_{11} — compactness of a system; K_{12} — requirement for new materials and technologies at creation of system.

These twelve quality criteria of further were united into hierarchical structure shown in a Fig. 2.5. The main goal in this task (focus) was formulated as follows: "To reveal the most perspective devices from the point of view of perfection".

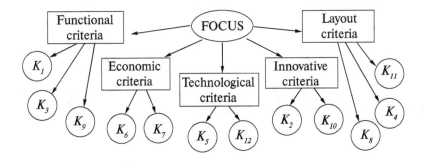

Fig. 2.5. Quality criteria hierarchy for the analysis of the development
of pneumatic dampers

Results of marginal analysis

The analytic hierarchy processes (AHP) is based on pair comparisons of
objects, on formation of pair comparisons matrixes and on subsequent calculation of the main eigenvectors for these matrixes, which are interpreted as
vectors of priorities for considered objects [5, 6]. For the calculation of the
generalized estimations for alternatives, which are at the lowermost hierarchy
level (is not shown in a Fig. 2.5), the procedure of linear additive convolution
on hierarchy is applied.

At the first stage the alternatives priorities vectors for all criteria in hierarchy were computed. Experts estimated the superiority of concrete alternatives
by criteria during filling the pair comparisons matrixes. The importance of all
criteria was accepted identical. As a result the tendencies of change of priorities
of groups of criteria in time (Fig. 2.6) were established. The order of an ar-
rangement of alternatives in a Fig. 2.6 corresponds to time of their occurrence.

During the evolution there is an essential improvement of the functional,
layout and innovative criteria and deterioration of economic and technological
criteria. The analysis of pneumatic dampers by the innovation criteria permits
to reveal a unordinary situation, when criterion of novelty for later alternative
A_4 is worse, than for the previous prototype A_3. The components of an integrated priorities vector concerning the hierarchy's focus demonstrate, that the
situations are probable, when earlier designs are more effectively by the generalized additive criterion than later inventions (A_2 better, than A_3 and A_4). The
established facts enable to influence on decision making, therefore, the approach considered allows to increase validity of the decisions at a choice of
rational variants in view of the tendencies of evolution

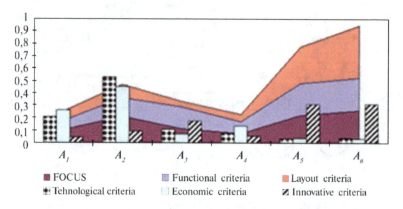

Fig. 2.6. The change of criteria groups for alternatives
which have appeared in different moments of time

During the study of designs evolution the marginal analysis was carried out by means of AHP. The purpose of such analysis consists in revealing criteria, which are most desirable for the improvements in the future. At the filling of pair comparison matrixes the expert should answer questions: "How much an improvement of one characteristic is more preferably commensurable improvement of another?". The received priorities enable to estimate the importance of criteria during development of devices of the considered class. Improvements of a system's quality by one criteria is usually accompanied by deterioration of their estimations by another. In this connection it is interesting to reveal criteria, the deterioration by which are admitted in the certain degree. In a Fig. 2.7. The priorities of criteria groups concerning their contribution to an main goal and marginal priorities showing a desire of improvements and an admissibility of possible deterioration are given. The groups are located in decreasing order of priorities concerning focus of hierarchy. The marginal priorities of groups for improvements have another order: the improvements by layout criteria are a little more important, than the improvement of functional parameters, and improvement of economic parameters is more important than improvement of innovation criteria. Most important criteria for the progress are functional, layout and innovative. From the point of view of the inventor some deterioration of innovation and economic criteria are admitted, but the deterioration of functional and layout criteria are unacceptable. This result coincides with results of the analysis of evolution (Fig. 2.6).

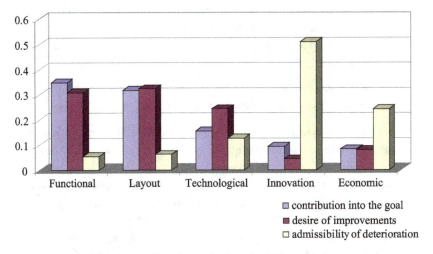

Fig. 2.7. The results of marginal analysis for criteria groups

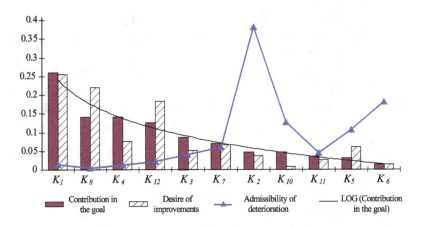

Fig. 2.8. The results of marginal analysis of development criteria

The results of the marginal criteria analysis are given in a Fig. 2.8. They show, that the deterioration of innovation criteria (K_2, K_{10}) and a cost (K_6) are admitted. The deterioration of vibroisolation quality (K_1), spatial orientation (K_8) and frequencies spectra reorganization (K_4) practically are inadmissible. Most urgent tasks are improvement of K_1, K_8 and adaptability to manufacture (K_{12}), then a reduction of complexity (K_5) and operational expenses (K_7) and also increasing of reliability of systems (K_3).

The researches show, that the marginal analysis of quality criteria allows to receive the authentic forecasts of development of TS of a researched class. Thus it is possible to reduce expenses of work and time for the analysis of the patent information.

2.3. A choice of a perspective system for vibration isolation in conditions of varying environment

Our report is devoted to the applications of Analytical Hierarchy and Network Processes in engineering designing, where decision-making and forecasting are the principal problems in the initial stages.

We researched different approaches to these problems, such as fuzzy sets, logic reasoning, utility theory and AHP, developed by Thomas Saaty. We assume the last methodology is the most suitable for the problem-solving in the first stages of engineering designing. We had developed some versions of software for AHP and ANP. Among them there is a program system for decision-making with dynamic judgements.

We would like to show the results of the practical problem, which is connected with a choice of a principal type of the vibration isolation system (VIS) in the first step of the projection.

In a such problem it should be taken into account the probable changes of requirements to the object being designed during time. The engineering requirements vary because the environment of the designed system changes. These changes cause the modifications of the experts' judgements and the priorities of the task units.

ANP is a good tool for an estimation of the task units significance, when experts' preferences are constant.

Let us consider the example, where the VIS producer should choose a perspective type of VIS for equipping of vehicle. Graph of influences is shown in the Fig. 2.9. In this task it was necessary to fill in 95 pair comparison matrixes.

The sequential raising of the supermatrix in integer degrees has resulted to the vector of limiting impact priorities (Fig. 2.10).

The greatest impact into main goal have the following units:

2.3 — competitiveness;

1.3 — VIS controlled;

2.2 — production growth;

2.4 — investments;

2.1 — profit.

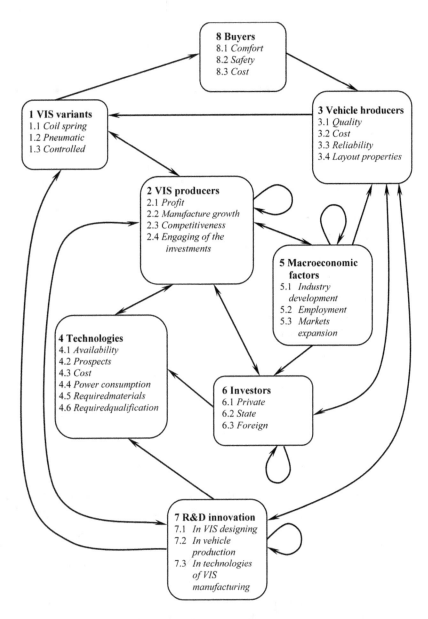

Fig. 2.9. The network structure for the task of forecasting a perspective VIS

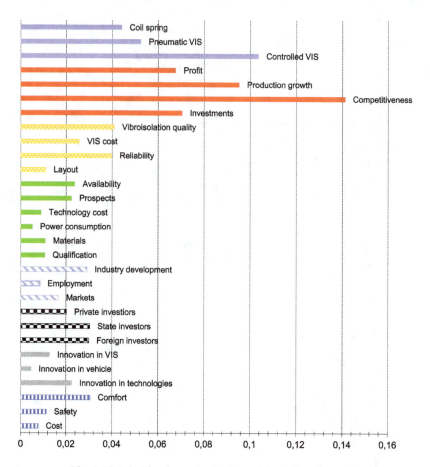

Fig. 2.10. Limiting impact priorities of the task units

The most influential cluster is VIS producers, then follow the type of VIS and cluster of the vehicle producers (Fig. 2.11). The main requirements of vehicle producers to VIS are vibroisolation quality and reliability. The most important technologies factors are availability and prospects. Impact priorities of the state and foreign investors essentially exceed the private ones. Main requirement of vehicle buyers to VIS is comfort. Impact priorities of macroeconomic and R&D innovations are small. The strongest macroeconomic factor is industry development, and the most essential innovation factor is progress in technologies.

Limiting impact priorities

Cluster 1	1.1 Spring	1.2 Pneumatic	1.3 Controlled			
Type of VIS	0.0441	0.0524	0.1035			
Cluster 2	**2.1 Profit**	**2.2 Growth**	**2.3 Competitiveness**	**2.4 Investments**		
Purposes of VIS producers	0.0676	0.0952	0.1413	0.0704		
Cluster 3	**3.1 Quality**	**3.2 Cost**	**3.3 Reliability**	**3.4 Layout properties**		
Requirements of vehicle producers	0.0409	0.0258	0.0398	0.0112		
Cluster 4	**4.1 Availability**	**4.2 Prospects**	**4.3. Cost**	**4.4 Power consumption**	**4.5 Materials**	**4.6 Qualification**
Technologies parameters	0.0238	0.0224	0.0091	0.0053	0.011	0.0108
Cluster 5	**5.1 Development**	**5.2 Employment**	**5.3 Market expansion**			
Macroeconomic factors	0.0292	0.0086	0.0167			
Cluster 6	**6.1 Private**	**6.2 State**	**6.3 Foreign**			
Investors	0.0202	0.0304	0.03			
Cluster 7	**7.1 In VIS**	**7.2 In vehicle**	**7.3 In technology**			
R&D innovations	0.0129	0.0047	0.0225			
Cluster 8	**8.1 Comfort**	**8.2 In vehicle**	**8.3 Cost**			
Requirements of vehicle buyers	0.0306	0.0047	0.0079			

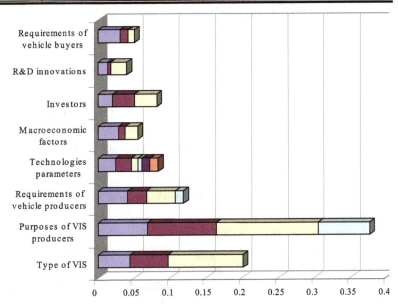

Fig. 2.11. Limiting impact priorities for the cluste

2.4   Expert Preferences Varying in Time

We have solved this task by another way, using AHP with dynamic judgements. At first we solved the static task for a choice of the best type of VIS at the present moment t_0. The hierarchy of the problem is shown in the Fig. 2.12. The first level contains main factors. They are macroeconomics, investment climate, R&D innovations and requirements of the vehicle buyers.

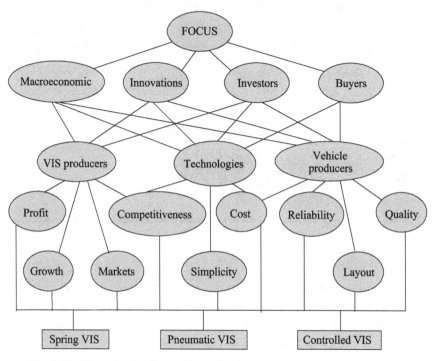

Fig. 2.12. Hierarchy for the problem of a choice of a perspective VIS type

At the second level there are main actors for the problem of a VIS manufacturing, namely VIS producers, vehicle producers and technologies parameters. The set of criteria for a choice of VIS is at the third hierarchy level.

The outcomes of the static task are brought in the Fig. 2.12. The most influential factors at the present moment are investment climate and macroeconomics.

For VIS producers the maximum priority has profit; for vehicle producers the most important criteria are the cost and layout properties.

Priorities vectors for criteria in the static task

	Coil spring	Pneumatic	Controlled
Profit	0.648	0.230	0.122
Growth	0.143	0.429	0.429
Competitiveness	0.075	0.333	0.592
Markets	0.109	0.582	0.309
Quality	0.066	0.319	0.615
Cost	0.751	0.178	0.070
Reliability	0.637	0.105	0.258
Layout	0.105	0.258	0.637

Priorities vectors for alternatives in the static task

	Coil spring	Pneumatic	Controlled
Profit	0.648	0.230	0.122
Growth	0.143	0.429	0.429
Competitiveness	0.075	0.333	0.592
Markets	0.109	0.582	0.309
Quality	0.066	0.319	0.615
Cost	0.751	0.178	0.070
Reliability	0.637	0.105	0.258
Layout	0.105	0.258	0.637

Coil spring is the best from point of view the profit, cost, reliability and manufacture simplicity, therefore it is the best concerning the hierarchy focus.

VIS controlled is the best in terms of the following criteria: production growth, competitiveness, vibroisolation quality and layout. It has the second place. And pneumatic VIS is good for production growth and marketing. It is the latter.

Next step in the problem solving was the revealing of varying judgements. We assumed the preferences of the alternatives concerning the criteria remain constant in future Fig. 2.13. These are the pair comparison matrixes with dynamic judgements. The filling of these matrixes was fulfilled as follows. There were selected $(n-1)$ cells in the matrix, where the functions describing the preferences changes were formed. The preferences values in the start moment t_0 were equal to ones in the static task. After that the values for other (n^2-2n-1) preferences were calculated at the base of the functions given. Such cells are marked as *Auto*. Thus there was no problem with consistency during a solution of the dynamic task. The forming of functions was produced with the help developed software (Fig. 2.14, 2.15).

FOCUS	Macroeconomic	Innovations	Investments
Macroeconomic	1	$1/0.25e^{0.6t}$	Auto
Innovations	$0.25e^{0.6t}$	1	$0.2-0.18t+0.15t^2$
Investments	Auto	$1/(0.2-0.18t+0.15t^2)$	1
Buyers	$0.2-0.05t+0.08t^2$	Auto	Auto

VIS producers	Profit	Growth	Competitiveness	Markets
Profit	1	$1/(0.2+0.05t+0.025t^2)$	$1/0.333e^{0.43t}$	$1/0.333e^{0.43t}$
Growth	$0.2+0.05t+0.025t^2$	1	Auto	Auto
Competitiveness	$0.333e^{0.43t}$	Auto	1	Auto
Markets	$0.333e^{0.43t}$	Auto	Auto	1

Vehicles producers	Quality	Cost	Reliability	Layout
Quality	1	$0.333+0.4t+0.04t^2$	$3-1.15t+0.18t^2$	$0.333+0.15t$
Cost	$1/(0.333+0.4t+0.04t^2)$	1	Auto	Auto
Reliability	$1/(3-1.15t+0.18t^2)$	Auto	1	Auto
Layout	$1/(0.333+0.15t)$	Auto	Auto	1

Fig. 2.13. The dynamic pair comparison matrixes

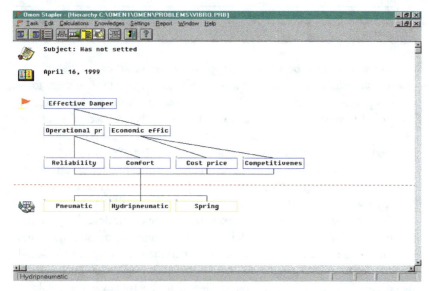

Fig. 2.14. Screen form for building of a hierarchy

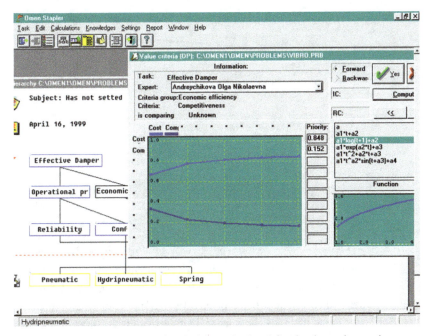

Fig. 2.15. Screen of result priorities calculated for the dynamic matrix

In the Fig. 2.16, 2.17 one can see the outcomes of the dynamic task. The first graph demonstrates the changes of the factors priorities. We can see that priorities of innovation and buyers requirements will increase in Russia in future. The influence of macroeconomic and investments will decrease.

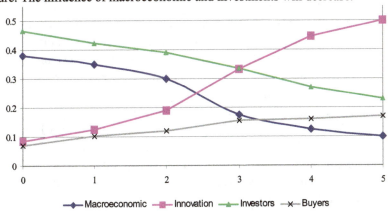

Fig. 2.16. The changes of factor's priorities in time

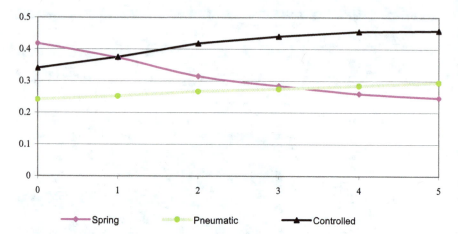

Fig. 2.17. The changes of alternative's priorities in time

It is interesting to note the modifications of alternatives priorities concerning the hierarchy focus. Coil spring moves from the first place to the latter. The best in future will be VIS controlled, pneumatic VIS moves to the second place.

Both considered methods show that VIS controlled is the most perspective system from points of view corresponding to different aspects of designing.

The results obtained supplement each other and allow to reveal the contradictions in expert information.

2.5   About some features of AHP/ANP applications

Introduction

The evolution of AHP/ANP methodology occurs in different ways; the most important of them are the substantiation of its fundamentals, the comparing and combining with other decision-making methods, the exploring of its opportunities by examples of applications. The last item is the most diverse and complex, so as applications have the specificity that takes main attention, therefore a careful analysis of AHP/ANP applications is the urgent and interesting problem. Here it is interesting not so much the problems, which were solved with use of AHP/ANP, as the procedure of problems solving. We do not claim to do exhaustive analysis of AHP/ANP applications in this paper, but we would like to notice some features in problem statements, results' interpretations and difficulties, which can arise.

Brief review of AHP/ANP applications

AHP is the analytical tool for decision-making problems, which should be represented by the hierarchy, containing the set of alternatives at the bottom level, the main goal at the top and a number of the sets of criteria, subcriteria, factors, actors, etc. at the intermediate levels [7, 8]. The AHP applications, as a rule, have traditional statement of the problems — choose the best variant from the given set of alternatives in terms of goal, taking into consideration a structured set of criteria, factors and actors [8-11]. The particular class of applications are decision-making problems with use BOCR-analysis (Benefits, Opportunities, Costs, Risks), which contain a set (usually four) of hierarchies and include a procedure of the synthesis of global priorities [12]. It's amazing that a number of applications of marginal analysis [7] is negligible, while it can give valuable results [13]. Unfortunately, up today there is not available software for AHP with dynamic judgments, which is a powerful tool for forecasting. Because of this, applications of this technique are scarce [14].

Important advantages of AHP are good understandability and interpretability of the results. These advantages sometimes create impression of seeming simplicity that lead to mistakes, which, as a rule, arise from imperfect representation of the problem and from the invalid choice of measurement method for each criterion.

ANP gives the opportunity to take into consideration mutual influences of criteria and alternatives; therefore it enables to diversify problems' statements [12]. Besides decision-making problems with dependence we can state the problems of researching of influence and/or forecasting of possible consequences of such influences. ANP gives the opportunity to find out the elements, which accumulate influences, and to interpret their limit priorities as impact of main goal [11]. Further we describe the features of ANP applications for researching of influences in difficult practical problems.

ANP as a researching tool

Analytic Network Process is a powerful tool for system analysis and qualitative simulating. One of its main advantages is that it can be applied under uncertainty, when other techniques do not work. ANP enables to describe the problem by the qualitative attributes such as clusters, nodes and relations between them. After that one can use quantitative data in the form of expert judgments for an experimental evaluating of mutual influences of the elements. Thus we have an opportunity to explore complex problem and to obtain unobvious results by the experimenting with the model thereby to achieve the better understanding of the problem. The researcher can reveal not only the elements (nodes and clusters), which accumulate influences, but also the elements, which are the most influential [15]. In such problems a researcher should formulate his goals, but he can do without the special cluster, containing alternatives, because his interests are wider than alternatives. He has concern in the revealing of all nodes and clusters, which accumulate influence and influence other elements. Besides he can be interested in the addition and deletion of some elements and relations between them to understand the real problem better. Below we describe these research procedures by short examples.

Revealing of the most influential elements

When we want to research influences in a complex problem, first of all we have to build a connected network that shows these influences. We shall demonstrate the procedure by the example of researching financial crisis [16]. Network model, describing this problem, is shown in the Figure 2.18, where one can see the cluster-source *Government* and the cluster-sink *Macrofactors*. The goal was to answer the questions "What effect will have the actions are being taken by the government (the nodes of the cluster Government) on other clusters and nodes?" and "What government's actions are the most influential?" When filling the matrixes for the network in the Fig. 2.18, experts should answer the question "What of two compared nodes (clusters) the analyzed node (cluster) influence more and how much more?" As result we had got pair comparison matrixes, like the following:

Comparing by the cluster Banks	Banks	Producers	Population	Sc&Tech	Macrofactors	w
Banks	1	2	3	9	5	0,4574
Producers		1	2	5	3	0,087
Population			1	3	2	0,1497
Sc&Tech				1	1/2	0,2572
Macrofactors					1	0,0487

Limit priorities of the nodes are brought in Fig. 2.18, where we can see zero values for the nodes of the cluster *Government*. As well we were interested in answering the question "What of the government's steps will have the most influence?", therefore we had turned up network and had passed to the inverted task that is shown in Fig. 2.19.

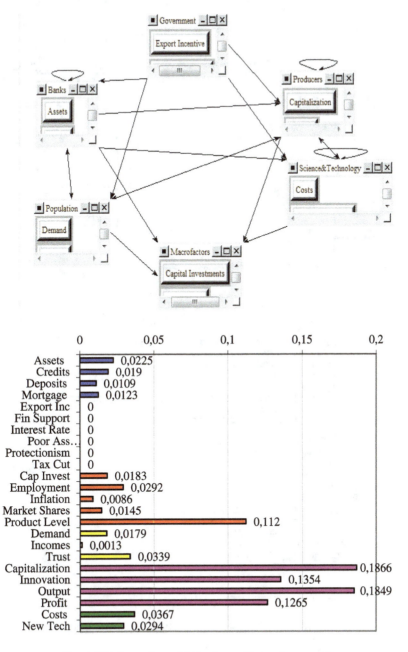

Fig. 2.18. Network model for the problem of researching
of financial crisis and limit priorities of the nodes

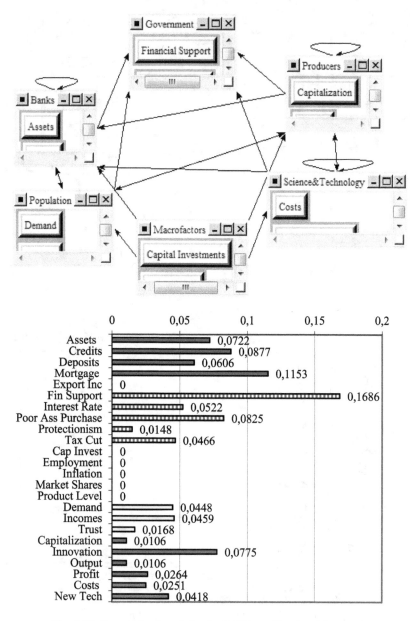

Fig. 2.19. Inverted network for the problem of researching
of financial crisis and limit priorities of the nodes

In Fig. 2.19 we can see reverse direction of arrows. Note, this is not meant that influence direction has changed; we had to do that owing to use ANP software [16] to fill pair comparison matrixes, which contain answers the question "What of two compared clusters (nodes) influence the analyzed cluster (node) more, and how much more?" Here is the example of a matrix

Comparing by the cluster Banks	Banks	Government	Population	w
Banks	1	2	3	0,4574
Government		1	2	0,087
Population			1	0,1497

Let's compare Fig. 2.18 and Fig. 2.19. In Fig. 2.18 cluster *Banks* influence clusters *Producers, Population, Sc&Tech, Macrofactors* anditself, i.e. *Banks*, therefore the first matrix has dimension of five and expresses influence of *Banks* other clusters. In turns, in Figure 2.18 we can see that cluster *Banks* is influenced by the clusters *Government, Population* and by itself, i.e. *Banks*. The last matrix shows, how these clusters influence cluster *Banks*. To do such comparison with use ANP software we had to change arrows' directions. We had done pair comparison matrixes for all remaining clusters and nodes likewise. Limit priorities of the nodes for the inverted task are brought in Fig. 2.19, where one can see zero values for the nodes of cluster *Macofactors*, and non-zero values for the nodes of cluster *Government*. Thus it is possible to evaluate, what of the government's actions will have the most effect for researched model.

We would like to notice one important aspect in influences analysis that is connected with a sign of influence, which can be positive or negative. In general, one should not represent positive and negative influence in one network, as then the results will not be interpreted. In such cases one can construct two networks, which will show positive and negative influences separately, and then it is possible to generalize limit priorities of the same elements like BOCR technique.

Experimental research of network structure

Here we want to show the procedure of the network creation, which usually causes difficulties. The problem is to evaluate efficiency of expense items of state budget in Russian Federation. This urgent problem is complicated by non-transparency and political circumstances. We use the real data from open sources (http://www.minfin.ru/ru) about expense items of state budget for 2013 year. The simplest network for the problem is shown in Fig. 2.20, 2.21 which shows a sharing of budgetary funds. Main goal was to answer question "What part of budgetary funds is being accumulated in the elements (nodes, clusters)?"

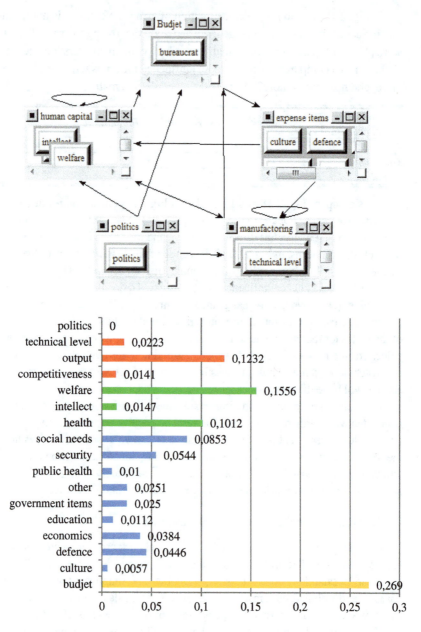

Fig. 2.20. Network for the researching of efficiency of the budgetary
funds' sharing of and limit priorities of nodes

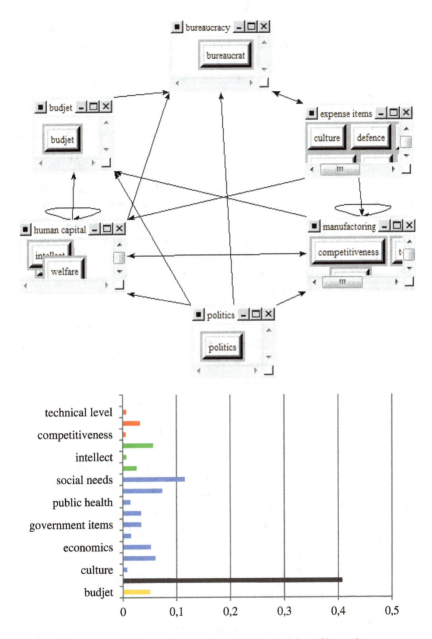

Fig. 2.21. Changed network and limit priorities of its nodes

We can see that 27% should return to *Budget* through the tax, which come from *Manufacturing* and *Human capital* clusters, and zero value for cluster-source *Politics*. Cluster *Manufacturing* contains three nodes — *competitiveness, technical level* and *output*, which has the greatest limit priority. *Human capital* is characterized by *health, welfare* and *intellect*, which has the least part of budget funds. Mutual influences of the elements one can see in supermatrix, which is brought in Appendix 1. The accordance of normalized priorities of elements of cluster Expense items with real data are shown in Fig. 2.22. We can see that it is very good, but the real financing of manufacturing and human capital as well as return to budget poorly correspond with reality. We cannot have sufficient tax proceeds, when the most part of people has small incomes and a lot of manufacturers are very close to bankruptcy. The base of state budget consists of the tax proceeds from oil and gas sales as well as other minerals. In addition, Russia today has very high level of corruption and improper use of budgetary funds. To take into consideration these aspects we have added into network one cluster *Bureaucracy*, containing a single node. *Bureaucracy* is intermediate between *Budget* and real recipients of budget funds. Most of them have conflict of interests, when making decisions about the financing. Feedback between *Expense items* and *Bureaucracy* simulate corruption scheme named backoff (otkat in Russian). The model with this change and the limit priorities for its nodes are shown in Fig. 2.21.

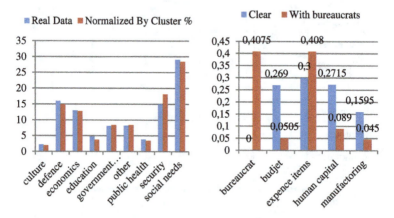

Fig. 2.22. The comparison normalized limit priorities of expense items with real data (at the left) and comparison of limit priorities of clusters for two models (at the right)

We can see that the backoff exceeds 40% while the return to budget has dropped up to 5%. Impact to *Manufacturing* and *Human capital* is appreciably reduced too. The comparison of limit priorities of the clusters is shown in Fig. 2.22 that demonstrates reallocation of budgetary funds for benefit of bureaucracy and increasing of expense items, which are not connected with manufacturing and human capital.

This example illustrates the research procedure that can take place in the development of ANP application. Step-by-step complication of the network model enables to understand a difficult problem and to obtain the results, explaining reality.

Conclusion

This paper is an attempt to review main opportunities that AHP/ANP gives to researchers. In the teaching and consulting on AHP/ANP applications the most important and difficult steps are connected with the problem statement. Besides decision-making problems ANP can be used as the simulating tool that enables to research significant relations and influences in complex systems.

What will be with copyright in internet?
The search of decision with analytic network process

Introduction

The appearance of Internet has changed the world and has stated before mankind a number of new problems. In particular, the economics of knowledge does not submit to classical economic laws, which are focused on a market exchange of material assets. The knowledge (information) has an important feature, which is connected with the possibility of making the unlimited number of copies. This feature essentially distinguishes the information from tangible (material) resources. The dissemination of knowledge differs from the mechanism of a commodity-money exchange. The evolution of computers and the Internet appearance practically has reduced to zero the costs on copying of the information, in this connection the level of a piracy (copyrights violation) has increased. The aggravation of punishments for a copyright violation results in the contradiction with other human rights, such as the information right, the education right, the publication right etc. At the moment all over the world there are debates, what should be done for the copyright protection in the Internet [17-20]. We have made an attempt to systematize and to analyze the known to us data and opinions in this field with application of ANP [21] and ANP software [22].

Problem statement

The main goal of the research is to find out the best way of copyright protection. We consider this problem, taking into account the categories of Benefits, Costs and Risks. We resign the category Opportunities because its priority less than others. Moreover, it can include a lot of fantastic variants, which are ill-defined, so no use to carry out their quantitative analysis.

At the first step it is necessary to form the Alternative's cluster, which will contain the different measures for the regulation of Internet-content. There are two mainstreams in the numerous discussions of this problem, the first of them declares free use of Internet-content and the second urges to aggravate the punishment for copyright violation [23-25]. Back to the Future: Can. At this, there are ideas to punish customers, site owners and providers. Free use of content is very advantageous for customers, but it causes a question: "Who will pay content's creation?" In the attempts to answer this question one can see the following variants:

- Sponsoring of creators of Internet-content, for example, as well as in Renaissance.

- Content's creators have other sources of income, a lot of leisure-time and don't aim to earn livelihood with Internet-content. At the moment this way seems fantastic, we name it *Change of Commodity-Money Paradigm*, but we think that Internet makes us do it in future.

- *Voluntary payment for Internet-content*. This idea is proposed both by the researchers [26-28] (and by some creators, which test it experimentally).

- *Tax upon data media* or *tax upon incoming Internet traffic*, which will be distributed between creators. Such schemes already are used in some countries (for example, in Sweden), and there are countries that plan to implement them (for example, Russia).

Apart from above mentioned measures, there is one else, which is connected with development of *new technologies for copyright protection*. As well as in the armament industry, if new weapon appears, then the appropriate defense enginery is developed sooner or later. Thus, we shall research ten alternatives that will be included into networks for Benefits, Costs and Risks.

Benefits Network

The main actors in Internet are Providers, Consumers (users) and Content Creators. When Benefits Network was being constructed, our goal was to understand, what alternatives would ensure the greatest benefits for considered actors with taking into account their mutual influence. The Benefits Network is shown in Fig. 2.23, where one can see all clusters and the nodes, which they include.

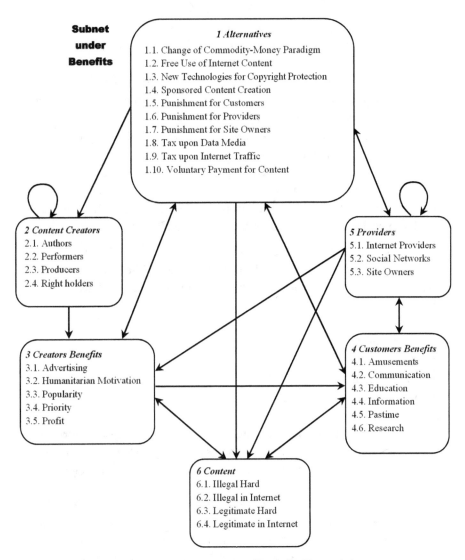

Fig. 2.23. The structure of Benefits Network

Cluster Providers is represented by Internet Providers, Site Owners and Social Networks. We think these actors above all influence the allocation of the Internet content and access of users to it. The influence of providers expresses their benefits and, in turn, the nodes influencing Providers affect the Providers' benefits. Therefore, the special cluster for Providers' benefits is not made.

Cluster Content Creators include Authors, Performers, Producers and Right holders. Such composition is caused by the variety of content. Creator's Benefits contains the following nodes:

- Advertising — creators are interested in informing users on their creations.
- Humanitarian Motivation — many talent people need in the creation and publishing their creations regardless of rewards.
- Popularity — this benefit is especially inherent to creators of the content for mass consumption.
- Priority — who is the first and who is most quotable — these problems are very significant for authors.
- Profit — this node is the most important for Producers and Right holders. It can be the main motive for many Authors and Performers too.

Instead of cluster Customers we use the cluster Customer's Benefits, because there is not a sense to consider different groups of the consumers in this research. These benefits correspond to different kinds of user's activity in Internet. Here they are:

- Amusements;
- Communication;
- Education;
- Information;
- Pastime;
- Research.

Cluster Content includes four categories formed on the base of attributes Legitimacy and Media type. This research is an attempt to look at the problem as whole, therefore content was not differentiated by functions, although it will be interesting to do in future.

The relations between clusters and nodes correspond to influence, preference or importance. We suppose the alternatives influence all the clusters and their elements. In turn, the elements (nodes) of the alternative's cluster are influenced by the clusters Creators Benefits, Customers Benefits and Providers. Content influence the benefits for creators and customers and so on.

Cost's Network

The subnet under Costs is shown in the Fig. 2.24. It contains six clusters: Alternatives, Content, Content Creators, Creators Costs, Customers Costs and Providers. New clusters in comparison with Benefits subnet are Creators Costs and Customers Costs. Main costs of creators are Knowledge, Money and Time.

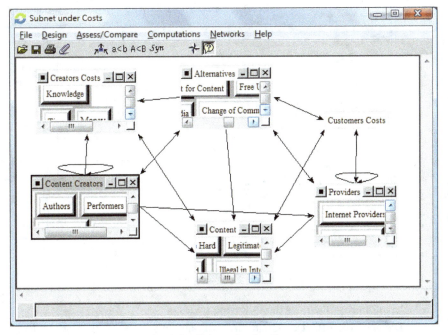

Fig. 2.24. Subnet for the Costs

We consider the following main costs of the customers:

- Downloading — payment for content downloading.
- Extended Services — payment for additional services given by providers.
- Hindered Access to Content may be caused either by too high cost or by other circumstances.
- Internet Connection — payment for log-in.
- Internet Traffic — payment for traffic.
- Unwanted Advertising — this issue means intangible costs of the customers, which are connected with forcible marketing. Note, that this node deserves a special attention, because it touches a very urgent problem of gibberish information.

Risk's Network

Risk's network is shown in Fig. 2.25. It contains the following clusters: Alternatives, Content, Content Creators, Providers, Creators Risks, Customers Risks and Providers Risks. Let consider the last three clusters in detail.

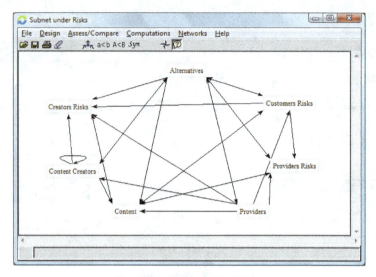

Fig. 2.25. Subnet under Risks

Creators Risk includes the following nodes:

- Disincentive Effect on Creativity. Non-authorized use of the content can deprive of the authors of creative stimulus.
- Financial Loss can take place, if creators invest money in their products, but the customers don't pay for them.
- Lack of Dialog. The excessive protection of content from non-authorized use can result in lack of dialogue with the consumers.
- Obscurity. The creators, consciously limiting the field of distribution of their products, have a risk to remain unknown.
- Plagiarism. This and the next item don't need comments.
- Unprofitability.

We single out the following main risks for the customers:
- Civil Liability.
- Criminal Liability.
- Hindered Access to Content.
- Increase of Information Cost.
- Internet Disconnection.

The main risks for providers are:
- Civil or Criminal Liability.
- Clients Loss.
- Reduction in Income.

Discussion of the results

At first we have collected expert judgments and have done pair comparisons of clusters and nodes in every network. After that the overall results were obtained.

Benefits

The limiting priorities for the benefits network are shown in Fig. 2.26. One can see that the best alternatives are Free Use of Internet Content and Sponsored Content Creation. Let examine this result. We can see that the consumers' benefits have the greatest priority. It means that the consumers' benefits to the greatest degree accumulate influence of researched elements of the problem. In other words, benefits, first of all, are the consumers' benefits. It follows from the structure of the network of mutual influences, but is not someone's opinion. Such result can be explained by the fact that benefits of creators and providers arise only then, when the consumers gain if getting of their products and services.

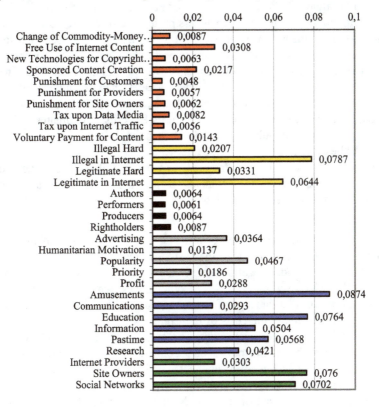

Fig. 2.26. Limiting priorities for benefits network

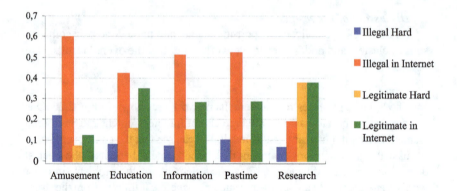

Fig. 2.27. Preference of the content's types for the customers

Content is the second cluster on the importance, at this a share of Internet-content is almost 73 % of the accumulated influence, and 40 % from it is illegal content. No wonder that the consumers prefer free-of-charge downloading of the Internet-content, if it is possible. In a Fig. 2.27 one can see, that for all purposes, except researches, consumers prefer the illegal Internet-content.

The third cluster on importance is Providers, among which Site Owners and Social Networks have priorities twice greater, than Internet Providers.

The cluster Content Creators in the least degree is influenced by other elements, which influence the cluster Creators Benefits. The greatest priorities among them have Popularity and Advertising, the Profit is on the third place.

The best alternative is Free Use Internet Content, and then Sponsored Content Creation and Voluntary Payment for Content follow. These alternatives are more preferable for the customers. The priorities of alternatives connected with punishment, are much smaller.

Costs

The distribution of limiting priorities of the clusters for costs network is shown in Fig. 2.28. In terms of the costs the cluster Content is the most important, and the node Illegal in Internet has the greatest priority in this cluster (it nearly twice exceeds priorities of other nodes, which are approximately equal). It means that this type of content results in the highest costs. The costs in this network imply the costs of the Content Creators, Customers and Providers, which influence each other. The greatest contribution to the overall costs is brought by the Customers, then Content Creators and Providers follow. Main costs of the customers are connected with the payment for content downloading and with intangible costs from unwanted advertising. The most important costs for Content Creators are Money and Knowledge put in content.

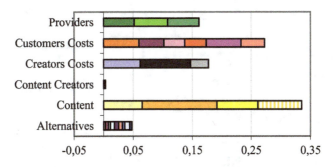

Fig. 2.28. Limiting priorities of the clusters for the Costs network

The analysis of alternatives shows that the Tax upon Internet Traffic has the greatest costs, next three alternatives connected with punishments follow. Let's try to explain these outcomes with help of Fig. 2.29. The alternative Free Use of Internet Content has the greatest costs for the Content Creators, but the costs of Providers and Customers for it are rather less in comparison with others. Tax upon Internet Traffic has high costs of the customers and social networks, but not for Content Creators and Site Owners. The alternatives connected with punishments are characterized by high costs of the customers and providers. As the total influence of the customers and providers more than twice surpasses the influence of the Content Creators, so these alternatives become the leaders on costs.

Limiting priorities of alternatives normalized by cluster are brought in Table 2.1. Multiple-aspect analysis with use of ANP shows that alternative having maximum benefits, is characterized by low costs, and vice versa high-cost alternatives have small benefits.

Risks

Limiting priorities of the nodes in the Risks network are shown in Fig. 2.30. Influence of risks is substantially accumulated in the clusters Alternatives and Content. The most risky types of Content are Illegal Hard and Illegal in Internet. The least risky category is Legitimate Internet content. The Providers have the highest risks among the actors, after them the Content Creators follows; the Customers' risks take the third place. The maximum risk for providers is reduction in incomes, for Content Creators — financial losses and unprofitability, for the customers — civil liability for breach of copyrights and increase of information cost.

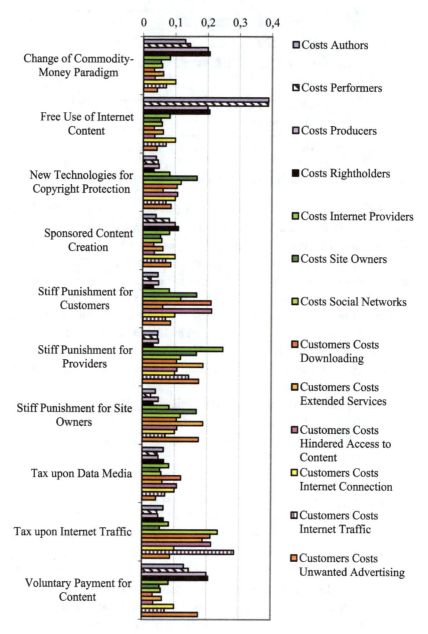

Fig. 2.29. Alternatives' priorities with respect to influencing nodes

Table 2.1. Normalized limiting priorities of Alternatives

Alternatives	Costs 0,2	Benefits 0,4	Risks 0,4
Change of Commodity-Money Paradigm	0,05974	0,07752	0,07224
Free Use of Internet Content	0,06065	0,27443	0,10379
New Technologies for Copyright Protection	0,10038	0,05655	0,08558
Sponsored Content Creation	0,06472	0,19306	0,06871
Punishment for Customers	0,13097	0,04248	0,1338
Punishment for Providers	0,14299	0,05045	0,13917
Punishment for Site Owners	0,1231	0,05528	0,13292
Tax upon Data Media	0,0812	0,0726	0,08028
Tax upon Internet Traffic	0,15959	0,05005	0,0956
Voluntary Payment for Content	0,07664	0,12759	0,08791

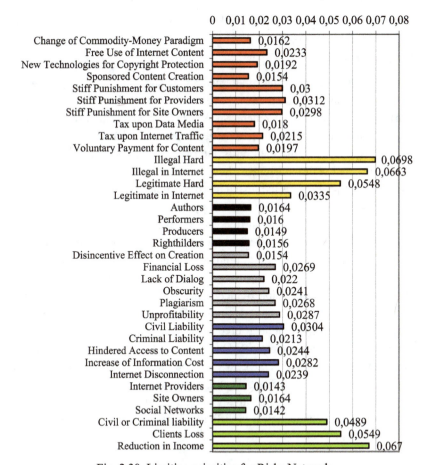

Fig. 2.30. Limiting priorities for Risks Network

151

Leaders over the risks among alternatives are the alternatives connected with punishments, after them Free Use of Internet Content follows. Sponsored Content Creation is the least risky alternative.

Generalized Results

Final step of research is the synthesis of priorities of alternatives and the obtaining of generalized result. Limiting priorities of alternatives with respect to benefits, costs and risks normalized by cluster are brought in Table 2.1 and in Fig. 2.31. We have used the following formula for the synthesis of generalized result:

$$w_{A_i}^G = p_B w_{A_i}^B - p_C w_{A_i}^C - p_R w_{A_i}^R ,$$

where p_B, p_C, p_R — priorities of Benefits, Costs and Risks respectively; $w_{A_i}^B$, $w_{A_i}^C$, $w_{A_i}^R$ — normalized limiting priorities of i's alternative by Benefits, Costs and Risks respectively; $w_{A_i}^G$ — generalized priority of i's alternative.

The generalized priorities of alternatives are shown in Fig. 2.32, where we can see that only three alternatives have positive generalized priorities, particularly Free Use of internet Content, Sponsored Content Creation and Voluntary Payment for Content, which is near-zero. Other alternatives have negative overall priorities, because their costs and risks surpass their benefits. Alternatives connected with punishments have minimum values. This outcome is in conflict with the opinions expressed by some public figures, which insist on a aggravation of the punishments for a copyright breach. We think obtained results are reasonable because, in first, we can explain them due to application of ANP, and, in second, they can be supported by the following considerations.

As digital content can be unlimited replicated, any punishments do not guarantee it from non-authorized use. The Internet is a self-organizing network structure, for which a principle of hierarchical management is not fitted. Therefore a complete control for the use of the information which has appeared in a world wide web is impossible. Moreover, Internet makes accessible the confidential data, which are not protected by copyright, to anyone. A bright example is the history with a site Wiki Leaks. On the other hand, there are technical opportunities to watch over a behavior of the users of the Internet, but their implementation is connected with a violation of human rights and with large expenses. In this connection it is difficult to imagine, that the piracy can be eradicated completely.

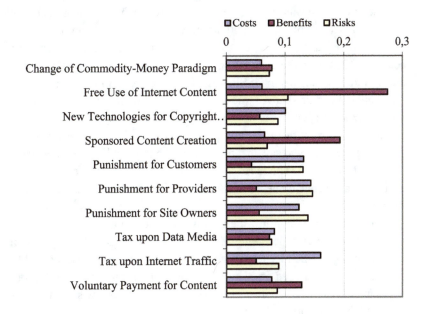

Fig. 2.31. Limiting priorities of alternatives normalized by cluster

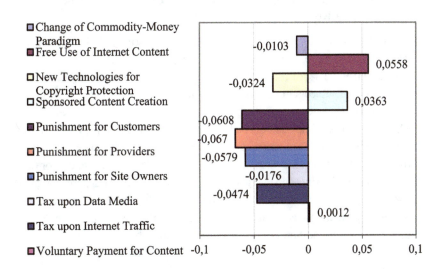

Fig. 2.32. Synthesized priorities of alternatives

The alternative way is connected with the research of the reasons of a piracy and a creation of such conditions, at which it becomes minimal. The reasons of a piracy are caused not only by poverty of the customers, but also that content differs from the material goods in consumers' representation. One of the well-known slogans in USSR was "The art belongs to the people". Note, that there is a certain share of true in it. But besides money, authors need in the popularity and respect of public. The users satisfy a number of their needs with the help of Internet; they regularly pay to providers, but can break the copyrights. It is necessary to say, that the users of the Internet have grand problems connected with a huge volume of the gibberish information; therefore an urgent challenge is the development of the means for effective search and filtration of Internet content.

These arguments confirm the results obtained with the help of network model. In engineering designing there is a good heuristic rule: "If you can't change an object, then try to change its environment". We think it should be applied to the researched problem in the following form: "If we can't protect copyright in Internet, then it is necessary to change the society so that the need in copyright protection vanishes.

Choice with Considering of Requirements of Decision-makers and Alternatives

In decision-making problems it is accepted to assign a set of alternatives (objects) and one or more decision-makers (subjects), which should choose the best alternative using a set of relevant criteria. Sometimes it is difficult to select the objects and the subjects in the socio-economical systems, as the participants of decision-making process simultaneously choose each other. Examples of such tasks are: a choice of the business partners, a selection of the employees to a firm, a choice of strategy of enterprise development and so on. The solving of similar problems by traditional methods of the Decision Theory may lead to the conflicts between the participants and the ignoring of essential information describing various kinds of the relations between the subjects and the objects of a choice.

We propose a new approach to the problems of collaborative choice [29] based on a representation of the expert information by the sets of properties and the requirements, which subjects make to other participants of decision-making process. The representation of information in terms of properties and requirements (demands) enables to separate the objective features of the decisions (properties) from subjective preferences of the decision-makers (requirements). It gives an opportunity for the application of different methods for information processing during a formation and analysis of collaborative decisions, and also an opportunity for the development of intelligent software based on structured knowledge bases containing the objective data, subjective preferences, the rules for formation and evaluation of possible decisions, and the rules for the probable conflicts' resolution.

In the problems of collective choice the participants can make demands not only to alter-natives being chosen, but also to each other. Sometimes these requirements and the mutual influences determine a group choice, which can differ from the outcomes obtained without considering of such information. The approach taking into account mutual requirements of the choice subjects gives the results more feasible in practice. Besides, it enables to find out the reasons explaining why the group sometimes can choose alternative, which is not being the best objectively. At last, in collaborative decision-making problems we can generate and ex-amine the various sets of complex alternatives. For example, when organizing of a joint enterprise one should consider a set of combinations, which include various output kinds being produced, industrial partners, investors, different technologies etc. Such problems emerge in virtual enterprises, both in a stage of their organization, and in a stage of functioning.

Let's consider an example of the collaborative decision-making problem, where the enterprise — producer chooses the output kind for manufacturing with considering of probable consumers, investors and accessible technologies. The structure of the task is presented in a Fig. 2.33.

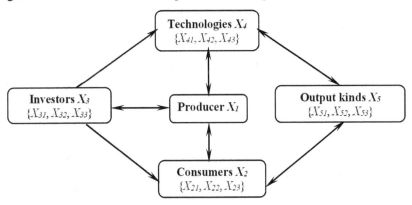

Fig. 2.33. Mutual requirements' graph for the collaborative
decision-making problem

The arrows in the Fig. 2.33 correspond to the requirements directions. Each element of the task is described by a set of properties, which may be expressed by numerical, fuzzy or verbal ratings. Each subject can make some demands to others. Requirements may be expressed by equalities, inequalities or ranges. The degree of requirement satisfaction is calculated as a measure of similarity to the value of appropriate property. To estimate a degree of compliance over all requirements, which a subject make to another, the weighed sum is used. The outcomes of problem solving are the values of generalized measure of mutual requirements compliance for each possible combination, which can be calculated as following:

$$F(d_z) = \prod_{\substack{i=1 \\ i \neq j}}^{N} \left[\sum_{k=1}^{K_{ij}} w_k^j S_k (R_{Y_ik}^j, P_{Y_jl}) \right]^{v_i}, \quad d_z \in D,$$

where $D = X_1 \times X_2 \times \ldots \times X_N$; N — the number of subjects; $R_{Y_ik}^j - k$'s requirement, which a subject Y_i make to l's property of subject Y_j (P_{Y_jl}); K_{ij} — the number of requirements from i's subject to j's; w_k^j — a weight factor for k's requirement of i's subject; v_i — a weight factor of i's subject; $S_k (R_{Y_ik}^j, P_{Y_jl})$ — a measure of similarity of $R_{Y_ik}^j$ to P_{Y_jl}. The way of calculating of similarity measures depends on a form of representation of properties and requirements [29].

In the task shown in Fig. 2.33, producer X_1 simultaneously should make a choice of an output kind from the set X_5, main consumers for his output from the set X_2, a technology for manufacturing his output from X_4 and investors from X_3. Let X_1 produces vibroprotection systems and considers the following alternatives: X_{51} — air damper; X_{52} — spring damper and X_{53} — controlled VPS. Properties of these alternatives and requirements to them are brought in Table 2.2.

We can see, that the most VPS properties are expressed by the orderable verbal ratings, except $P_5(X_{5j})$, and the most requirements are formulated as inequalities. For such case $S_k (R_{Y_ik}^j, P_{Y_jl})$ is calculated as an inclusion measure. We don't adduce here the tables for the others choice subjects because of limited size of this paper.

The outcomes are shown in a Fig. 2.34. The best variant of collaborative decision possesses the maximal value of the generalized measure of the mutual requirements compliance. This variant includes Air damper (X_{51}) manufactured with technology X_{44}, which suits to consumer X_{21} and to investors X_{31}, X_{33}. Note, that all variants containing the investor X_{32} possess small values of generalized measure of mutual requirements compliance. The consumer X_{23} needs in VPS of very high quality, but producer X_1 can't turn out such technique. The consumer X_{22} doesn't require very high quality of damping, therefore he can buy both spring and air damper. Finally, the rational choice for producer is the purchasing and tuning of the technology X_{44} for manufacturing of air damper X_{51} with attracting of the investors X_{31} and X_{33}. So the producer should direct his attention to consumers X_{21} and X_{22}.

Table 2.2. Representation of properties and requirements Properties of VPS X_5

		Quality	Reliability	Cost	Layout	Type of VPS	Spatial orientation	The number of frequencies
		$P_1(X_{5j})$	$P_2(X_{5j})$	$P_3(X_{5j})$	$P_4(X_{5j})$	$P_5(X_{5j})$	$P_6(X_{5j})$	$P_7(X_{5j})$
VPS	X_{51}	High	Middle	Middle	Middle	Pneumatic	Middle	Some
	X_{52}	Middle	High	Low	Low	Spring	Middle	One
	X_{53}	High	High	High	High	Controlled	High	Much
		Requirements to X_5						
		$R_1(X_{ij}, X_5)$	$R_2(X_{ij}, X_5)$	$R_3(X_{ij}, X_5)$	$R_4(X_{ij}, X_5)$	$R_5(X_{ij}, X_5)$	$R_6(X_{ij}, X_5)$	$R_7(X_{ij}, X_5)$
Consumer	X_{21}	Not less than High	Not less than Middle	Not more than Middle	Not less than Middle	—	Not less than Middle	One or more
	X_{22}	Not less than Middle	Not less than High	Not more than Middle	Not less than High	—	Not less than Middle	Restricted spectrum
	X_{23}	Not less than High	Not less than High	Not more than High	Not less than High	—	Not less than High	Wide spectrum
Technology	X_{41}	—	—	—	—	Spring	—	—
	X_{42}	—	—	—	—	Pneumatic	—	—
	X_{43}	—	—	—	—	Controlled	—	—
	X_{44}	—	—	—	—	Pneumatic	—	—

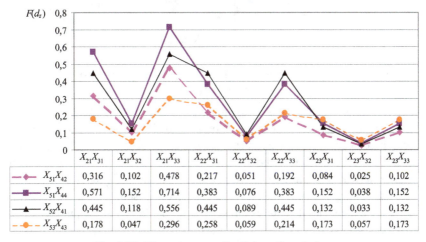

$F(d_z)$	$X_{21}X_{31}$	$X_{21}X_{32}$	$X_{21}X_{33}$	$X_{22}X_{31}$	$X_{22}X_{32}$	$X_{22}X_{33}$	$X_{23}X_{31}$	$X_{23}X_{32}$	$X_{23}X_{33}$
$X_{51}X_{42}$	0,316	0,102	0,478	0,217	0,051	0,192	0,084	0,025	0,102
$X_{51}X_{44}$	0,571	0,152	0,714	0,383	0,076	0,383	0,152	0,038	0,152
$X_{52}X_{41}$	0,445	0,118	0,556	0,445	0,089	0,445	0,132	0,033	0,132
$X_{53}X_{43}$	0,178	0,047	0,296	0,258	0,059	0,214	0,173	0,057	0,173

Fig. 2.34. The outcomes of collaborative choice

Note, the approach considered includes a procedure of the decision synthesis, but not only the task of decision analysis. It may be generalized to the case, when a structure of the decision synthesized can be modifiable. For example, in considered problem the decision variants can include several investors, consumers and so on.

Principles of the Compromise and Conflicts Resolution

We suppose the modern DSS should contain the set of the decision-making methods, which are destined for the certain classes of the tasks. Besides that, a decision-maker should have an opportunity to obtain the outcomes according to various compromise principles used for calculation of a generalized ratings of alternatives quality. It is especially important in the problems of collective or cooperative decision-making. Sometimes the use of different compromise principles helps to make the correct choice. For example, a Fig. 2.35 demonstrates the overall ranking of three alternatives (B1, B2, B3) for three participants with use of different compromise principles. The analysis of these bar charts indicates the most reasonable choice is B3.

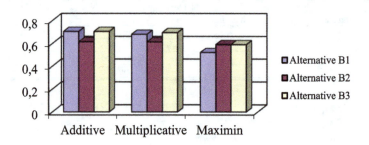

Fig. 2.35. An example of the ranking of alternatives with use of different compromise principles

The conflicts resolution between the participants of a collective choice is possible with use of dialogue procedures for a modification of the requirements and their weights. Note, the information representation in form of the requirements makes a collective choice more clear and helps to solve a problem of manipulation by preferences. The decision-makers preferences characterize the relationship between alternatives and subjective aspirations of participants, i.e. they are not simple entities on the nature. Manipulating the preferences, a person can advisedly deform the subjective information, pursuing own goals. When the information used for decision-making is divided into objective (properties) and subjective (requirements) components, the choice subject operates only with his requirements. In a searching for a compromise with other participants, decision-maker can change weight factors of the requirements, make his demands softer or stronger, refuse some requirements and add new ones. Thus the information on alternatives properties remains constant.

Venture capitalists decision making: applying analytic network process to the startups evaluation introduction

The startup market is highly competitive and the percentage of companies that prosper is small. In the early stage of development, startups often experience various difficulties including a financial gap that limits the company's ability to innovate and commercialize its products [30]. The success or failure of a new business is often dependent on overcoming a series of potential barriers, e.g. limited human capital management capabilities, high uncertainty in terms of product and market, volatile development process, weak partnership ties [31].

There is enough research to support the idea that start-ups that are supported by Venture Capital (VC) generally tend to be more successful than those that do not receive VC support [32- 34]. Undoubtedly, Venture Capitalists (VCs) play the most crucial role in identifying and financing new and highly innovative firms [35]. Moreover, Savaneviciene, Venckuviene and Girdauskienea (2015) conclude that VC is a catalyst for startups to overcome the "valley of death".

While some researchers suggest using statistics to make better VCs decisions, others mention the importance of intuition, arguing that most business decisions are made in the face of uncertainty and these uncertain situations have too many unknowns and complexities to lend themselves to statistical analysis [36-38]. Zacharakis and Meyer [39] suggest that although the expert VC's intuition is valuable it often leads to biased results.

In this article, in order to join different approaches to VCs decision making, we synthesize analytical and heuristic approaches through applying Analytic Network Process (ANP) methodology. An example of comparative evaluation of four Russian e-commerce startups is considered. The proposed ANP model represents problem complexity as a network structure with dependences and feedbacks between decision criteria and alternatives. Based on VCs judgments that are checked for consistency, the ANP approach helps choose the best startup for funding or estimate the target startup versus other startups. ANP makes it possible to make decisions under risks as it allows examining the problem from different angles, e.g. benefits, opportunities, and risks (Saaty 2008a). To implement ANP model Multichoice software has been developed.

Venture capitalists decision making

In the area of VC investment decision methods are used both as tools to evaluate startups, and as tools to analyze in order to identify the factors that drive financial decisions. VCs decision criteria have faced numerous challenges with identifying the economic value of a new venture. A number of studies have produced empirically derived lists of the principle evaluation criteria. The earlier VC research mostly agreed on six criteria: management skill and experience, venture team, product attributes, market growth and size, and expected returns [40-42,]. Subsequent works have also acknowledged the importance of passion in entrepreneurship.

Initial research used post hoc surveys and interviews to collect data on VCs' self-reported decision policy for decisions made in the past. This reliance on retrospective and self-reported data may have generated biased results. Zacharakis and Meyer [39] support the fact that people are poor at introspection and often suffer from recall and post-hoc rationalization biases among others. Therefore, real-time methods such as Verbal Protocols and Conjoint Analysis are more appropriate and eliminate these biases.

Verbal Protocols are real-time "think aloud" observations of VCs screening a potential deal [43]. Different research studies have used Verbal Protocols to understand information in the actual decision process [39-42].

Conjoint Analysis is a technique that assesses decision criteria (attributes) and their significance in the judgment, and how these attributes affect the judgment and the relative importance of each attribute in the decision process [44]. Conjoint Analysis has been used in many studies and gains a deeper understanding of the VC decision process [45, 46].

Another attempt at accomplishing some improvement in the VCs decision process was proposed by Zacharakis and Meyer [47]. They introduced actuarial decision aides that are models that decompose a decision into component cues and recombines those cues to predict the potential outcome. Actuarial models include environmental and bootstrapping models, where the former employ discriminant or regression analysis on actual decision data. Shepherd and Zacharakis [48] proposed that bootstrapping models hold considerable potential for improving VCs decision accuracy.

In any case, for evaluating new ventures not all the VCs are able to follow the same investment decision process [35]. VCs are individuals with their own unique experience, perspective and business priorities, so they do not evaluate startups the same way. Some VCs give more importance to the entrepreneur's characteristics, while others are more intrigued with financial and marketing perspectives. Monika and Sharma [35] highlight that VCs follow the multi-criteria perspective for taking investment decision.

Using heuristics

It is well recognized in the decision-making literature that decision makers are not perfectly rational, but "boundedly rational", which means that when individuals make decisions, their rationality is limited by the tractability of the decision problem, the cognitive limitations of their minds, and the time available to make the decision [49]. Tversky and Kahneman [50] showed that people making decisions under uncertainty rely on a limited number of heuristic principles, which leads to systematic errors.

Zacharakis and Meyer [47] suggest that a VC is apt to assess the success of a current venture prospect by how similar it is to a past success when analyzing VCs decision making. In this assessment, VCs use a representativeness heuristic, which may lead to severe errors [50]. Likewise, if a VC utilizes a satisfying heuristic it may eliminate potentially profitable investments [47]. While assessing decision criteria, VCs may tend to underweight the more important criteria and overweight the less important criteria [49].

Thus, biases and heuristics significantly affect the behavior of VCs. Bias factors include risk perception, overconfidence, inconsistency and habit and framing [48, 51, 52]. All considerations about applying heuristic rules and intuition in VCs decision making imply simplification of the decision process and inconsistent of human judgments.

Woike, Hoffrage, and Petty [53] compared simple heuristics with machine learning and regression models and showed that simple heuristics is competitive with more complex VCs decision strategies. However, is it possible to synthesize analytic and heuristic approaches? Could we apply heuristics without sufficient reduction of the complexity of the problem? This article contributes to answering these questions.

Multi-criteria decision analysis

Due to the complex nature of VCs decision, we suggest that multi-criteria decision analysis (MCDA) methods can help find the best investment strategy. MCDA is devoted to supporting and aiding VCs in situations in which multiple conflicting decision factors (objectives, goals, criteria, etc.) must be considered simultaneously.

There is a vast body of literature on the use of multi-criteria methodologies in financial decision-making, such as project financing, financial performance evaluation, investment selection, extension of credit, and foreign direct investment; however much less is reported on applications of MCDA to VC portfolio selection [54-57]. In recent research, Pakizeh and Hosseini [58] propose PROMETHEE method; Afful-Dadzie, Oplatková, and Nabareseh [59] apply Fuzzy PROMETHEE for selecting startup businesses; Beim and Lévesque consider MAVT. Lu and Shen [60], Su, Jiang, and Ma [61] and Gui-lan [62] evaluate investment risks of VC company based on Analytic Hierarchy Process (AHP). Shijian and Yinyan [63] apply AHP-Fuzzy evaluation methods to evaluate VC project. Wiratno, Latiffianti, and Wirawan [64] apply ANP for selection of business funding proposals. Among the existing methods, ANP is one that considers dependences between decisions criteria [65] (Saaty, 1996). In light of research on MCDA in making VCs decisions, we consider ANP as a decision aid for VCs in understanding the complexities of the decisions they face.

Model construction and results

ANP Model

The ANP model may be constructed after the screening stage of investment where the number of initially available alternatives has been reduced. In our study, four Russian e-commerce startups (let us identify them as A, B, C, and D) are subjected to deep analysis with ANP.

Startup A is a coffee service for drivers, a small chain of stores that offers snacks, tea and coffee to go. Drivers can make an order and pay in advance via a mobile app, and then just pick up in order to save time.

Startup B is a time bank, a reciprocity-based work trading system in which hours are used as currency. With time banking, a person with one skill set can bank and trade hours of work for equal hours of work in another skill set instead of paying or being paid for services.

Startup C is an organic food delivery online service. The service integrates products from different stores to help people buy any organic food without an extra charge for delivery from different shops.

Startup D is an online store for renting sporting goods and equipment (skiing, skates, snowboards, bicycles, etc.). The service allows people to rent goods for the whole season and thereby solves the problem of storing goods in the apartment at the time of the year when they are not being used.

In order to make a comprehensive decision, an investor should take into account the startups performance and development prospects, as well as current and expected risks.

The model included two network structures:

1. Benefits- Opportunities network- This combines all criteria of efficiency and potential of the startups. We consider Benefits and Opportunities within one network structure as benefits criteria have always had an impact on opportunities criteria.

2. Risks network- This includes the most important current and expected risk factors.

These network structures are combined in the control hierarchy for evaluating the networks contribution to the final decision. Each network contains selection criteria, relationship among criteria, and the submitted funding proposals.

Decision criteria of the networks were chosen based on Macmillan [40], Robinson [41], Hall and Hofer [42] and on criteria used in the most popular Russian startups competition — School of a Young Billionaire, organized by Forbes Russia Magazine [66].

The network of Benefits-Opportunities (Fig. 2.36) includes six decision clusters which include the following: Growth for the last year, Society, Team, Promotion, Prospects, Production. Each of the clusters has its own specified criteria (nodes).

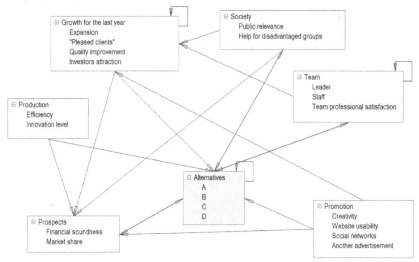

Fig. 2.36. Benefits-Opportunities network

The network of Risks (Fig. 2.37) includes four clusters which include the following: Competition, Commercial risks, Operational risks, and Other risks.

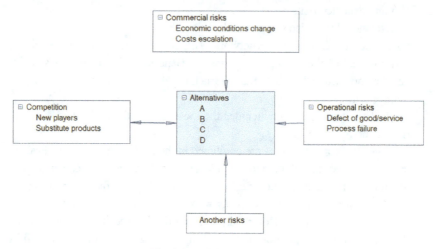

Fig. 2.37. Risks network

To combine and evaluate a network's contribution to the final decision, the control hierarchy is built (Fig. 2.38). Considered networks are evaluated in terms of the Company's profit, the Company's competitiveness, and Improving societal well-being.

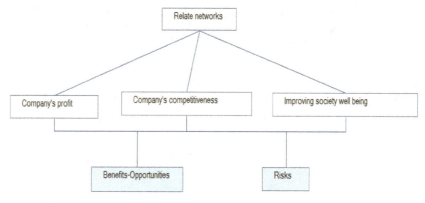

Fig. 2.38. Control hierarchy

The result of the ANP algorithm is to find a startup with the highest ratings in terms of benefits-opportunities and risks priorities ratio. As a result, the selected startup will be the most attractive to receive funding.

Results

The model is built in Multichoice, which is a new software for MCDA based on the ANP/AHP [67]. All pairwise comparison matrixes are filled by one expert, the investor concerned (for more details on the methodology of building pairwise comparisons see Saaty (2008b)). In this study, we do not consider the case of multiple experts, although this may be done (for more details see Saaty [68]).

For the network of Benefits-Opportunities, thirty-seven pair comparison matrixes are filled: 6 for cluster comparisons, and 31 for nodes comparisons. The results of evaluating the startups by each decision criteria of Benefits-Opportunities network are shown in Fig. 2.39.

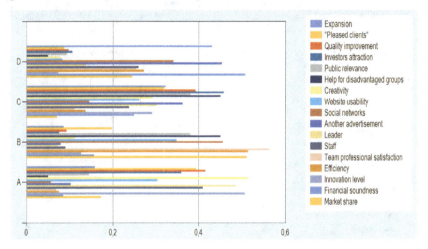

Fig. 2.39. Results of pairwise comparisons of the startups by each node of the Benefits-Opportunities network

Further relative measurements of the influence of elements within the Risks network are considered. Eleven pair comparison matrixes for nodes are filled by the very same expert. The results of evaluating the startups by each decision criteria of the Risks network are shown in Fig. 2.40.

The priority vectors that are obtained are then combined in a supermatrix and weighted in a weighed supermatrix. After the limit supermatrix is calculated, cluster limit vectors are normalized.

Limit normalized by cluster priorities of startups in Benefits-Opportunities network is shown in Fig. 2.41.

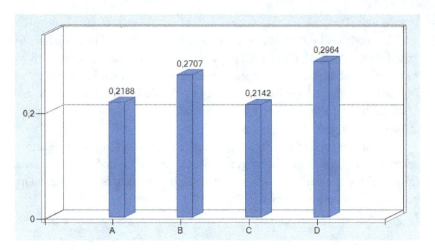

Fig. 2.40. Results of pairwise comparisons of the startups by each node
of the Risks network

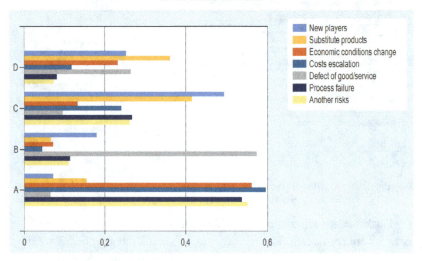

Fig. 2.41. Limit normalized by cluster priorities of the startups
in Benefits-Opportunities network

To analyze the obtained priorities of alternatives within the Benefits-Opportunities network (Fig. 2.41), one should take into account that according to the network's structure (Fig. 2.36) clusters Prospects, Growth for the last year and Team have the highest weights because they accumulate their significance through all links coming into them.

As shown in Fig. 2.39, startup D has the highest node priorities of the "significant" clusters: Expansion (cluster Growth for the last year) — 0.43, Financial soundness (cluster Prospects) — 0.51. The B startup also has the highest node priorities of the "significant" clusters: Team professional satisfaction (cluster Team) — 0.56, Market share (cluster Prospects) — 0.51. Therefore, these startups are the best in terms of Benefits-Opportunities that is shown in Fig. 2.41.

Limit normalized by cluster priorities of startups in the Risks network is shown in Fig. 2.42.

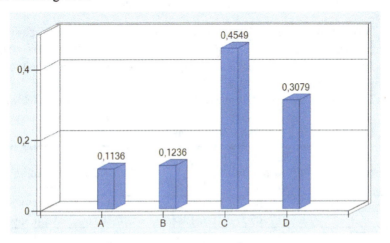

Fig. 2.42. Limit normalized by cluster priorities of the startups
in Risks network

One always should take into account a network's structure for analyzing the obtained priorities. According to the structure of the Risks network (Fig. 2.37), only the Competition cluster accumulates the importance. Therefore, the priorities of the startups by nodes of the Competition cluster are more significant in making the final result. As shown in Fig. 2.42, startup C has the highest priority (0.45) in the Risks network due to its highest nodes priorities of the "significant" cluster Competition.

To obtain priority ratings for the Benefits-Opportunities and Risks networks of the model, they are evaluated by selecting the appropriate rating category from a defined linguistic scale on each criterion of the control hierarchy. In the study, a "High", "Middle", and "Low" linguistic scale is used.

The results of networks linguistic evaluation in control hierarchy (Fig. 2.38) are shown in Table 2.3.

Table 2.3. Linguistic estimation of networks by the criteria of control hierarchy

Crion	Benefits-Opportunities	Risks
Company's profit	High	High
Company's competitiveness	High	Middle
Improving society well being	High	Low

Preferences for linguistic categories obtained by pairwise comparisons and equal:

$$w^{HIGH} = 0.56, \quad w^{MIDDLE} = 0.32, \quad w^{LOW} = 0.12.$$

Priorities of the criteria of control hierarchy are obtained from pairwise comparisons and equal: $P^{REVENUE} = 0.1$, $P^{COMPETITIVNESS} = 0.23$, $P^{WELLBEING} = 0.67$.

Thus, the final weights of Benefits-Opportunities network (w^{BO}) and Risks network (w^R) are: $w^{BO} = 0.73$, $w^R = 0.27$.

The results of multiplicative and additive composition are shown in Table 2.4.

Table 2.4. Synthesis results

Alternatives	Benefits-Opportunities (0,7262)	Risks (0,2738)	Multiplicative	Additive
A	0,2188	0,1136	0,2658	0,2824
B	0,2707	0,1236	0,3031	0,3597
C	0,2142	0,4549	0,179	0,0685
D	0,2964	0,3079	0,2522	0,2894

According to the synthesis results, startup B seems to be the most attractive for funding. The startup is an example of a good balanced alternative that is placed second in terms of Benefits-Opportunities and Risks and first in overall ranking. All alternatives have positive priority at additive composition, which means that they carry benefits-opportunities higher than risks. Sensitivity analysis shows that the final startup's priorities are stable to the 5% changes of elements priorities in the networks and to the 5% changes of networks weights.

Discussion

Practical implementation issues. The goal of this paper is to improve VCs decision making by synthesizing analytical and heuristic approaches. The proposed ANP methodology is a useful decision aid for VCs that helps to valuate selected ventures.

The commonly used valuation techniques in corporate finance (e.g. discounted cash flow method, earning multiple method and net asset method, etc.) depend on strict assumptions and require information that new ventures typically cannot provide (such as accounting information). Hence, their applicability is severely limited in valuating early-stage new ventures and both venture capitalists and entrepreneurs are frustrated by huge variance of valuations computed from the extant methods for the same new venture [36]. Uncertainty and risk related to product creation and commercialization, human resource management issues, lack of technological knowledge etc. are inherent features for startups.

Thus, VCs must make their decision under uncertainty and risk without a sufficient amount of financial records. All these facts are major requisites for using heuristic rules in evaluation, and as a result in valuation of startups. On the other hand, although the expert VC's intuition is valuable, it is often biased resulting in suboptimal decisions [47].

The proposed ANP methodology makes it possible to assess all criteria that are valuable for VCs without sufficient simplification of the problem. ANP startups ratings may be used as weights for determining startups valuation. For example, a target startup may be included in an ANP model with an already funded similar start up in order to determine an appropriate valuation of the target. The valuation of the considered startup will be determined through final weights of the alternatives. Thus, the ANP approach may considerably extend the scope of comparative valuation methods.

Furthermore, the problem of evaluating startups arises not only in the case of their valuation, but also occurs in the selection of winners at startup competitions. At some competitions, the startups may be very different from each other, so the right evaluation of the competitors may be a very complicated task. Since winners experience a positive effect of visibility and reputation, a fair and impartial selection of a winner is the best guarantee for adequate funding.

The proposed ANP model uses one expert who is responsible for model building and making comparisons. However, the ANP may be also applied in the case where a group of experts dealing with framing a constructed network structure. Aczel and Saaty [69] proved that the unique way to combine reciprocal individual judgments into a corresponding reciprocal group judgment is by using their geometric mean.

Limitations

As with any methodology, ANP/AHP has its possible limitations. The first one concerns the number of included criteria and alternatives. ANP/AHP does not work optimally in the case where the number of alternatives is large; therefore, it cannot be applied at the screening stage of investment. Therefore, at first, VCs must screen the hundreds of proposals by using, for example, actuarial decision aides or simple heuristic rules [47, 53]. Those ventures that survive the initial stage can then be subjected to deep analysis with ANP.

Another approach that works with a large number of items, for example, is to use an extension of AHP structuring by incorporating it into another method of prioritization known as Best-Worst scaling [70].

Zacharakis and Meyer [47] also conclude that as more information is available to the decision, the VC's predictive accuracy substantially decreases. Although this statement relates to heuristic decision making, it partly concerns ANP too. In spite of the fact that ANP helps to analyze complex VC decision problems through including as many network structures, decision criteria and interactions between them as needed, when the number of criteria is large, the amount of time needed to complete the pairwise comparison will be considerably long. Furthermore, pairwise comparison value might be inconsistent due to this massive number of comparisons. As a result, quality of perception of the comparisons will be reduced. To solve this problem, different ways to improve the consistency of judgements have been discussed [71, 72]. Another solution is to use incomplete pairwise comparisons [73, 74]. Therefore, it is the expert's responsibility to determine the degree of the model's complexity that would make ANP more applicable.

In spite of the requirement that an allowable consistency ratio must be not more than about .10, the requirement of 10% cannot be made smaller, such as 1 or 0.1%, without trivializing the impact of inconsistency. Saaty [75] noticed that inconsistency itself is important because without it new knowledge that changes, preference cannot be admitted. Assuming that all knowledge should be consistent contradicts experience, which requires continued revision of understanding.

The second limitation of building effective ANP models involves the fact that feedback on the quality of VC's decision is slow in coming [47]. It generally takes 7 years to identify the portfolio winners, and 2 to 3 years to identify the losers [76]. Thus, slow feedback makes it difficult to adjust ANP approach for VCs in their decision processes.

Conclusion. The research was aimed at applying ANP to evaluate and select startup businesses for funding. We proposed the idea that to be transparent and understandable, VCs should not collapse the complexity of the decision process into a simplistic scheme. VCs should decompose judgments through elaborate structures and organize their reasoning and calculations in sophisticated ways. Experience indicates that it is not very difficult to do this although it takes more time and effort. Indeed, we must use feedback networks to arrive at the kind of decisions needed to cope with the future [77].

Thus, ANP deliberately synthesizes heuristic and analytic approaches and considerably extends the idea of making business decisions under uncertainty. ANP allows considering the complexity of the problem and uses expert's pairwise comparisons based on heuristics. In ANP, heuristics is used without reducing the complexity of the task and thus helps to avoid the systematic error. On the other hand, ANP is not a heuristic method; it is a mathematical theory that makes it possible to deal with all kinds of dependence and feedback between decision criteria and alternatives and examines the problem from different angles (in our study these are Benefits-Opportunities and Risks).

Despite the potential benefits of applying the ANP methodology in VCs decision-making process, Shepherd and Zacharakis [78] mentioned that, "VCs rarely use decision aids and thus may be missing an opportunity. We hope that the proposed example of applying the ANP in VCs decision making and the developed Multichoice decisions software encourages researchers to further explore ANP in the area of VC investment decisions. We expect that applying heuristics as part of the analytical process will lead to other results than using heuristics per se. However, this statement must be proved in future research.

Application of Analytic Network Process to a forecasting of oral health

Introduction

Analytic Network Process developed by Thomas L. Saaty [11] can be successfully applied to forecasting a functional state of various forms of human physiological activity using the knowledge accumulated by skilled doctors and physiologists. In this paper we consider the problem of modeling of oral health, taking account of a number of external and internal factors.

The forecasting of the onset and development of dental diseases is an urgent problem in modern dentistry, as the incidence of dental caries and periodontium pathologies is very high among the human population and their clinical course is progressive. Usually a disease forecasting is based on clinical presentations of an action of various adverse factors on hard tooth tissues and on periodontium. As is known, caries and inflammatory diseases of periodontium are caused by both local and general risk factors [79, 80].

The well known general risk factors are: content of fluorine in water; a daily diet; stresses; somatic diseases, which give rise to abnormalities of endocrine regulation, immunity and metabolism.

In this research we take into consideration the following local factors: the presence of carbohydrate food debris; the presence of microorganisms in the dental deposit; the abnormal composition and properties of the oral fluid. Besides, the resistance of hard tooth tissues (full value of structure, chemical composition, genetic code) is important for the onset of caries.

Analytic Network Process (ANP) proposes a constructing of a qualitative model describing an influence of external factors upon the system under study, and also interdependence of the system's elements. Such a model can be built with use of knowledge of high-skilled experts; and it represents the linguistic description of basic components, elements and factors, as well as a description of a meaning and directions of influence flows in the system researched. The influence of different factors upon the system's elements (or a mutual influence of internal elements) can be of ambiguous semantics, therefore at initial stage of research, one should precisely formulate a main goal, in terms of which the basic categories of the task will be determined: criteria, components or clusters, elements, judgments.

Constructing a network model

The main goal of this research is to find out the factors, which make the greatest impact into oral health. The results of scientific research, published scientific works [80-84], as well as the experience of applied medicine were used to single out 15 major factors influencing an oral health. These factors were grouped into the following 7 clusters.

1) Life-support conditions. This term reflects external influence of environmental factors upon a human organism, in particular, upon oral health. The most important factors among them are represented by the following elements of this cluster:

1.1. Nutrition compound (foodstuff composition; amount of consumed carbohydrates; softness or hardness of food);

1.2. Ecology of life (chemical composition of air and water, including content of fluorine in water; geoclimatic conditions of existence);

1.3. Social conditions (sanitary conditions depending on social environment and personal income).

2) Oral hygiene. Main external factors determining oral hygiene are:

2.1. Skills of proper tooth brushing;

2.2. Regularity of dental inspections;

2.3. Quality of hygienic means used.

Training patients to brush teeth properly and an individual selection of hygienic means for oral cavity decrease the risk of dental diseases

3) Status of dental health. This cluster characterizes the current state of oral cavity conditioned by all external and internal influences, as well as by case history of a patient. There are two main elements here:

3.1. State of teeth;

3.2. State of periodontium.

State of teeth (presence of carious cavities, poor-quality tooth stoppings and dental deposits) in many respects determines the state of periodontium (onset and progress of gingivitis and periodontitis). Besides, the onset of periodontium diseases can be associated with dental anomalies and deformation, errors during prosthetic alignments, and also with dental traumas. Inflammatory diseases of periodontium influence both the general health of the human organism and the state of teeth. A formation of bone recesses at periodontitis finally results in loosening of teeth, while etiological microbe agent promotes caries of hard tooth tissues.

4) General health status. This cluster characterizes the influence of basic parameters of human health on the state of oral cavity. Among these parameters we consider the following elements:

4.1. Hormonal status;

4.2. Age;

4.3. Level of immune reactivity.

We suppose these parameters of the general health have important influence on oral health and their further detailed elaboration is not expedient.

5) A type of blood circulation is one of major internal factors influencing dental and periodontium health [80]. We shall examine integrated influence of this factor without detailing it by a set of elements and we shall presume that various types of blood circulation (eukinetic, hyperkinetic, hypokinetic) influence a state of other systems by different ways.

6) A type of vegetative regulation determines vascular tone, secretion of salivary glands, and also blood supply to teeth and periodontium. This cluster, as well as previous (a type of blood circulation), is considered at the generalized level, i.e. it is submitted by a single element. An influence of a vegetative regulation type (sympathotonic, normotonic and vagotonic) upon a general health of human organism as a whole and, in particular, upon an oral health is beyond question and it is described in a number of scientific works [80-82].

7) Salivation system. This cluster is detailed by a set of the following elements, whose influence upon oral health is well known [79, 83]:

7.1. Saliva secretion rate;

7.2. Salivation character (qualitative and quantitative saliva composition).

Such factors as ethnic features, professional insalubrities, harmful habits etc. were not taken into account in the model because of their insignificant influence in comparison with the factors described above.

After the allocation of basic elements and clusters it is necessary to ascertain connections between them. The graph of clusters interaction is shown in a Fig. 2.43 where the arrows specify influence directions. The arrow from one cluster to another testifies that all or some elements in the first cluster influence all or some elements in the second cluster. The loops of a feedback (internal cycles) correspond to mutual influence between the elements in one cluster. In addition to internal cycles, there can be external cycles formed by connections between different clusters. The examples of external cycles in a Figure 2.43 are the closed contours formed by the clusters $3-4-3, 4-6-4, 4-6-5-7-3-4, 4-7-3-4$ etc. Let's consider in detail the meaning and direction of the connections between the clusters in a Fig. 2.43.

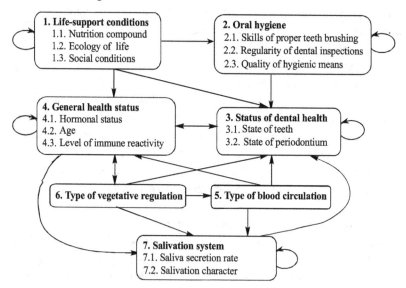

Fig. 2.43. The influence graph describing a state of oral health

The first cluster's elements (Life-support conditions) noticeably influence a Status of dental health (cluster 3) and a General health status (cluster 4). Besides that, to a lesser degree, they influence each other, and some of them (Social conditions and Ecology of life) influence the elements of the second cluster (Oral hygiene). The most important influences of the first cluster's elements are the following ones: Social conditions → Nutrition compound, Social conditions → Quality of hygienic means, Nutrition compound → State of teeth, Ecology of life → Level of immune reactivity.

It is obviously, that the elements of second cluster (Oral hygiene) influence a State of dental health (cluster 3). A loop of a feedback at the second cluster is explained by an assumption, that a Regularity of dental inspections is under influence of other elements of this cluster.

In the third cluster a State of teeth (presence of cavities, stoppings, teeth congestion) in many respects determines a State of periodontium, which, in turn, influences a State of teeth, i.e. the elements of this cluster influence each other. It's clear that the third and fourth clusters are interdependent, as insufficient mastication of food, presence of chronic infections' foci, and inflammations in oral cavity influence a General health status.

In turn, the fourth cluster's elements (Hormonal status, Age and Level of immune reactivity) influence a Status of dental health. Except direct affecting, a General health status marginally influences a Status of dental health through the seventh cluster (Salivation system). The type of vegetativeregulation depends on elements of the fourth cluster, namely, a type can change with age, after sustained diseases and stresses.

The type of blood circulation influences a General health status, a Status of dental health (particularly a State of periodontium) and a Salivation system, as cardiovascular system provides a necessary level of vital activity and is the indicator of a human organism's adaptability.

The type of vegetativeregulation influences a Type of blood circulation, a Salivation system, a Status of dental health and a General health status. The intensity of these influences may be different, but the fact of their existence is beyond question.

The elements of the seventh cluster (Salivation system) mutually influence each other and also a Status of dental health.

The following step of this research is to find out the relative intensity of influence for all elements of the system examined. Further, on the base of constructed model, limiting priorities of the elements are calculated. These priorities characterize a contribution of every element into main goal being formulated.

Revealing of relative intensity
of influence for clusters and their elements

In ANP an intensity of influence is being estimated by the experts with use of pairwise comparison's procedure and the fundamental ratio scale [11]. Pair comparison technique is the most universal method of measurements, as it can be applied at absence of any scales and standards, in particular at a measurement of intangible attributes. Comparing two objects with respect to a common attribute (criterion, property) the expert estimates a relative preference of one object over another, choosing a suitable estimation from the fundamental scale. The expert's comparisons of homogeneous objects with respect to each criterion are put in reciprocal matrix of pairwise comparisons.

For each pairwise comparisons matrix the right eigenvector is calculated, which is interpreted as the vector of relative priorities of the elements compared. The calculation of the normalized eigenvector for any pairwise comparisons matrix with dimension of n generally enables to change (n^2-n) judgments to n estimations expressed by the numbers from a continuous interval [0, 1]. Calculation of eigenvalue for any matrix of pair comparisons gives an opportunity to check out the expert's judgments in terms of consistency and transitivity [11]. For our model (see Fig. 2.43), it was necessary to fill 35 pairwise comparisons matrixes for elements and 7 matrixes for clusters. The latter were used for a calculation of the clusters' weight factors. The network model in a Figure 2.43 can be presented by the following matrix:

Clusters	1	2	3	4	5	6	7
1	1	0	0	0	0	0	0
2	1	1	0	0	0	0	0
3	1	1	1	1	1	1	1
B= 4	1	0	1	1	1	1	0
5	0	0	0	0	0	1	0
6	0	0	0	1	0	0	0
7	0	0	0	1	1	1	1

The unit elements in the matrix B testify that the cluster specified at the top (identifier of a column) influence the cluster specified to the left (identifier of a row). For each column of this matrix the matrix of pairwise comparisons of corresponding clusters was filled. At filling of matrixes, experts answered a question: "What of two compared clusters (specified at rows) the given cluster (at the top of column) does influence more, and how much more?" or a question

"What of the compared clusters does contribute into the given cluster more, and how much more?" At answering these questions, the experts used estimations from the fundamental ratio scale. For example, influence of the first cluster (Life-support conditions) upon other clusters is represented by the following matrix:

$$
A_1 = \begin{array}{c|cccc|c}
\mathbf{1} & 1 & 2 & 3 & 4 & W \\
\hline
1 & \mathbf{1} & 1 & 1/3 & 1/5 & 0.100 \\
2 & 1 & \mathbf{1} & 1/3 & 1/5 & 0.100 \\
3 & 3 & 3 & \mathbf{1} & 1/2 & 0.283 \\
4 & 5 & 5 & 2 & \mathbf{1} & 0.517 \\
\end{array}
$$

The elements of the first cluster influence each other and also the elements of the second, third and fourth clusters (see the first column in the matrix B). Let's consider the explanation of experts' estimations in the matrix A_1 containing clusters' pairwise comparisons obtained at answering the question "What of two clusters the first cluster (Life-support conditions) does influence more, and how much more?". We can see the first cluster's elements make significant impact into the fourth cluster and some less impact into the third cluster.

The second column of the matrix B testifies that the cluster Oral hygiene influences itself and the third cluster, thus the pairwise comparisons matrix A_2 looks like:

$$
A_2 = \begin{array}{c|cc|c}
\mathbf{2} & 2 & 3 & W \\
\hline
2 & \mathbf{1} & 1/5 & 0.167 \\
3 & 5 & \mathbf{1} & 0.833 \\
\end{array}
$$

We can see that the factors of Oral hygiene influence a Status of dental health more, than each other.

Others 5 pairwise comparisons matrixes for clusters were similarly filled. Obtained priorities vectors were used for forming of the following matrix of clusters' weight factors:

$$
D = \begin{array}{c|ccccccc}
 & 1 & 2 & 3 & 4 & 5 & 6 & 7 \\
\hline
1 & 0.1 & 0 & 0 & 0 & 0 & 0 & 0 \\
2 & 0.1 & 0.167 & 0 & 0 & 0 & 0 & 0 \\
3 & 0.283 & 0.833 & 0.8 & 0.125 & 0.143 & 0.09 & 0.5 \\
4 & 0.517 & 0 & 0.2 & 0.5 & 0.286 & 0.051 & 0 \\
5 & 0 & 0 & 0 & 0 & 0 & 0.606 & 0 \\
6 & 0 & 0 & 0 & 0.125 & 0 & 0 & 0 \\
7 & 0 & 0 & 0 & 0.25 & 0.571 & 0.253 & 0.5 \\
\end{array}
$$

The next step is a filling of pairwise comparisons matrixes for elements of clusters and calculation of their priorities. Let's consider this procedure on the example of the first cluster, which contains the following elements: 1.1. — Nutrition compound; 1.2 — Ecology of life; 1.3 — Social conditions. These elements influence each other and also the elements of the second, third and fourth clusters. Some of them don't influence elements in other clusters. So, a Nutrition compound does not influence Ecology of life and Social conditions, however two the last factors influence other elements in the first cluster. We have the following pairwise comparisons matrixes for the first cluster's elements:

$$C_{112} = \begin{array}{c|cc|c} \mathbf{1.2} & 1.1 & 1.3 & W \\ \hline 1.1 & 1 & 5 & 0.833 \\ 1.3 & 1/5 & 1 & 0.167 \end{array} \qquad C_{113} = \begin{array}{c|cc|c} \mathbf{1.3} & 1.1 & 1.2 & w \\ \hline 1.1 & 1 & 5 & 0.833 \\ 1.2 & 1/5 & 1 & 0.167 \end{array}$$

These matrixes demonstrate that Ecology of life influences Nutrition compound much more strongly, than Social conditions, and Social conditions influences Nutrition compound more strongly in comparison with Ecology of life.

The second cluster's elements are influenced by all elements of the first cluster except Nutrition compound. Thus, Ecology of life (1.2) influences a Regularity of dental inspections (2.2) much more strongly, than other elements of the second cluster. The factor Social conditions (1.3) influences a Quality of hygienic means (2.3) in a greater extent than others and nearly does not influence a Skills of proper teeth brushing (2.1). These influences are represented by the following matrixes:

$$C_{212} = \begin{array}{c|ccc|c} \mathbf{1.2} & 2.1 & 2.2 & 2.3 & w \\ \hline 2.1 & 1 & 1/7 & 1 & 0.111 \\ 2.2 & 7 & 1 & 7 & 0.778 \\ 2.3 & 1 & 1/7 & 1 & 0.111 \end{array} \qquad C_{213} = \begin{array}{c|ccc|c} \mathbf{1.3} & 2.1 & 2.2 & 2.3 & w \\ \hline 2.1 & 1 & 1/4 & 1/8 & 0.077 \\ 2.2 & 4 & 1 & 1/2 & 0.308 \\ 2.3 & 8 & 2 & 1 & 0.615 \end{array}$$

Nutrition compound (1.1) and Ecology of life (1.2) influence the elements of the third cluster (Status of dental health). The following matrixes contain estimations of intensity of their relative influence:

$$C_{311} = \begin{array}{c|cc|c} \mathbf{1.1} & 3.1 & 3.2 & W \\ \hline 3.1 & 1 & 5 & 0.833 \\ 3.2 & 1/5 & 1 & 0.167 \end{array} \qquad C_{312} = \begin{array}{c|cc|c} \mathbf{1.2} & 3.1 & 3.2 & w \\ \hline 3.1 & 1 & 3 & 0.75 \\ 3.2 & 1/3 & 1 & 0.25 \end{array}$$

We can see from these matrixes that the elements of the first cluster influence a State of teeth more strongly, than a State of periodontium.

All elements of the first cluster influence the elements of the fourth cluster (General health status). These influences are brought in the following matrixes:

$$C_{411} = \begin{array}{c|ccc|c} \mathbf{1.1} & 4.1 & 4.2 & 4.3 & w \\ \hline 4.1 & 1 & 5 & 1/2 & 0.319 \\ 4.2 & 1/5 & 1 & 1/9 & 0.066 \\ 4.3 & 2 & 9 & 1 & 0.615 \end{array} \qquad C_{412} = \begin{array}{c|ccc|c} \mathbf{1.2} & 4.1 & 4.2 & 4.3 & w \\ \hline 4.1 & 1 & 3 & 1/3 & 0.231 \\ 4.2 & 1/3 & 1 & 1/9 & 0.077 \\ 4.3 & 3 & 9 & 1 & 0.692 \end{array}$$

$$C_{413} = \begin{array}{c|ccc|c} \mathbf{1.3} & 4.1 & 4.2 & 4.3 & w \\ \hline 4.1 & 1 & 3 & 1/2 & 0.3 \\ 4.2 & 1/3 & 1 & 1/6 & 0.1 \\ 4.3 & 2 & 6 & 1 & 0.6 \end{array}$$

The matrixes above testify that Nutrition compound (1.1) exerts the most important influence on a Level of immune reactivity (4.3), lesser on a Hormonal status (4.1) and nearly does not influence Age (4.2). Ecology of life (1.2) and Social conditions (1.3) influence the elements of fourth cluster similarly.

The pairwise comparisons matrixes for estimation of influence of the elements from other clusters were similarly formed. The priorities vectors computed for these matrixes were put in the unweighted supermatrix for this network task, which is shown in Table 2.5. Expert judgments in all matrixes had a good consistency (index of a consistency did not exceed 0.02).

Calculation of limiting priorities for the factors

When elements in a complex system influence each other their priorities constantly change, therefore one can say the considered task becomes dynamic. We are interested with a long-term forecast of oral health and with a limit result of mutual influencing of the factors considered. The ANP enables to find out, whether there is a steady limit state for a network model with feedback and also to calculate limiting priorities for all elements and clusters.

If the sums of elements in every column of a supermatrix are equal to unity, then speak that the matrix is stochastic by columns. The consecutive raising of a stochastic matrix into integer powers results in a finite limit, which, generally speaking, may be non-unique. To make a supermatrix stochastic one can multiply its blocks corresponding to the clusters by the cluster's weight factors shown in a matrix D. The result is a weighed supermatrix, which is brought in Table 2.6. The raising of this matrix into high powers has resulted in a steady solution, which is a square matrix with identical columns, whose elements do not change at the further increasing of the exponent. These are the limiting priorities of the elements. We can see them in Table 3 and interpret as the factors' contributions into main goal.

Table 2.5. Unweighted supermatrix

	1			2			3		4			5	6	7	
	1.1	1.2	1.3	2.1	2.2	2.3	3.1	3.2	4.1	4.2	4.3	5	6	7.1	7.2
1.1	0	0.833	0.833	0	0	0	0	0	0	0	0	0	0	0	0
1.2	0	0	0.167	0	0	0	0	0	0	0	0	0	0	0	0
1.3	0	0.167	0	0	0	0	0	0	0	0	0	0	0	0	0
2.1	0	0.111	0.077	0	0.75	0.25	0	0	0	0	0	0	0	0	0
2.2	0	0.778	0.308	0.875	0	0.75	0	0	0	0	0	0	0	0	0
2.3	0	0.111	0.615	0.125	0.25	0	0	0	0	0	0	0	0	0	0
3.1	0.833	0.75	0	0.75	0.833	0.833	0	1	0.167	0.5	0.25	0.2	0.25	0.75	0.333
3.2	0.167	0.25	0	0.25	0.167	0.167	1	0	0.833	0.5	0.75	0.8	0.75	0.25	0.667
4.1	0.319	0.231	0.3	0	0	0	0.222	0.236	0	0.667	0.833	0.236	0.25	0	0
4.2	0.066	0.077	0.1	0	0	0	0.111	0.082	0.25	0	0.167	0.082	0.069	0	0
4.3	0.615	0.692	0.6	0	0	0	0.667	0.682	0.75	0.333	0	0.682	0.681	0	0
5	0	0	0	0	0	0	0	0	0	0	0	0	1	0	0
6	0	0	0	0	0	0	0	0	1	1	1	0	0	0	0
7.1	0	0	0	0	0	0	0	0	0.25	0.75	0.333	0.25	0.75	0	1
7.2	0	0	0	0	0	0	0	0	0.75	0.25	0.667	0.75	0.25	1	0

Table 2.6. Weighted supermatrix

	1			2			3		4			5	6	7	
	1.1	1.2	1.3	2.1	2.2	2.3	3.1	3.2	4.1	4.2	4.3	5	6	7.1	7.2
1.1	0	0.083	0.117	0	0	0	0	0	0	0	0	0	0	0	0
1.2	0	0	0.023	0	0	0	0	0	0	0	0	0	0	0	0
1.3	0	0.017	0	0	0	0	0	0	0	0	0	0	0	0	0
2.1	0	0.011	0.011	0	0.125	0.042	0	0	0	0	0	0	0	0	0
2.2	0	0.078	0.043	0.146	0	0.125	0	0	0	0	0	0	0	0	0
2.3	0	0.011	0.085	0.021	0.042	0	0	0	0	0	0	0	0	0	0
3.1	0.295	0.212	0	0.625	0.694	0.694	0	0.8	0.021	0.063	0.032	0.029	0.083	0.375	0.167
3.2	0.039	0.071	0	0.208	0.139	0.139	0.8	0	0.104	0.063	0.094	0.115	0.067	0.125	0.333
4.1	0.206	0.119	0.216	0	0	0	0.044	0.047	0	0.333	0.416	0.067	0.013	0	0
4.2	0.043	0.04	0.073	0	0	0	0.023	0.017	0.125	0	0.083	0.023	0.004	0	0
4.3	0.397	0.358	0.432	0	0	0	0.133	0.136	0.375	0.167	0	0.195	0.035	0	0
5	0	0	0	0	0	0	0	0	0	0	0	0	0.606	0	0
6	0	0	0	0	0	0	0	0	0.125	0.125	0.125	0	0	0	0
7.1	0	0	0	0	0	0	0	0	0.063	0.187	0.083	0.143	0.19	0	0.5
7.2	0	0	0	0	0	0	0	0	0.187	0.063	0.167	0.428	0.063	0.5	0

Results discussion

The outcomes shown in Tables 2.6, 2.7 and in Fig. 2.44, 2.45 suggest to conclude the following assertions about mutual influencing of external and internal factors:

- Life-support conditions have the most important influence on a State of teeth, a Level of immune reactivity and a Hormonal status.
- Oral hygiene strongly influences a State of teeth and less a State of periodontium.
- The elements of Dental health status noticeably affect each other. To a lesser degree they influence a Level of immune reactivity.
- Hormonal status has the most appreciable influence on a Level of immune reactivity, Salivation character and a State of periodontium.
- Age noticeably influences a Hormonal status, Saliva secretion rate, Level of immune reactivity and Vegetative regulation type.
- A Level of immune reactivity appreciably affects a Hormonal status and Salivation character.
- A Blood circulation type strongly influences Salivation character and less influences a Level of immune reactivity and a State of periodontium.
- A Vegetative regulation type governs a Blood circulation type. Besides, it noticeably influence Saliva secretion rate.
- The elements of Salivation system noticeably affect each other. They also have some influence on a Dental health status such that a Saliva secretion rate affects a State of teeth, and Salivation character — a State of periodontium.

The priorities shown in Tables 2.5, 2.6 can be considered as expert estimations of an influence intensity for the set of the examined factors at the present moment. Limiting priorities (see Table 2.7) can be interpreted as predictable values of the examined factors' contribution into main goal, in our case into oral health. The factors having high values of a limiting priority in a greater extent determine the purpose, as in the limit accumulate into itself the influence of other factors. In other words, data from Table 2.7 (and stripy columns in a Figures 2.44) correspond to the elements, which concentrate influence of all examined factors. It is easy to note, the elements of a Dental health status make the greatest impact into main goal, furthermore, the limiting priority of a State of periodontium is a little bit more, than priority of a State of teeth. The limiting priorities of the clusters are shown in a Figure 2.45 where the stripy columns correspond to the integrated contribution of every cluster into main goal.

181

Table 2.7. Limiting priorities of the elements and clusters

1			2			3		4			5	6	7	
0			0			0.56		0.237			0.018	0.03	0.155	
1.1	1.2	1.3	2.1	2.2	2.3	3.1	3.2	4.1	4.2	4.3	5	6	7.1	7.2
0	0	0	0	0	0	0.276	0.284	0.087	0.032	0.118	0.018	0.03	0.071	0.084

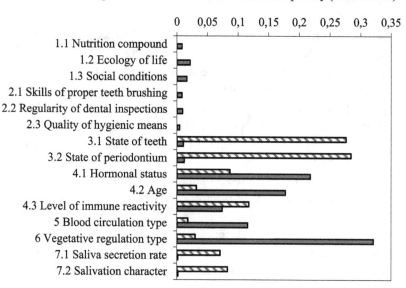

Fig. 2.44. Limiting outcomes for the network model

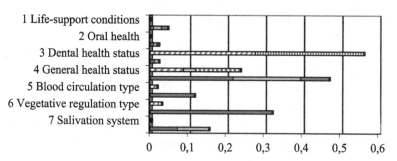

Fig. 2.45. Limiting outcomes for the clusters

We can see that the contribution of the third cluster (Dental health status) exceeds 50 %. The third rank among all clusters' elements (see Figure 2.44) has a Level of immune reactivity, being the element of the fourth cluster (General health status), which takes the second place among all clusters (see Figure 2.45). Another element of this cluster — Hormonal status, — has the fourth rank. The element Age is the least significant in the fourth cluster; it can be explained by negligible influence on it of other factors. The Salivation system has the third rank among clusters, and its elements are at the fifth and sixth places (see Figure 2.44). The Salivation character is slightly more significant than Saliva secretion rate. The fourth place among the clusters occupies a Type of vegetative regulation followed by a Type of blood circulation. The limiting priorities of the elements from the first and the second clusters equal to zero. This fact can be explained that external factors are not influenced by other elements, therefore there is no accumulation of influence in them. The node corresponding to the first cluster in a Figure 1 is a source; and the node, which corresponds to the second cluster, is a flow element with a loop of a feedback.

The first cluster is a powerful source influencing other clusters; only 10% of its influence makes up a feedback. The contribution of this cluster's elements into main goal comes through the third and fourth clusters indirectly (see above matrix D). The second cluster gets about 10% of the first cluster's influence, and only 16.7 % of this value comes back through a feedback into second cluster. The contribution of the second cluster's elements into main goal is come through the third cluster (Dental health status).

In order to find out the elements, which have the greatest influence upon oral health, we inverted this task by transposing the matrix B. At that it was necessary to fill the set of new pairwise comparisons matrixes, asking the experts a question: "What of two analyzed factors (clusters, elements) influence the given factor (cluster or element) more?" For example, "What of the elements of a Dental health status (State of teeth or State of periodontium) does influence a Level of immune reactivity more?" The supermatrix of the inverted task is shown in Table 2.8. Its columns show the influences of the factors specified in rows (at the left) upon the element being the heading of a column. The raising of this matrix into high powers enables to compute the limiting priorities of influence of the examined factors upon all elements of the model. These priorities called as limiting influence priorities are represented in Table 2.9 and in a Fig. 2.44, 2.45.

Table 2.8. The weighed supermatrix of the inverted task

	1			2			3		4			5	6	7	
	1.1	1.2	1.3	2.1	2.2	2.3	3.1	3.2	4.1	4.2	4.3	5	6	7.1	7.2
1.1	0	0	0	0	0.071	0.071	0.039	0.039	0.019	0	0.027				
1.2	0.2	0	0	0	0.214	0.071	0.013	0.013	0.056	0	0.054	0	0	0	
1.3	0.8	0	0	0	0.214	0.357	0.006	0.006	0.019	0	0.014				
2.1	0			0	0.333	0.167	0.176	0.176	0			0	0	0	
2.2				0.75	0	0.333	0.062	0.062							
2.3				0.25	0.167	0	0.033	0.033							
3.1	0			0			0	0.272	0.026	0	0.013	0	0	0	
3.2							0.272	0	0.026	0	0.04				
4.1	0			0			0.064	0.122	0	0	0.324	0	0.571	0.097	0.097
4.2							0.02	0.03	0.324	0	0.108		0.286	0.016	0.016
4.3							0.128	0.06	0.108	0	0		0.143	0.048	0.048
5	0			0			0.03	0.03	0.155	0.368	0.155	0	0	0.083	0.083
6	0			0			0.037	0.037	0.266	0.632	0.266	1	0	0.582	0.583
7.1	0			0			0.078	0.029	0			0	0	0	0.174
7.2							0.039	0.087						0.174	0

Table 2.9. Limiting priorities for the inverted task

	1			2			3		4			5	6	7	
	0.0458			0.0219			0.0224		0.47			0.116	0.321	0.0033	
	1.1	1.2	1.3	2.1	2.2	2.3	3.1	3.2	4.1	4.2	4.3	5	6	7.1	7.2
1.1	0	0	0	0	0	0	0.008	0.008	0.008	0.008	0.008	0.008	0.008	0.008	0.0083
1.2	0	0	0	0	0	0	0.021	0.021	0.021	0.021	0.021	0.021	0.021	0.021	0.0214
1.3	0	0	0	0	0	0	0.016	0.016	0.016	0.016	0.016	0.016	0.016	0.016	0.0161
2.1	0	0	0	0	0	0	0.008	0.008	0.008	0.008	0.008	0.008	0.008	0.008	0.0081
2.2	0	0	0	0	0	0	0.009	0.009	0.009	0.009	0.009	0.009	0.009	0.009	0.0093
2.3	0	0	0	0	0	0	0.004	0.004	0.004	0.004	0.004	0.004	0.004	0.004	0.0045
3.1	0	0	0	0	0	0	0.010	0.010	0.010	0.010	0.010	0.010	0.010	0.010	0.0104
3.2	0	0	0	0	0	0	0.012	0.01	0.01	0.012	0.01	0.012	0.012	0.012	0.012
4.1	0	0	0	0	0	0	0.218	0.21	0.21	0.218	0.218	0.218	0.218	0.218	0.218
4.2	0	0	0	0	0	0	0.177	0.177	0.177	0.177	0.177	0.177	0.177	0.177	0.1776
4.3	0	0	0	0	0	0	0.074	0.074	0.074	0.074	0.074	0.074	0.074	0.074	0.0744
5	0	0	0	0	0	0	0.115	0.115	0.115	0.115	0.115	0.115	0.115	0.115	0.1159
6	0	0	0	0	0	0	0.320	0.320	0.320	0.320	0.320	0.320	0.320	0.320	0.3207
7.1	0	0	0	0	0	0	0.001	0.001	0.001	0.001	0.001	0.001	0.001	0.001	0.0015
7.2	0	0	0	0	0	0	0.001	0.001	0.001	0.001	0.001	0.001	0.001	0.001	0.0018

The outcomes of the inverted task reveal the most influential of the factors examined. The obvious leader among them is the Type of vegetative regulation with the limiting priority 0.3207, the second is a Hormonal status (0.218), and the third is Age (0.1776). The distribution of clusters' integrated priorities is shown in a Fig. 2.45 where we can see that the greatest influence upon oral health has a General health status (cluster 4) followed by the Type of vegetative regulation and the Type of blood circulation behind it.

The influence of external factors (cluster 1 and 2) is less significant that is coordinated with up-to-date concepts in dentistry science [79, 81].

The Table 2.9 demonstrates that external factors collected in the first and second clusters are not influenced by internal ones. At the same time the limiting priorities of influence of each factor upon all other elements become the same. The general physiological factors (clusters 4, 5, 6) have the most important influence upon oral health and others elements of the model. The influence of Life-support conditions (cluster 1) less, than total influence of above mentioned factors approximately in 10 times . The second cluster (Oral hygiene) and the third cluster (Dental health status) have small and close limiting priorities of influence, and the seventh cluster (Salivation system) is nearly insignificant.

The results obtained are based on the study of pathological processes in the oral cavity in connection with other organism systems and a human environment. They are well matched with intuitive concepts of the experts, have reasonable interpretation, and enable to make a detailed forecast substantiation. The intermediate results also are of interest, as enable to analyze an opportunity of interaction of elements considered. The application of ANP gives an opportunity to estimate a contribution of the examined external and internal factors into the oral health status and to predict their influence in view of feedback in open physiological system.

The conclusion that the health of oral cavity is governed by the elements of a Dental health status is trivial and validates the expert information used. New results are the relative priorities describing influence intensity and impact into oral health of such factors as immunity level, hormonal status, vegetative regulation type, blood circulation type, and parameters of salivation system. These results are of a special interest of dentists and physiologists. The influence of the elements of a General health status is very strong; it's an order greater than the influence of external conditions. Let's note that the small limiting priorities of influence of the external factors should not be interpreted as the evidence of their insignificance. The cyclic character of mutual influence between the functional systems in human organism promotes the increasing of limiting priorities of these factors. For example, the elements of the third cluster (Dental health status) influence parameters of a General health status (cluster 4), which, in turn, influence a Dental health status, i.e. the influence in the cycle is gradually increased up to some limiting value. The clusters 1 and 2 representing external conditions are not included in cycles, therefore their impact into a Dental health status and into a General health status is distributed in the system and appears indirectly. This implies that the conditions of life-support and oral hygienic factors become more important when physiological parameters of the human organism are abnormal. In other words, people with immunodeficiency or with abnormalities of blood circulation, hormonal status and vegetative regulation are influenced by ecology, diet and social conditions in greater degree. Therefore they should care for the oral cavity more attentively and take preventive restorative measures.

The application of ANP to a problem of oral health forecasting has a number of advantages, in particular the following:

- An opportunity to build a model on the base of the expert information with taking into consideration the intangible factors and qualitative parameters;
- Considerable time saving and more wide area of the application in comparison with statistical models based on the empirical data;
- An opportunity to check out different hypotheses about a structure and intensity of influences at the various sets of the factors.

References of chapter 2

1. Keeney R.L., Raiffa H. *Decisions with Multiple Objectives: Preferences and Value Tradeoffs*, New York: John Willey & Sons, 1976.
2. Moulin H. *Axioms of Cooperative Decision Making*, Cambridge: Cambridge University Press, 1988.
3. Saaty T.L. *Decision Making With Dependence And Feedback: The Analytic Network Process*, Pittsburgh: RWS Publications, 2001.
4. Saaty T.L. *Fundamentals of Decision Making and Priority Theory with the Analytic Hierarchy Process*, Pittsburgh: RWS Publications, 1994.
5. Andreichicov A.V. and Andreichicova O.N. (2001) "A choice of a perspective system for vibration isolation in conditions of varying environment", *Proceedings of the Sixth International Symposium on the Analytic Hierarchy Process ISAHP'2001*, Bern, 13-24.

6. Andreichicova O.N. "A New Approach to the collective choice problem based on the compliance of mutual requirements of the participants", *Software and Computer Systems*, 2001, No. 3, p. 24-27 (in Russian).

7. Saaty, T.L. (1980) *The Analytic Hierarchy Process*. McGraw–Hill, New York NY.

8. Saaty, T.L. (1994) *Fundamentals of Decision Making and Priority Theory with the Analytic Hierarchy Process*. Pittsburg, PA: RWS Publications.

9. Saaty, T.L., Vargas L.G. (1994) *Decision Making in Economic, Political, Social and Technological Environments with the Analytic Hierarchy Process*. Pittsburg, PA: RWS Publications.

10. Saaty, T.L. (1999) *Decision Making for Leaders: The Analytic Hierarchy Process for Decisions in a Complex World*. Pittsburg, PA: RWS Publications.

11. Saaty, T.L. (2001) Decision Making with Dependence and Feedback: The Analytic Network Process. Pittsburgh, PA: RWS Publications.

12. Saaty, T.L. (2005) *Theory and Applications of the Analytic network Process: Decision Making with Benefits, Opportunities, Costs, and Risks*. Pittsburg, PA: RWS Publications.

13. Andreichicov A.V., Andreichicova O.N. (2003) The Analysis of the Technical Systems' Evolution. *Proceedings of the 7th International Symposium on the Analytic Hierarchy Process* (ISAHP'2003), August 7-9, 2003, Bali, Indonesia, p. 121-126.

14. Andreichicov A.V., Andreichicova O.N. (1999) Intelligent software based on AHP. *Proceedings of the Fifth International Symposium on the Analytic Hierarchy Process* (ISAHP'99), August 12-14, 1999, Kobe, Japan, p. 393-398.

15. Andreichicova O.N., Radyshevskaya T.N. (2009) An application of the Analytic Network Process to researching oral health. *International Journal of the Analytic Hierarchy Process*, vol. 1, issue 1, 2009, pp. 45-60, http://ijahp.org.

16. Andreichicova O.N., Andreichicov A.V. (2009) Analytic Network Process as Qualitative Simulating Tool: Researching of Financial Crisis. *Proceedings of 10th International Symposium on the Analytic Hierarchy/Network Process Multi-criteria Decision Making* (ISAHP'2009), July 29 — August 1 2009, University of Pittsburgh, Pittsburgh, Pennsylvania, USA, www.isahp.org

17. Brown M.F. (2003). *Who Owns Native Culture?* Cambridge: Harvard University Press
18. Caves R.E. (2000). *Creative Industries: Contracts between Art and Commerce.* Cambridge, MA: Harvard University Press.
19. Colston C. & Middleton K. (2005). *Modern Intellectual Property Law.* Cavendish Publishing, UK.
20. Cowen T. & Michael F. Brown. (2004). Who Owns Native Culture? *Journal of Cultural Economics, vol. 28, Issue 4,* 317–323.
21. Saaty, T.L. (2001). Decision making with dependence and feedback: The analytic network process. Pittsburgh, PA: RWS Publications.
22. Super Decisions software (2009). Software for the ANP, downloaded from the website http://www.superdecisions.com.
23. Bainbridge D.I. (2009). *Intellectual Property.* Harlow, England; New York: Pearson Longman.
24. Liebowitz S.J. (2003). Back to the Future: Can copyright owners appropriate revenues in the face of new technologies? *The Economics of Copyright: Recent Developments and Analysis.* Cheltenham: Edward Elgar Publishing.
25. Towse R. (2001). *Creativity, Incentive and Reward: an economic analysis of copyright and culture in the Information Age.* Cheltenham: Edward Elgar.
26. Hansen T.B. (1997). The Willingness-to-Pay for the Royal Theatre in Copenhagen as a Public Good. *Journal of Cultural Economics, vol. 21,* 1–18.
27. H. Olsson. (2000). *The Role of Copyright and Future Challenges to Creators, Industry, Legislators and Society at Large — Inventors' and Creators' Rights as Basic Human Rights.* WIPO/IP/HEL/00/15, Available from URL: http://www.wipo.int.
28. Woodhead R. (2000). *Tipping — a method for optimizing compensation for intellectual property.* Available from URL: <http://www.tipping.self-promotion.com/>.
29. Andreichicova O.N. "A New Approach to the collective choice problem based on the compliance of mutual requirements of the participants", *Software and Computer Systems,* 2001, No. 3, p. 24-27 (in Russian).
30. Hudson, J. Khazragui, H.F. (2013). Into the valley of death: Research to innovation. *Drug Discovery Today, 18(13-14),* 610-613. Doi: https://doi.org/10.1016/j.drudis.2013.01.012

31. Fielden, S. L., Davidson, M.J., Makin, P.J. (2000). Barriers encountered during micro and small business start-up in North-West England. *Journal of Small Business and Enterprise Development,7(4),* 295-304. Doi: https://doi.org/10.1108/EUM0000000006852

32. Gompers, P. A., Lerner, J. (2004). *The venture capital cycle (Second edition).* Cambridge, MA: MIT Press.

33. Chemmanur, T., Krishnan, K., Debarshi K. Nandy. (2008). How does venture capital financing improve efficiency in private firms? A look beneath the surface. *Review of Financial Studies,24(12),* 4037-4090. Doi: https://doi.org/10.1093/rfs/hhr096

34. Bertoni, F., Colombo, M.G., Grilli, L. (2011). Venture capital financing and the growth of high-tech start-ups: Disentangling treatment from selection effects. *Research Policy,40(7),* 1028-1043. Doi: https://doi.org/10.1016/j.respol.2011.03.008

35. Monika, D., Sharma, A.K. (2015). Venture capitalists' investment decision criteria for new ventures: A review." *XVIII Annual International Conference of the Society of Operations Management (SOM-14). Procedia — Social and Behavioral Sciences,189,* 465-470. Doi: https://doi.org/10.1016/j.sbspro.2015.03.195

36. Miloud, T., Aspelund, A., Cabrol, M. (2012). Startup valuation by venture capitalists: an empirical study. *Venture Capital: An International Journal of Entrepreneurial Finance,14 (2-3),* 151-174. Doi: https://doi.org/10.1080/13691066.2012.667907

37. Narayanasamy, C., Hashemoghli, A., Rashid, R.M. (2012). Venture capital pre-investment decision making process: An exploratory study in Malaysia. *Global Journal of Business Research, 6(5),* 49-63.

38. Mousavi, S., Gigerenzer, G. (2014). Risk, uncertainty, and heuristics. *Journal of Business Research, 67,* 1671-1678. Doi: https://doi.org/10.1016/j.jbusres.2014.02.013

39. Zacharakis, A.L., Meyer, G.D. (1998). A lack of insight: Do venture capitalists really understand their own decision process?" *Journal of Business Venturing,13(1),* 57-76. Doi: https://doi.org/10.1016/S0883-9026(97)00004-9

40. MacMillan, I.C., Zeman, L., SubbaNarasimha. P.N. (1987). Criteria distinguishing unsuccessful ventures in the venture screening process. *Journal of Business Venturing, 2(2),* 123-137. Doi: https://doi.org/10.1016/0883-9026(87)90003-6

41. Robinson, R.B. (1987). Emerging strategies in the venture capital industry. *Journal of Business Venturing,2(1),* 53–77. Doi: https://doi.org/10.1016/0883-9026(87)90019-X

42. Hall, J. Hofer, C.W. (1993). Venture capitalists' decision criteria in new venture evaluation. *Journal of Business Venturing,8(1),* 25–42. Doi: https://doi.org/10.1016/0883-9026(93)90009-T

43. Landström, H. (2007). *Handbook of Research on Venture Capital.* Edward Elgar Publishing.

44. Shepherd, D.A., Zacharakis. A. (1999). Conjoint analysis: a new methodological approach for researching the decision policies of venture capitalists. *Venture Capital,1(3),* 197-217. Doi: https://doi.org/10.1080/136910699295866

45. Hsu, D. K, Haynie, J.M., Simmons, S.A., McKelvie, A. (2014). What matters, matters differently: a conjoint analysis of the decision policies of angel and venture capital investors. *Venture Capital,16(1),* 1-25. https://doi.org/10.1080/13691066.2013.825527

46. Zacharakis, A., Shepherd, D.A. (2004). A non-additive decision-aid for venture capitalists investment decisions. *European Journal of Operational Research,* 162, 673–689. Doi: https://doi.org/10.1016/j.ejor.2003.10.028

47. Zacharakis, A.L., Meyer, G.D. (2000). The potential of actuarial decision models: Can they improve the venture capital investment decision?" *Journal of Business Venturing,15(4),* 323-346. Doi: https://doi.org/10.1016/S0883-9026(98)00016-0

48. Zacharakis, A., Shepherd, D.A. (2001). The nature of information and overconfidence on venture capitalists' decision making. *Journal of Business Venturing,16(4),* 311-332. Doi: https://doi.org/10.1016/S0883-9026(99)00052-X

49. Simon, H. A. (1957). *Models of Man.* New York: Wiley & Sons.

50. Tversky, A. Kahneman, D. (1974). Judgment under uncertainty: Heuristics and biases. *Science, New Series, 185(4157),* 1124-1131. Doi: 10.1126/science.185.4157.1124

51. Dimov, D., Shepherd, D.A., Sutcliffe, K.M. (2007). Requisite expertise, firm reputation, and status in venture capital investment allocation decisions. *Journal of Business Venturing,22(4),* 481-502. Doi: https://doi.org/10.1016/j.jbusvent.2006.05.001

52. Mitteness, C., Sudek, R., Cardon, M.S. (2012). Angel investor characteristics that determine whether perceived passion leads to higher evaluations
of funding potential. *Journal of Business Venturing,27(5)*, 592-606. Doi:
https://doi.org/10.1016/j.jbusvent.2011.11.003

53. Woike, J.K., Hoffrage, U., Petty, J.S. (2015). Picking profitable investments: The success of equal weighting in simulated venture capitalist decision making. *Journal of Business Research,68(8)*, 1705–1716. Doi:
https://doi.org/10.1016/j.jbusres.2015.03.030

54. Beshah, B., Kitaw, D. (2013). AHP application in a financial institution.
International Journal of the Analytic Hierarchy Process,5(1), 54-71. Doi:
http://dx.doi.org/10.13033/ijahp.v5i1.135

55. Bhandari, A., Nakarmi, A. (2016). A financial perfomance evaluation of
commercial banks in Nepal using AHP model. *International Journal of
the Analytic Hierarchy Process, 8(2)*, 318-333.Doi: http://dx.doi.org/
10.13033/ijahp.v8i2.368

56. Saracoglu, B.O. (2015). An AHP application in the investment selection
of small hydropower plants in Turkey. *International Journal of the
Analytic Hierarchy Process,*
7(2), 211-239. Doi: http://dx.doi.org/10.13033/ijahp.v7i2.198

57. Beim, G., Lévesque, M. (2004). Selecting projects for venture capital funding: A Multiple Criteria Decision approach. *Technical Memorandum Number 791*, Weatherhead School of Management, Case Western University.

58. Pakizeh, K., Hosseini, M. (2015). Venture capital investment selection
based on PROMETHEE. *Applied Mathematics in Engineering,
Management and Technology, 3(1)*, 566-572.

59. Afful-Dadziea E, Oplatková,a, Z.K., Nabareseh, S. (2015). Selecting startup businesses in a public venture capital financing using Fuzzy PROME-
THEE. *19th International Conference on Knowledge Based and Intelligent Information and Engineering Systems. Procedia Computer
Science,60*, 63-72. Doi: https://doi.org/10.1016/j.procs.2015.08.105

60. Lu, Z., Shen, Y. (2011). The study on venture capital project appraisal
using AHP-Fuzzy comprehensive evaluation methods. *International Journal of Advancements in Computing Technology,3(8)*, 50-56.

61. Su, H., Jiang, R. Ma, X. (2009_. Risk evaluation of venture capital based
on AHP and grey relational analysis methods. *International Conference
on Information Management, Innovation Management and Industrial Engineering, 2009*, 316-320. Doi: 10.1109/ICIII.2009.536

62. Gui-lan, Hu. (2011). An improved AHP-based evaluation study on the investment risk of venture capital company. *Fourth International Symposium on Knowledge Acquisition and Modeling,2011*, 17-20. Doi:10.1109/KAM.2011.12

63. Shijian, F. Yinyan, C. (2015). AHP-Fuzzy comprehensive evaluation model of venture investment and financing system: Based on the case of incubation base in Anhui. *Canadian Social Science,11(1)*, 148-153.

64. Wiratno, S., Latiffianti, E., Wirawan, K.K. (2015). Selection of business funding proposals using analytic network process: a case study at a venture capital company." *Industrial Engineering and Service Science. Procedia Manufacturing* 4: 237-243. Doi: https://doi.org/10.1016/j.promfg. 2015.11.037

65. Saaty, T. L. (1996). *Decision making with dependence and feedback: The Analytic Network Process*. Pittsburgh: RWS Publications.

66. Forbes, R. (2017). *School of a young billionaire*. http://www.forbes.ru/school

67. Milkova, M., Andreichikova, O. (2016). Software announcement: Multichoice as new software for decision making with Analytic Network Process. *International Journal of the Analytic Hierarchy Process,8(2)*, 388-400.Doi: http://dx.doi.org/10.13033/ijahp.v8i2.413

68. Saaty, T.L. (2010). *Principia mathematica decernendi: Mathematical principles of decision making: Generalization of the Analytic Network Process to neural firing and synthesis*. Pittsburgh, PA: RWS Publications.

69. Aczel, J., Saaty, T. (1983). Procedures for synthesizing ratio judgments. *Journal of Mathematical Psychology,27(1)*, 93-102. Doi: https://doi.org/ 10.1016/0022-2496(83)90028-7

70. Lipovetsky, S. (2016). AHP structuring in best-worst scaling and the secretary problem. *International Journal of the Analytic Hierarchy Process, 8(3)*, 502-513. Doi: http://dx.doi.org/10.13033/ijahp.v8i3.332

71. Saaty, T.L. (2003). Decision-making with the AHP: Why is the principal eigenvector necessary. *European Journal of Operational Research,145*, 85-91. Doi: https://doi.org/10.1016/S0377-2217(02)00227-8

72. Koczkodaj, W.W., Szybowski. J. (2016). The limit of inconsistency reduction in pairwise comparisons. *International Journal of Applied Mathematics and Computer Science,26 (3)*, 721–729.Doi: https://doi.org/ 10.1515/amcs-2016-0050

73. Fedrizzia, M., Giove S. (2007). Incomplete pairwise comparison and consistency optimization. *European Journal of Operational Research, 183(1)*, 303-313. Doi: https://doi.org/10.1016/j.ejor.2006.09.065

74. Bozóki, Sándor, János, Fülöp, Rónyai, L. (2010). On optimal completion of incomplete pairwise comparison matrices. *Mathematical and Computer Modelling, 52 (1-2)*, 318-333. Doi: https://doi.org/10.1016/j.mcm.2010.02.047

75. Saaty, T.L. (2013). On the measurement of intangibles. A principal eigenvector approach to relative measurement derived from paired comparisons. *Notices of the AMS, 60(2)*, 192-208.

76. Timmons, J.A. Spinelli, S. (2004). *New venture creation: Entrepreneurship for the 21st century.* Boston: McGraw-Hill/Irwin.

77. Saaty, T.L., Vargas. L.G. (2006). *Decision making with the Analytic Network Process: economic, political, social and technological applications with benefits, opportunities, costs and risks.* New York: Springer.

78. Shepherd, D.A., Zacharakis, A. (2002). Venture capitalists' expertise: A call for research into decision aids and cognitive feedback. *Journal of Business Venturing, 17(1)*, 1-20. Doi: https://doi.org/10.1016/S0883-9026(00)00051-3

79. Leont'ev V.K., Shestakov V.T. and Voronin V.F. (2003) *Estimation of the basic directions of dentistry development*, Moscow: Medical book (in Russian).

80. Rybakov A.I. and Chelidze L.N. (1990), *Anatomico-physiological features of an oral cavity and their significance in a pathology*, Tbilisi: Metsnierba (in Russian).

81. Eriksen H.M. and Bjertness E. (1991), "Concepts of health and disease and caries prediction: a literature review", *Scand. J. Dent. Res.*, 99 (6), 476-483.

82. Hollister M.C. and Weintraub J.A. (1993), "The association of oral status with systemic health, quality of life and economic productivity", *J. Dent. Educ.*, 57 (12), 901-912.

83. Borovskiy E.V. and Leont'ev B.K. (1991) *Biology of an oral cavity*, Moscow: Medicine, (in Russian).

84. Andreichicova O.N. and Radyshevskaya T.N. (2003) "Application of Analytic Network Process for a forecasting of basic systems' health in the human organism", *Information Technologies*, 7, 45-53 (in Russian).

CHAPTER 3.Intelligent System for Strategic Decisions

*Background.*There are many computer programs that implement different methods of decision making. Overview of software products showed, that some of them are more versatile and allow conducting evaluation in a variety of ways (Web-HIPRE, Logical Decisions, etc.), while others are soft shells and provide analytics with tools for creation and optimization of high-grade expert systems (FuzzyTECH). However, the integration of decision-support tools in the control loops, and enterprise information systems requires solving a number of problems, which are caused by the following factors:

- predominantly collective nature of decisionmaking activities;
- asynchronous flow of individual processes in coordination process;
- sharing common data warehouses of enterprise information system;
- duplication of information and the emergence of contradictions in databases and knowledge bases of different decision-making methods;
- lack of experience in choosing the right decision-support tools for the user.

The vast majority of application systems are oriented to support the process of individual decisionmaking.

At the same time, the work of experts and decision-makers (hereinafter-DM) in the groups has long been a standard. At the same time the practice of simultaneous presence of experts in large groups is gradually being replaced by asynchronous communication via network technologies. Such an option removes a number of temporal and spatial constraints, and in some cases saves financial resources of the company. Tools of decision-making theory are consistently brought in line with group methods and are designed for different types of tasks. However, the wide availability (including among inexperienced users) generates a problem of selecting an optimal set of mathematical methods and software tools for the implementation of an integrated intelligent decision support system (hereinafter-DSS).

3.1. Methods

Methods of analysis of networks and hierarchies

Both indicated methods belong to the class of multi-criteria methods and are used under conditions of uncertainty. The method of network analysis (MNA) is a generalization of the method of hierarchy analysis (MHA) for network structures with feedback. This allows acting with mutual dependence criteria by preference. MHA can be used when the elements of a model are independent. For these approaches, a clear graphical representation of the problem of choice is characteristic because of the decomposition of the latter into the components (target, policy, factors, actors, alternative, etc.). Another advantage is the way of preference revelation through pairwise comparisons.

Implementation of the method of network analysis includes the following basic steps:

1. Construction of the network structure.To do this, the elements of decision- making tasks are clustered, and arbitrary links between clusters are allowed. Formation of clusters and links is considered as informal procedure and is carried out by experts and DM on the basis of knowledge about the specifics of the problem being solved. Combining elements into clusters helps to reduce the dimension of the model and improve the consistency of judgments. The network shows the impact of clusters on each other as far as an achievement of a global goal is concerned. Benefits, costs, opportunities, risks, and so on could be considered as that goal.

2. For a network a binary impact matrixis built:

$$B = \{b_{ij}\} = \begin{cases} 1, & \text{if } i \text{ depends on } j \\ 0, & \text{otherwise} \end{cases}$$

Matrix B is checked for transitivity. If check is negative a network should be corrected. To normalize a network reachability matrix is used, which is obtained by raising a matrix $(E + B)$ into integer powers k until the condition is fulfilled $(E+B)^k \cong (E+B)^{k+1}$, where E is unity matrix.

3. Prioritization of cluster elements. The elements of each cluster are compared in pairs with respect to each element of a cluster affecting it. In this case, experts estimate the intensity of the influence of some elements on the other. The resultsof the comparison are entered into the matrix of pairwise comparisons (hereinafter-MPC). Principal eigenvectors of MPC are interpreted as vectors of priorities of compared elements.

4. On the basis of the matrix B and the calculated vectors of priorities of cluster elements a supermatrix of network task Wis built. Its columns are formed by major eigenvectors of MPC.

5. Prioritization of clusters based on pairwise comparisons. Comparison of clusters is carried out as described in paragraph 3, or with respect to only a

specified purpose or set of elements of a special management hierarchy, which details the maingoal (in the second case, a set of supermatrices for elements of managing hierarchy is formed).

6. Bringing a supermatrix (or some of them) to a stochastic form by rationing. To do this, the priorities of cluster elements are multiplied by the priorities of the clusters.

7. Analysis of the structure of the supermatrix and the choice of method for calculating marginal priorities. For a primitive stochastic supermatrix marginal priorities are calculated as

$$W^{\infty} = \lim_{k \to \infty} W^{k}$$

8. If the main purpose is detailed by hierarchy, contraction of derived vectors of priorities is carried out.

The calculated values of marginal priorities are interpreted as the contribution of the corresponding elements in the main goal for a certain period of prediction (until expressed preferences change). Solution of networking tasks enables to come reasonably to the problem of determining the importance of the criteria in the choice tasks. In particular, the sum of marginal priorities of cluster elements shows the extent of the combined effect of the latter (the contribution to the main goal).

Obviously, the result of the analysis is essentially dependent on the reliability and consistency of expert assessments. Therefore, the steps of filling the matrix of pairwise comparisons and clusters are key. In these approaches tools to assess the homogeneity of expert judgments are provided.

When filling MPC an expert answers to the following questions: «Which of two elements being compared is more important or has greater impact?», «Which of two elements being compared is more probable?», «Which of two elements being compared is more preferable?», and «What is this preference?»

Comparison of criteria usually involves comparing their degree of importance regarding the purpose of the study. It is also taken into account, which of the alternatives is more preferable, or more probable ona particular criterion, as well as to which extent one object is more preferable than another.

After filling each MPC, verification of transitivity and uniformity of judgment and calculation of the vector of priorities for elements- «childs» in relation to the element- «parent» is conducted.

PRIME method

The main function of the method (Preference Ratios In Multiattribute Evaluation) is that, unlike MHA or fuzzy inference, information about preferences can be set using intervals.

Sometimes DM does not know the exact count of his own preferences or extraction of the exact values is too complicated and time consuming. In such situations, it is possible to use the inaccurate value judgments in the form of intervals. With their help the weights of criteria and levels of attributes of alternatives are determined. After analyzing, not single assessments, but their possible ranges are appointed for alternatives. Search for the best solution is carried out through a set of decision rules or dominant analysis. Inaccurate value judgments are quite suitable for group decision-making. Individual opinions of different actors can be combined by constructing unified interval estimates from private estimates.

The characteristic features of PRIME method are:
- use of the difference of attribute values for the establishment of an order of alternatives preference;
- refusal to use numerical measurement scales;
- representation of preference relations of DM in the form of precise and imprecise assessments, as well as a direct comparison of the alternatives in relation to objectives (holistic comparisons).

Then the authors consider the fundamentals of the method.

The evaluation function of the additive nature has a form:

$$V(x) = \sum_{i=1}^{N} w_i v_i^N (x_i) = \sum_{i=1}^{N} v_i (x_i)$$

where N is a number of attributes in the hierarchy of a problem, x_i — value of an attribute X_i of the alternative, $v_i(x_i) = w_i * v_i^N(x_i)$ — normalized weighted value corresponding to the value of x_i. Let x_i* and x_i^0 denote the best and the worst values obtained by the attribute X_i. For a normalized evaluation function we have:

$$\begin{cases} v_i^N (x_i^0) = 0 \\ v_i^N (x_i^*) = 1 \end{cases}$$

In the assumption that $v_i(x_i^0) = 0$, the overall evaluation can be expressed in the form:

$$V(x) = \sum_{i=1}^{N} v_i(x_i) = \sum_{i=1}^{N} \left[v_i(x_i^*) - v_i(x_i^0) \right] \left[\frac{v_i(x_i) - v_i(x_i^0)}{v_i(x_i^*) - v_i(x_i^0)} \right] = \sum_{i=1}^{N} w_i v_i^N(x_i)$$

Then it becomes possible to express the weights of attributes and normalized evaluation function using the difference in values:

$$w_i = v_i(x_i^*) - v_i(x_i^0)$$

$$v_i^N(x_i) = \frac{v_i(x_i) - v_i(x_i^0)}{v_i(x_i^*) - v_i(x_i^0)} = \frac{v_i(x_i) - v_i(x_i^0)}{w_i}$$

At the same time the condition should be satisfied:

$$\sum_{i=1}^{N} v_i(x_i^*) = \sum_{i=1}^{N} w_i = 1$$

Obtained evaluations of values' differences are sufficient to support conclusions about the preferences of the decision maker, taking into account:

1. Ordinal ranking.

We assume that the decision maker prefers x_i^j as compared to x_i^k. From this it follows that: $v_i(x_i^j) - v_i(x_i^k) > 0$.

That is, the ranking gives rise to a number of linear restrictions in relation to single evaluation functions of attributives.

2. Determination of ratios of differences of values (numerical ranking). Let L and U be respectively lower and upper limits of the ratio of the differences of values:

$$L \leq \frac{v(x_j) - v(x_k)}{v(x_l) - v(x_m)} \leq U$$

From this it follows that:

$$\begin{cases} -v(x_j)v(x_k) + L(v(x_l) - v(x_m)) \leq 0 \\ v(x_j) - v(x_k) - U(v(x_l) - v(x_m)) \leq 0 \end{cases}$$

3. Direct comparison of alternatives in relation to objectives (holistic comparisons). In comparisons of this type techniques of ordinal and numerical ranking are applied to the evaluation function of the objectives. For example, if DM considering a purpose oi, prefers the value x^1 as compared to x^2, it indicates that: $v_{oi}(x_{oi}^1) - v_{oi}(x_{oi}^2) > 0$, where v_{oi} is a function of an overall evaluation as to the purpose oi, and x_{ai}^i — the value of the alternative $i \in \{1,2\}$ in relation to the purpose oi.

198

Ranking of alternatives

To adjust the evaluation function the results of a direct comparison can also be used. For example, bycorrelating $v_i(x_i^j)$ with the best and the worst values x_i^* and x_i^0:

$$L \leq \frac{v_i(x_i^j) - v_i(x_i^0)}{v_i(x_i^*) - v_i(x_i^0)} \leq U$$

Attribute weights are traditionally determined using SWING method. The algorithm consists of two phases:

1. One of the attributes with the highest level of importance gets its evaluation as 100 points.

2. The remaining attributes in turn are compared with the most important one. According to the results for each of them a range of values of importance is assigned $[L, U]$.

Received suggestions of experts on the ranges of values of importance generate inequations:

$$\frac{L}{100} \leq \frac{w_i}{w_{ref}} \leq \frac{U}{100} \Leftrightarrow \frac{L}{100} \leq \frac{v_i(x_i^*) - v_i(x_i^0)}{v_{ref}(x_i^*) - v_{ref}(x_{ref}^0)} \leq \frac{U}{100}$$

At the last stage of the analysis by PRIME method synthesis of priorities of alternatives is carried out. By solving the linear programming tasks from inequations generated by experts we receive:

1. Interval evaluations of alternatives.

$$V(x) \in \left[\min \sum_{i=1}^{N} v_i(x_i), \max \sum_{i=1}^{N} v_i(x_i) \right]$$

2. Intervals of attributes weights.

$$w_i \in \left[\min\{v_i(x_i^*) - v_i(x_i^0)\}, \max\{v_i(x_i^*) - v_i(x_i^0)\} \right]$$

3. Structures of preferences.

Absolute and paired dominations are distinguished. The alternative x^j is more preferable than the alternative x^k in the sense of absolute domination, if the intervals of their values do not overlap. That is the smallest value x^j exceeds the maximum value of the alternative x^k:

$$\min \sum_{i=1}^{N} v_i(x_i^j) > \max \sum_{i=1}^{N} v_i(x_i^k)$$

The alternative x^j is more preferable than the alternative x^k in the sense of paired domination if:

$$\max\left(V(x^k)-V(x^j)\right)<0 \Leftrightarrow$$

$$\max\left(\sum_{i=1}^{N}v_i(x^k)-\sum_{i=1}^{N}v_i(x^j)\right)=\max\left(\sum_{i=1}^{N}w_i\left(v_i^N(x^k)-v_i^N(x^j)\right)\right)<0$$

In other words, for any fixed set of weights wi normalized (weighted) minimum value of the alternative x^k is higher than the maximum normalized (weighted) value x^j. It should be noted that the paired domination is less stringent than the absolute. In addition, the paired one for x^k and x^j are worth checking only if $\max(V(x^j))>\max(V(x^k))\geq\min(V(x^j))>\min(V(x^k))$.

If the first inequation is not satisfied, then regardless of further adjustments to the model of preferences, evaluation of the alternative x^j cannot exceed the value of x^k. When the second inequation is not satisfied, then x^j dominates x^k absolutely.

Finally, if the last inequation is not satisfied, then there are such values of weights w_i $i = 1..., N$, at which the value of x^k is higher than the value of x^j. Consequently, the situation of domination may occur or be excluded completely, depending on the interval of estimates when the condition is not satisfied.

4. The results of the application of logical rules.

Rule maximax reveals an alternative with the maximum possible value, maximin — with the maximum lower bound of the evaluation. Rule minimax regret finds an alternative for which the maximum possible value of importance loss (and hence the error
of its selection as dominant) is minimal:

$$\max_{j, j\neq k}\left[\max\left(\sum_{i=1}^{N}v_i(x_i^j)-\sum_{i=1}^{N}v_i(x_i^k)\right)\right]$$

Rule of central values reveals an alternative with the maximum average value of the estimation interval. Thus, PRIME method has a strong mathematical foundation. Simulation or statistical tools are not used. Conclusion on the basis of logical rules allows determining the non-dominated alternatives, even in situations where other methods based on preference relations, are powerless.

Methods of ELECTRE family

This family focuses on solving problems of multicriteria choice with a given set of alternatives.

These methods are based on relative determining of the quality level of alternatives on criteria, i. e. quality of alternatives on many criteria is represented not in the form of a generalized quantitative evaluation, but on the basis of detection of conditions of superiority of one alternative over another.

The traditional formulation of the problem of decision-making is as follows. There are n criteria, measuring scales for alternatives quality on these criteria (usually quantitative), criteria weights (usually integers), a finite set of alternatives and their evaluation according to the criteria.

We introduce the following notations: $A = \{A1, An\}$ — a set of alternatives; $I = \{K1, \ldots, Kn\}$ — set of criteria, according to which each alternative $Ai \in A$ can be evaluated. A set I can be divided into three subsets (classes):

$I^+ \left(A_i, A_j\right)$ — a subset of criteria according to which A_i is more preferable than A_j;

$I^= \left(A_i, A_j\right)$ — a subset of criteria according to which A_i is equivalent with A_j;

$I^- \left(A_i, A_j\right)$ — a subset of criteria according to which A_j is more preferable than A_i.

Supposing that it is possible to determine the relative importance of each of these subsets, which is characterized by three numbers:

$$P^+ \left(A_i, A_j\right), P^= \left(A_i, A_j\right), P^- \left(A_i, A_j\right).$$

We introduce a threshold c and we assume that Ai is superior to Aj, if the condition is satisfied

$$c\left[P^+ \left(A_i, A_j\right), \ P^= \left(A_i, A_j\right), \ P^- \left(A_i, A_j\right)\right] \geq c.$$

The left side of this inequation is called the index of consent, the right — the threshold of dissent.

In ELECTRE-I method the index of consent is defined as the sum of $P^+ \left(A_i, A_j\right) + P^= \left(A_i, A_j\right)$ or in the form:

$$\left(P^+ \left(A_i, A_j\right) + P^= \left(A_i, A_j\right)\right) / \left(P^+ \left(A_i, A_j\right) + P^= \left(A_i, A_j\right) + P^- \left(A_i, A_j\right)\right) \geq c.$$

To avoid the situation, when A_iRA_j and A_jRA_i (where R is a binary relation of superiority (preferences) defined on the set of alternatives A) are satisfied simulteneously, instead of the following condition can be used

$$P^+\left(A_i, A_j\right) / P^-\left(A_i, A_j\right) \geq c.$$

Thus, condition is recommended when the number of the matching evaluations in different embodiments is relatively small as compared to n, otherwise the condition is advisable.

In ELECTRE-II method the described approach and the condition are used. For practical calculations by the ELECTRE-I and ELECTRE-II methods we can take the expression:

$$P^*(A_i, A_j) = \sum_{i \in I^*(A_i, A_j)} p_i$$

where * is any symbol from the set $\{+, =, -\}$; p_i — weight, representing the importance of i-th criterion from the set I.

The condition (1) is necessary but insufficient to establish a relation of superiority in the pair (A_i, A_j).

Therefore the index of dissent is applied: $d(A_i, A_j) \leq d$, where d is a threshold of the index. Indexed condition takes into account the values of the differences between the estimates of the quality of alternatives according to certain criterion. And the index iscalculated by the formula:

$$d(A_i, A_j) = \max_{k \in I^-(A_i, A_j)} \frac{I_{A_j}^k - I_{A_i}^k}{L_k}$$

where $I_{A_i}^k, I_{A_j}^k$ are evaluations of alternatives A_i, and A_j to the criterion k; L_k — the value of the maximum gradation of the scale (its length), used to measure the criterion.

Hence, the ratio of preference for alternatives A_i and A_j is defined as follows:

$$AiRAj, \text{ if } c\left[P^+\left(A_i, A_j\right), P^=\left(A_i, A_j\right), P^-\left(A_i, A_j\right)\right] \geq c \text{ and } d\left(A_i, A_j\right) \leq d$$

Methods of the group ELECTRE imply formation of the core on the set of initial options (alternatives) A, all elements of which are incomparable (i. e., form a set of Pareto), and any option, not included in the core is dominated by at least one of its elements.

202

Narrowing of the core can be achieved by increasing the threshold value of the index of consent of the index c and decreasing the threshold of the index of dissent d. It should be noted that in the presence of Pareto-optimal alternative (which by all criteria is not
worse than other alternatives and is better on at least one criterion) a core is formed containing a single element, as this alternative dominates all the others.

3.2.　Software implementation of DSS

The structure of DSS is shown in Fig. 3.1. Database (DB) of the system contains a general description of the problem, hierarchical and network structures of criteria, results of a survey of experts and their correspondence, values of alternatives attributes (derived from the enterprise information system or entered directly by the administrator), and other information. Knowledge base (KB) includes practical problems, solved by various methods [1-5].

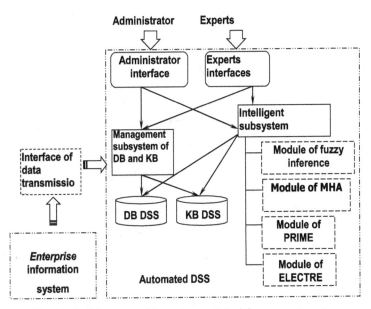

Fig. 3.1.Architecture of the automated decision support system
of the enterprise

Management subsystem of DB and KB base mainly allows the administrator to organize and coordinate the preparation of solutions. The access of experts in DSS is also performed through it. The use of passwords and assignment of access privileges ensure information security.

KB function is also implementation using inferences of the choice of the most optimal decision-making method for a particular situation. In accordance with this type of the problem, structure and nature of the problem data, the number of criteria, alternatives etc. are analyzed. At the request of the user evaluation can be conducted by several available methods. In this case, the final choice (the use of particular options) remains for a man.

Intelligent subsystem takes the original information from the database, generalized by the administrator, and adds formalized expert knowledge stored in KB. User interaction with DSS occurs through interface modules.

Data from the loops of the enterprise information system come automatically or on request from the administrator. They include accounting, finance, and management information of the current or past periods. Fig. 3.2 shows a scheme of decisionmaking process in the automated decision support system. At the first stage, the administrator receives a request from a user, defines a group of experts working on the problem. For them, access privileges, passwords and polling sequence (if required) are assigned.

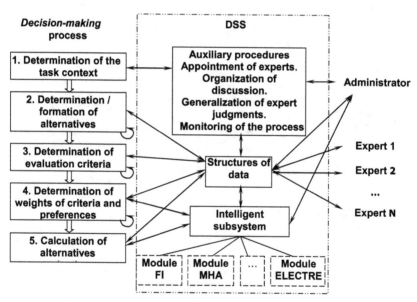

Fig. 3.2.Scheme of a process of multi-criteria decisionmaking
with the help of DSS

204

At the second stage a list of alternatives is determined and specified. This procedure, as well as the following two steps, is performed iteratively until an administrator records the achievement of consensus or the required number of votes.

For aggregation of collective assessments different principles of compromise are used: egalitarianism, utilitarianism, a fair compromise, etc. It takes less effort and time from participants of the process, than by consensus. However, it may not remove the conflict of goals or interests. The administrator eliminates data redundancy, for example, when it encounters exactly the same voting options.

Determination of the list of goals and criteria (third step) is usually faster. The proposed criteria represent views of different actors (individuals, influencing the decision-making process). Therefore, the inclusion of the maximum number of options for providing ensures a more comprehensive coverage of the problem. Discussions may arise with regard to the redundancy of attributes or their weak representativeness. At this stage the profile of the problem is finally formed, and an intelligent subsystem selects the optimal method of assessment. Then at the fourth stage standard questionnaires and forms are sent to the experts for entering the required information: final configuration of the model, criteria weights, degrees of alternatives preferences, etc.

Iterative implementation of the fourth stage becomes mandatory at the poor consistency or heterogeneity of judgments. If professionalism of experts varies widely, their opinions may be adjusted by weighting the ratings.

At the fifth stage, when all information is entered into databases and knowledge bases, estimates of alternatives is calculated by selected methods. User interfaces of DSS have to support a conclusion of the results in a convenient format for the decision maker: text or graphics.

Generalized functional model of DSS

In Fig. 3.3 it is represented as a directed graph. Each node corresponds to a logically complete procedure, implemented in the form of independent subprogram. Oriented edges of the graph indicate the direction of information transmission and the transition from one procedure to another. Situations of choice (when the user invokes a method of solving the problem) or branching of the processes are possible which are associated with test of logical conditions.

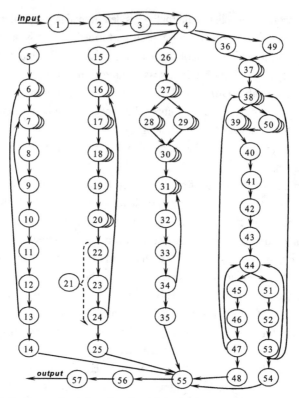

Fig. 3.3. Generalized functional model of DSS based on multi-criteria
methods of decision-making under uncertainty

Operation of the system begins with the activation of user interface modules and calling of lists of earlier introduced alternatives, objectives and methods. Output is possible at the logical conclusion of any of the stages. Support for asynchronous communication of participants of decision-making process enables to continue working on the task at any time, if its limit set by the administrator is not exceeded. At the same time an order for the basic procedures for each of the used methods is provided. Place of the procedure in the graph is determined by its serial number and generally is reduced to a few positions:

1. Input / editing descriptions of alternatives.
2. Input / editing goals and criteria of the task.
3. Automatic selection of solution methods by intellectual subsystem.
4. Selection of data from the enterprise information system.

The final stage of the work with the program is followed by:

1. Visualization of the results of evaluation by various methods.

2. Printing of reports.

3. Storage of the task environment in DB and KB, and the output from the system.

In Fig. 3.3 the nodes of the graph of the form mean information input procedures that may be performed repeatedly, depending on the number of voters. In the nodes (6, 16, 27, 37) experts complement the general structures of method models in accordance with their competencies (e. g., by functional area). Collaborative work together with the same area of the problem is possible. When creating hierarchies, trees purposes etc. using the database interface data on alternatives previously entered are used.

Reverse transitions from the latter to the initial procedures are performed, if it is necessary to specify the model. In the methods of MNA and MHA matrices of pairwise comparisons are adjusted again, if the calculation of the index of consent has given an unsatisfactory result. Transition (9–7) is activated when, after comparing the elements it is necessary to compare their clusters with each other. Algorithm procedure (7) is versatile, and a particular case is determined by transmission of relevant parameters.

In PRIME method branching (27–28, 29) is the user's choice of one or another way to specify criteria weights. Return to specify judgments (34–31) takes place not by the beginning of the chain, but by the step of quantitative preferences evaluation. Output of the cycle occurs when the degree of possible loss of significance becomes acceptable.

ELECTRE methods generally use single procedure. Last stages (45–47 and 51–53) are different. In ELECTRE profiles of categories (50) are described additionally. After this, assignment of preferences parameters (39) is carried out in the cycle according to the number of profiles. Return in case of model calibration may occur to the step of determining weights of criteria or determining the cutting off levelλ(in a procedure to eliminate uncertainty of preference relation — 44).

In case of fuzzy inference logging of judgment (21) is parallel to the procedures of fuzzification, actually output and defuzzification (22–24).

Conclusions

As the analysis of the functional model has shown, a clear distinction between modes of acquiring knowledge and consultations is obtained only for the class of ELECTRE and fuzzy inference methods. In the methods of PRIME, MNA and MHA introduction of new alternatives is associated with their additional comparing in relation to criteria of the next level. Even if the

207

number is not large, this procedure refers to a mode of acquiring knowledge and should be performed by experts.

Elimination of the mentioned problem is admissible in two ways. Firstly, experts can assess the maximum number of alternatives in advance. But such an approach is unacceptable in monitoring of business processes, as the number of potential states of the system is indefinite. Secondly, in MNA and MHA it is possible to apply the method of standards, which reveals quality levels on set criteria (standards) typical for the majority of alternatives. Obtained priorities of standards are associated with the proposed alternatives. Then the synthesis of quality values of the latter is perf ormed without additional analysis. This decision seems to be the most promising.

Ensuring support for consultations mode by PRIME method is only possible when using the utility function. Then this algorithm determines the upper and lower boundaries of preferences automatically without user intervention. Obviously, this approach is acceptable for attributes of quantitative nature. Comparison of qualitative characteristics is the prerogative of experts.

In conclusion it should be noted that these restrictions are relevant only for unskilled users. Application of DSS by experts does not exclude any methods and in any case greatly simplifies the decision-making process due to total or partial automation of its stages.

References of chapter 3

1. Raiffa, H. Decision Analysis: Introductory Readings on Choices Under Uncertainty [*Analiz reshenij (vvedenie v problemu vybora v uslovijah neopredelennosti)*]. Moscow, Nauka publ., 1990, 562 p.

2. Keeney, R.L., Raiffa, H. Decisions with multiple objectives: preferences and value tradeoffs [*Prinjatie reshenij pri mnogih kriterijah: predpochtenija i zameshhenija*]. Moscow, Radio i svjaz' publ., 1981, 486 p.

3. J. von Neumann., Morgenstern O. Theory of Games and Economic Behavior [*Teorija igr i ekonomicheskoe povedenie*]. Moscow, Nauka publ., 1970, 306 p.

4. Andreychikov, A.V., Andreichikova, O. N. System analysis and synthesis of strategic decisions in Innovation: Innovation Framework for Strategic Management and Marketing [*Sistemnyj analiz i sintez strategicheskih reshenij v innovatike: Osnovy strategicheskogo innovacionnogo menedzhmenta i marketinga*]. Moscow, Librokom publ., 2011, 248 p.

5. Andreychikov, A.V., Andreichikova, O. N. Strategic management in innovative organizations. System analysis and decision making [*Strategicheskij menedzhment v innovacionnyh organizacijah. Sistemnyj analiz i prinjatie reshenij*].Moscow, Infra-M publ., 2013, 396 p.